Witchcraft and Magic in Europe
The Twentieth Century

WITCHCRAFT AND MAGIC IN EUROPE

Series Editors
Bengt Ankarloo
Stuart Clark

The roots of European witchcraft and magic lie in Hebrew and other ancient Near Eastern cultures and in the Celtic, Nordic, and Germanic traditions of the continent. For two millennia, European folklore and ritual have been imbued with the belief in the supernatural, yielding a rich trove of histories and images.

Witchcraft and Magic in Europe combines traditional approaches of political, legal, and social historians with a critical synthesis of cultural anthropology, historical psychology, and gender studies. The series provides a modern, scholarly survey of the supernatural beliefs of Europeans from ancient times to the present day. Each volume of this ambitious series contains the work of distinguished scholars chosen for their expertise in a particular era or region.

Witchcraft and Magic in Europe: Biblical and Pagan Societies
Witchcraft and Magic in Europe: Ancient Greece and Rome
Witchcraft and Magic in Europe: The Middle Ages
Witchcraft and Magic in Europe: The Period of the Witch Trials
Witchcraft and Magic in Europe: The Eighteenth and Nineteenth Centuries
Witchcraft and Magic in Europe: The Twentieth Century

Witchcraft and Magic in Europe
The Twentieth Century

Edited by
BENGT ANKARLOO
and STUART CLARK

PENN

University of Pennsylvania Press
Philadelphia

First published 1999 by
The Athlone Press
1 Park Drive, London NW11 7SG

First published 1999 in the United States of America by
University of Pennsylvania Press
Philadelphia, Pennsylvania 19104–4011

British Library Cataloguing in Publication Data
*A catalogue record for this book is available
from the British Library*

Library of Congress Cataloging-in-Publication Data
Witchcraft and magic in Europe : the twentieth century / edited by
Bengt Ankarloo and Stuart Clark.
    p.   cm.
    Includes bibliographical references and index.
    ISBN 0–8122–3519–3 (hardcover : alk. paper). — ISBN 0–8122–1707–1
(pbk. : alk. paper)
    1. Witchcraft — Europe — History — 20th century. 2. Magic — Europe –
– History — 20th century. I. Ankarloo, Bengt, 1935–   .   II. Clark,
Stuart.
BF1584.E9W59   1999
133.4'3'0940904 — dc21   99–26081
                                                                CIP

Typeset by Ensystems, Saffron Walden, Essex
Printed and bound in Great Britain

Contents

Introduction

Bengt Ankarloo and Stuart Clark

This volume brings the History of Witchcraft and Magic in Europe up to the present day by surveying developments during the last century of the millennium. These display again the same two features that seem to have characterised witchcraft and magic, more than most cultural phenomena, down the ages — a capacity to adapt to and reflect contemporary needs and aspirations and yet, at the same time, an identity based on what are perceived to be highly traditional forms. It is as though they have survived for so long by being simultaneously responsive to the present and tied to the past; again and again, they are re-invented to provide answers to immediate problems, yet always with the reassurance — or perhaps threat — of a supposed continuity. Of course, these things are not necessarily the same to practitioners or believers and to observers (particularly historians). The answers may seem hollow and the continuity spurious to those who behave and believe differently. This differential in the way witchcraft and magic are viewed has been another constant element in both the history and the historiography of our subject and it is also illustrated in this volume.

Witchcraft and magic, then, are marked both by contemporaneity and by timelessness. The prognostications and prophylactics, the recipes and remedies, that have made up much of everyday magic have existed for so long because they have continued to seem efficacious in situations of practical need, but they have owed their transmission — and something of their status — to the traditionalisms of oral communication and to the re-cycling of texts that seem hardly to have changed. The magic of the magus has never ceased to appeal for its solutions to problems of power and knowledge and yet its literature, too, has been remarkably canonical and static. The early modern witch was the focus of fears that were largely the product of early modern conditions, while her identity — at least for intellectuals — was consciously fashioned from biblical law and history, classical poetry and legend, and medieval theology, as if there was no such thing as anachronism. Even today, the evil witch remains highly relevant to children's literature and the popular media even though she consists of archaisms.

The three studies that follow each testify to this abiding ambiguity and suggest ways to account for it, and even to resolve it. Nobody could suppose that the phenomena they describe are anything but embedded in twentieth-century life and thought. Modern pagan witchcraft, the subject of the first essay, must be seen in relation to many of the conventional features of contemporary religion and religious ritual, of notions of the self and of human abilities, and of attitudes to the world and its workings. Ronald Hutton explains that among its inspirations have been some of the most powerful impulses in modern culture – 'nostalgia for the natural and rural world, feminism, sexual liberation, dissatisfaction with established religious institutions and social norms, and a desire for greater individual self-expression and self-fulfilment.' (p. 59) It flourishes, therefore, because of its obvious relevance to contemporary lives and contemporary debates. The self-styled satanist groups examined by Jean La Fontaine in the second essay have also emerged as products of late second-millennium culture, even if in violent reaction against what they see as its repressive and authoritarian morality and social codes. Nor would the modern *myth* of satanism and of the satanic abuse of children – a very different thing altogether, as she decisively shows – be possible without the emergence of twentieth-century religious fundamentalism and, more precisely, public anxieties about parenting. It is true that this sense of contemporary relevance is weakest in the witchcraft cases discussed by Willem de Blécourt, who concludes our volume and our series. He concedes that one of the features of these episodes, confined as they largely are to remote rural areas, is their increasing marginality. The traces of the accompanying discourse, he suggests, may 'represent its last vestiges.' (p. 215) Even so, those who attacked the witch in the port of Naples in 1921, or who were consulting the witch-doctor Waldemar Eberling in the German village of Sarzbüttel before and during the 1950s, or who reluctantly confided their fears about bewitchment to the anthropologist Jeanne Favret-Saada in the Bocage around 1970 were all acting and speaking out of a conviction that witchcraft had a place in their lives and their social world. It is precisely this sense of having a place 'today', argues de Blécourt, that is threatened or denied whenever twentieth-century witchcraft is described as archaic or anachronistic.

And yet it is precisely the archaic that all these manifestations of witchcraft and magic in our century seem to exhibit. They *do* present themselves – or at least *are presented* – as timeless, or at least immemorial, not time bound. The clearest case, of course, is that of paganism, with its explicit debt to the religions of ancient Greece and Rome, its celebration of pagan deities and goddesses and the values associated with them, and, above all, its commitment to the view that the witches prosecuted during the early modern centuries were surviving practitioners of an 'old' religion, of which modern Wicca too is a further benign form. Everyone interested in the history of witchcraft knows of Margaret Murray's influence in this regard, particularly since the 1940s — although few, if any, will have realised that she considered herself a witch and even practised cursing! Here described as the 'godmother of Wicca' for her approving foreword to Gerald Gardner's *Witchcraft Today* (1954), her studies did more than anything else to create the impression of an age-old witch religion, continuous from pagan times and marked by veneration of a nature-god and by fertility rites. This was the religion whose twentieth-century discovery was announced in Gardner's book.

With satanism the situation is more complex. Unlike the modern pagans, none of the satanist groups that have actually existed in recent years has ever claimed continuity with demon-worshippers from the past. For these modern groups Satan certainly represents freedom from the constraining moralities of Christianity and the State, thus symbolizing rebelliousness, iconoclasm and hedonism. In this sense, therefore, it is true that satanism is still defined in opposition to Christianity. But, otherwise, its few devotees practice magic, not deity worship, and its only common philosophy seems to have been a form of social Darwinism. Instead, the element of timelessness here lies in the extraordinary persistence into the modern world of a mythology which attributes *to* twentieth-century satanism a kind of diabolism it has never exhibited. As previous volumes in this series have shown, Western Christianity rapidly developed a demonology in which human allies of Satan were thought to threaten the faithful by their secret organisation, their ritual celebration of demonism, and their magical powers. Of most relevance to the history of medieval heresy and early modern witchcraft, this demonology has nevertheless continued, even down to our own day, to generate myths which virtually replicate those of earlier centuries. Thus it is that in the twentieth century, organised satanism has again assumed a mythological significance — particularly, it seems, for Protestant fundamentalists and 'New Christians' — that bears little relation to either the actual practices, or even the very existence, of real satanists. Not only the latter, but pagans and Wiccans, astrologers and spiritualists, some forms of rock music, and even the Duke of Edinburgh (for his presidency of the World Wild Life Fund) have been attributed with aims similar to those of the sixteenth- and seventeenth-century sabbat goers. Like the accusers of heretics and witches in the past, the modern mythologisers have assumed both a continuous reality in the 'crimes' of devil-worshippers and also a uniform guilt.

The consequences for attitudes and, indeed, policies towards child abuse have been particularly profound and disturbing. Under the influence of this same lingering mythology — sometimes in the guise almost of a folk belief — the abduction and sexual abuse of children, because it is among the most horrendous and inhuman of late twentieth-century crimes, has been deemed to be carried out by ritual Satanists. Jean La Fontaine records here the nature and number of the allegations that have resulted, mainly in the USA and the UK. As in both the report commissioned from her by the UK Department of Health (published in 1994) and her recent monograph *Speak of the Devil: Tales of Satanic Abuse in Contemporary England* (Cambridge University Press; Cambridge, 1998) she is able to conclude categorically that 'independent material evidence to corroborate the accusations has never been found' (p. 129). While child abuse is, sadly, an all too real feature of modern life, the idea that it is sometimes a part of magical or religious rites inspired by Satanism remains a myth. More striking still in the context of this series, however, is the realization that the only 'evidence' that has emerged for it has been extracted from child victims or confessing adults by means of the same mixture of suggestion, pressure and willingness to take stories at face-value that must also have led to most of the witchcraft verdicts of early modern times too. Here again we seem to be faced with powerful continuities. But far from providing any retrospective 'proof' that real satanism lay behind the early modern trials, our twentieth-century experience of the workings of 'satanic abuse' mythology may finally be dispelling anything that remains of that wholly mistaken idea.

In Willem de Blécourt's essay the issue of whether continuity in witchcraft is a cultural phenomenon itself or simply a *perception* of a cultural phenomenon is again powerfully problematised. Here, however, the perceptions in question are those of academic researchers – above all, the folklorists, criminologists, and anthropologists who in the past have so often treated twentieth-century fears of *maleficium* merely as anachronisms. Indeed, de Blécourt makes an overwhelming case – hinging on the dilemmas faced by the anthropologist Jeanne Favret-Saada – for the way that scholarly study is always itself conceptually entangled with what it studies. Of course, refusing to treat such fears as exotic superstitions from the past does not preclude recognition of formal continuities or the extent to which similar fears would have been broadly intelligible to even our remote European predecesors. The four types of witchcraft he identifies – bewitching, unwitching, witching (securing wealth by witchcraft), and scolding – may manifest themselves differently in today's conditions but they are categories of behaviour that this series has found throughout Europe's history. The 'lived' context makes them intelligible in, and relevant to, the modern communities that experience them, yet nothing can lessen the shock that comes from reading Favret-Saada's now classic monograph, *Deadly Words: Witchcraft in the Bocage*, and recognizing from earlier centuries many of the situations she describes and much of the methodological ambiguities that arise in trying to grasp them. Even so, what cannot be doubted is that much of the modern research discussed by de Blécourt has, indeed, been premised on assumptions of atavism in witchcraft behaviour and discourse. What matters to him, instead, are the local inflections and the immediate context and these have all too often been obliterated by the very methods that have been adopted for recording and analysing modern witchcraft cases, the legend collections and indexes of the folklorists being the most obvious examples.

How then do we resolve the simultaneous presence of the contemporary and the archaic in twentieth-century witchcraft and magic? It may well be that there is no real ambiguity here at all. For what the essays in this volume point towards is the extent to which perceptions of continuity and timelessness are *themselves* the product of modern conditions and contemporary culture. However witchcraft and magic are represented, these representations are inescapably in and of the present; to perceive continuity in their history is, thus, in large part to reflect a contemporary desire to find it. As Ronald Hutton explains, the various cultural trends that have gone into the making of modern paganism invariably invested heavily – and retrospectively – in tradition. In his analysis, these include the development of secret societies in eighteenth- and nineteenth-century Britain (of which Wicca has been, in a sense, the latest), the continuing popular faith placed in the operative powers of magic, the emergence of a romantic style of folklore studies and of the Folklore Society itself, and the publication of anthropological theories like those of James Frazer and Edward Tylor. Gerald Gardner was an antiquarian and Margaret Murray both a Folklore Society member and a devoted Frazerian. Of the utmost significance, therefore, has been the way in which pagans, beginning in the 1970s and accelerating with the establishment of the Pagan Federation in 1988, have self-critically reworked their own history, recognised the metaphorical rather than literal nature of many of the key elements of the 'old' religion, and turned the 'Murray thesis' – discredited anyway by historians – into a foundation myth. In this sense, the academic and pagan worlds have lately come together, with Hutton's own research as a powerful example. Radical historicisation has thus at last removed the sense in which paganism's perception of its own past – particularly in the form established by Murray – has conflicted with its obvious rootedness in the present.

Those who have seen an almost medieval diabolism in twentieth-century satanism and paganism have, likewise, been influenced by the currents in modern religion most committed to fundamentalism, which, after all, is defined by the strict maintenance of what is most ancient in a practice or belief. In La Fontaine's analysis the rise of New Religious Movements since World War II has in fact been paralleled by the emergence of New Christians. Both have shared in a general religious revivalism but New Christianity has been marked by strict Biblicism, exclusivity, and the conviction of being 'engaged in a battle against all other religions which are tools of Satan' (p. 118). It is this sense of struggle, marked in some cases by millenialism, that has led to the re-invention of a mythology that attributes medieval dissent, early modern witchcraft, and twentieth-century religious experimentation (whether real or imagined) to the same transcendant and transhistorical demonism.

If we are to suppose that it is the insights of the historian and the anthropologist that can now expose these various perceptions of sameness as contemporary mythologies bred from modern social and cultural movements, then we must not forget too that such insights are themselves historically located. The relativism that has come to inform so much academic study in the era of post-modernity enables us to see how witchcraft and magic, and the opinions they provoke, are always related contingently to time and place. We are now better able to see difference than sameness in our relationships with 'other' cultures and other centuries, and to treat the desire for continuity as itself a cultural construction. For the time being, this governs the way we see the relationship between present and past; in the future, it will no doubt be re-thought. What cannot be doubted is that the way in which how we perceive the history of witchcraft and magic through the centuries and how we react to these things when we find them in our own world are inextricably bound up with each other.

PART 1

Modern Pagan Witchcraft

Ronald Hutton

In the history of European witchcraft and magic England traditionally occupies a marginal position. It features but seldom in studies of the subject during the ancient and medieval periods, and while it has abundant records for its share of the early modern witch trials, it remained both geographically and intellectually peripheral to them. It is therefore the more striking that when a historian considers the phenomenon of modern pagan witchcraft, the picture is exactly reversed. It is England which is the heartland, exporting ideas and practices to the rest of the British Isles and of Europe, and (above all) to North America. Twentieth-century pagan witchcraft, known in its most strongly established form as Wicca, is in fact the only religion which the English can claim to have given to the world. This is the more remarkable in that it is rooted in cultural trends which were themselves pan-European. The purpose of what follows is to identify those trends, to explain how and why they produced such a result in Britain alone, and to trace its subsequent development up to the present day.

SECTION 1

The Background to Pagan Witchcraft

SECRET SOCIETIES AND RITUAL MAGIC

One of the cultural trends in which twentieth century pagan witchcraft is rooted consisted of the eighteenth- and nineteenth-century manifestation of a central theme of the current series; the European tradition of learned ceremonial magic. The latter became caught up in one of the most remarkable and (until recently) least studied characteristics of Europe in the period between 1600 and 1800; a tremendous growth of secret societies, into which members were initiated upon an oath to observe the confidentiality of proceedings, and which incorporated an important element of ritual. The well-spring of these was Freemasonry, and David Stevenson has recently solved beyond reasonable doubt the question of its origins. He has shown that these lie in Scotland, at the end of the sixteenth century, where William Schaw, the royal Master of Works, either devised or supervised the development of the traditional trade craft of masons into a national network of permanent lodges. The latter were open to members who were not working masons, and their purpose was to build upon the medieval associations of masonry with sacred geometry and the arcane knowledge of ancient Egypt and King Solomon. These were mixed with Renaissance hermeticism, to produce a series of private and well-protected spaces in which ethics, symbols and mystical concepts could be discussed by members, and practical skills (such as the training of memory) imparted (Stevenson, 1988a, 1988b).

At the end of the seventeenth century the system spread to England, where it was fully developed by the 1720s, and during the course of the eighteenth century it was taken to France, and then to Germany, where it proved especially popular. In Britain it was valued above all as a means for Christians of all denominations to share a social and intellectual life in a hidden world beyond the reach of confessional strife. The European equivalents tended to be more concerned with its esoteric potential, and sometimes with that for subversive politics. Ritual tended to grow more elaborate, degrees of initiation to multiply, and the component of magical work and the claims to preserve ancient and esoteric knowledge to become more pronounced. In the process, many of the European societies broke any connection with the original Freemasonry. To historians, the descent is clear, but the new organisations often preferred to compete with the parent tradition, claiming to derive from the same old wisdom but to preserve the latter in a yet more direct and authentic form. From such roots came associations such as the Ancient and Accepted Rite, the Illuminati, and the Knights Templar and Rosicrucians of the late eighteenth century (Roberts, 1972; Partner, 1981; Stevenson, 1988a).

Certain features were already present in the masonic organizations of seventeenth-century Scotland which are especially important for the present subject, and which were merely elaborated during the subsequent 200 years of development in Britain. One was the insistence that they preserved knowledge and practices which had been handed down in secret from the most remote antiquity. At first this hidden tradition was linked mainly to Biblical characters and events, but as information about ancient civilizations increased, it was expanded to include the classical mystery religions. The whole body of supposed arcane learning was summed up under the simple label of 'the Craft', a relic of the Masons' origins in a medieval craft, or trade organization. Another major feature was the system of progressive initiation through degrees, which by the eighteenth century had been fixed in Britain as three, corresponding roughly to apprentice, journeyman and master. Another was the use of special marks and signs. From near the beginning one of the most important was the pentagram, the five-pointed star long prominent in the Western magical tradition. The triangle, square and hexagram were almost as important.

The earliest and most important of all masonic rituals was that of first-degree initiation, which developed slowly from the 1690s to take its final form about 100 years later. The candidate was 'properly prepared', that is blindfolded and bound with a special knot called the cable tow, which allowed him to be led easily. With his breast bared, he was taken to the door of the lodge, where a blade was pressed to his heart and removed when he made the correct ceremonial response. Once admitted, he was sometimes stripped naked and reclothed in a white robe. He was presented to the cardinal points of the compass, which stood for certain qualities; east for wisdom, west for strength, and south for beauty. Only the north was ignored, as the place of darkness. He then had to kneel and take the oath of secrecy, which included a recital of terrible penalties consequent upon any breach of it. He would then have read to him one or more of the documents which Freemasons called Charges, exhortations to ethical conduct, and be shown the 'working tools' suitable to his degree, a set of masonic implements, each of which had an important symbolic association. In addition, he would learn the ritual greeting and response of Freemasonry. This, then, was the basic structure, although some lodges elaborated it with further exhortations and ordeals. Many also incorporated riddles into the process, so that the postulant was initiated 'neither standing nor lying', 'neither naked nor clothed', 'neither bound nor free'. The higher degrees had their own admission ceremonies, and the postulant for these was never blindfolded.

The lodge usually had an altar in the centre, cubic in form and bearing the most important symbols and working tools. The lesser of these were kept at the three honoured cardinal points. The working space was consecrated before use, with corn, wine, oil and salt. In addition to special greetings, by 1696 Freemasonry had developed a distinctive embrace, called 'the Five Points of Fellowship', being 'foot to foot, knee to knee, heart to heart, hand to hand, and ear to ear'. The formal expression of assent to any action or proposition was 'so mote it be'. Some lodges had similarly standardized formulae to close proceedings, such as this, which ended second degree gatherings by the eighteenth century:

> 'Happy have we met,
> Happy have we been,
> Happy may we part,
> And happy meet again.'

All these trapping and actions (recorded in Slade, 1754; Cartwright 1947; Poole, 1951; Jones, 1956; Stevenson, 1988a) were built into the myth of immemorial antiquity which has been part of 'the Craft' from the beginning. It was merely elaborated with time, so that by the later nineteenth century Freemasonry was held by some of its spokesmen not to have derived from the ancient mysteries, but actually to have produced them, and to be older than civilization itself (Paton, 1873; Ward, 1921).

It is difficult to overvalue the importance of Freemasonry in nineteenth-century British culture. It was patronized by royalty, existed in every part of the nation and in town and countryside alike, and was an accepted part of local life; at the Scottish market town of Melrose during the mid-century, the local lodge laid on a public parade on the traditional fire festival of Midsummer Eve. Its officials were elected during the day, and when dusk came the members marched through the streets bearing torches and its banners, with a band playing (Dyer, 1876: 320–1). More significant still was the way in which masonic practice conditioned the way in which later associations and confraternities behaved. One example of this was provided by the early trade unions, the modern successors to the medieval 'crafts'. During the 1820s and 1830s many of these organized themselves in local lodges, coordinated by a Grand one on the masonic model. Like Masons, they invested in banners, robes and ritual regalia, and instituted ceremonies of initiation; two union members at Exeter were arrested by suspicious policemen on their way to a meeting with 'two wooden axes, two large cutlesses, two masks, and two white garments or robes, a large figure of Death with dart and hour-glass, a Bible and Testament.' (Pelling, 1976: 40).

More impressive still, and more enduring, was the influence of Free-masonry upon the friendly societies or benefit clubs and private insurance companies to provide working people with care in sickness and old age which appeared in large numbers all across Britain from the end of the eighteenth century; by the 1890s, they had at least four million members, compared to one and a half million trade unionists. Like masonry, they were found in town and country alike, so that over 100 were founded in the rural East Riding of Yorkshire in the years 1838–43 alone (Neave, 1991: 1). All the societies adopted the lodge system, and regalia such as sashes and banners. Some, however, rapidly developed into national associations with colourful titles and trappings, such as the 'Ancient Orders' of Foresters, Druids or Royal Shepherds, and the Society of Oddfellows. From Freemasonry these took a claim of immemorial antiquity; the Oddfellows claimed that they had been established by Roman soldiers, the Foresters included Alfred the Great among their earlier members, and the Druids named Noah as their founder.

They took over also the system of intitiation through degrees, and acceptance into the group with a ceremony which involved blindfolding and binding, an oath of secrecy, and some component of ordeal. Thus, around 1830 a candidate for initiation into the Shepherds was brought blindfolded into the lodge, to

> a rattling of chairs, shaking of sheet iron to imitation of thunder, clashing of swords, stamping of feet, upsetting of furniture and much more. . . . Then, in a sudden cessation, the beautiful words of the making would be heard in the otherwise silent gathering.

Ceremonies were further dramatized by the wearing of robes, usually in rich colours, the carrying of symbolic tools or weapons, and the use of sacred geometry; the Royal Antediluvian Order of Buffaloes always opened proceedings by forming a circle, as a symbol of brotherly love and equality. At times the mythology of the societies, to represent unbroken continuity from an ancient past, rebounded on them. One was at Huddersfield in 1833, where a clergyman warned the Oddfellows that they were 'worse than devils or infidels . . . if you do not foresake your badges which are emblems of wickedness . . . you will sink down to hell eternal' (Gosden, 1961: 127–34; Brown, 1982: 7–11.

In those parts of Britain where Freemasonry and Friendly Societies were weakest, the rural hinterland of Scotland, the masonic model evolved into its most bizarre popular form. The name 'Freemason' was itself English, and the original Scottish association had been called 'The Mason's Word', after the secret password which was one of its features (Stevenson, 1988a:

9). During the eighteenth century the grain millers of Scotland produced their own craft organization in imitation, The Miller's Word, to restrict entry to what had become a very desirable trade. It was likewise based upon a system of local groups with initiations, passwords and professional secrets, but was given an additional spice by holding meetings at night, and by spreading the beliefs that members acquired magical powers and paid for them by having to read the Bible backwards, three times over in three years. The initiation ceremony had come by the nineteenth century to include a strong element of deliberate blasphemy or mock-diabolism. The postulant had to bring a loaf, some jam and a bottle of whisky, as a mock-sacrament, and had to answer a parody of a catechism before a man impersonating a minister and standing before a bushel of corn representing an altar. At the climax, still blindfolded, he was told that he had to shake the Devil's hand, and was given stick or heated spade or a bullock's hoof to hold, while chains were clattered across the floor (McPherson, 1929: 292–3; Carter, 1979; 154–5).

In the early nineteenth century, horses began to replace the traditional oxen as the draught animals in the main agrarian areas of northern Scotland: the region west of Aberdeen and south of the Moray Firth, and Orkney. The skills required to manage them suddenly became much in demand, resulting in reputable and highly paid work. To train young men for it, regulate competition for it, and ensure that both services and rewards were maintained at a high level, a new secret society was formed, called The Horseman's Word. It rapidly became much more celebrated than the Miller's, being both numerically stronger (by 1880 three-fifths of farm-hands in arable areas worked with horses) and much less exclusive. The Horsemen took over the same structure of meetings and initiations, substituting their own craft knowledge, passwords, oaths and ordeals. The oaths varied, but were modelled quite recognizably on those of Freemasonry, with the same terrifying range of promised punishments in case of breach. The ordeals often included a trick whereby the postulant swore never to write or otherwise reveal the hidden word which was the symbol of the society's power. A short while later he was commanded to write it down, and flogged across back or knuckles if he was foolish enough to forget his oath and obey. The basis of the ceremony – the gifts of bread and whisky, the blindfolding of the postulant, the mock minister and catechism, and the encounter with the Devil – was taken straight from the Millers (McPherson, 1929: 290–2; Leask, 1933; Davidson, 1956; Henderson, 1962; Carter, 1979: 154–6).

During the course of the nineteenth century, the society spread out of its stronghold in the north-east, to most parts of Scotland and to large areas of eastern England where farms were either worked or leased by Scots (Davidson, 1956). As it Anglicized, it became known as The Society of Horsemen, but in all other respects remained the same (Davidson, 1956; Whitlock, 1992). In all its range, the organization absorbed and propagated much older skills and traditions; after all, a power over farm animals had been one of the immemorial attributions of witches and cunning men. During the late eighteenth century, a greater specialization appeared, in which individuals made a profession out of their particular ability to control horses. This was a truly international phenomenon, the most famous of such figures in Victorian England including Irishmen, Australians and Americans. As the century drew on, more was heard of the diffusion of this knowledge among fraternities of such specialists, known variously as the Horse Whisperers (a term imported from Ireland) or the Toadmen (who claimed to derive their power from a magical toad's bone, gained through a complex ritual). Although these disposed of the same sorts of training and lore as the Society of Horsemen, and are sometimes confused with it, they seem to have lacked its elaborate initiation ceremony (Youatt, 1859: 456–8; Evans, 1960: 239–71; Evans 1975: 29–35; Whitlock, 1992).

The striking diabolism of the Miller's and Horseman's Word may well have been a direct parody of the dominant presbyterian Christianity of the place and time; the meetings of the Horsemen were also characterized by hard drinking, and by jokes, songs and toasts which deliberately mocked conventional morality (Henderson, 1962). In this sense, it was a male anti-society, bent on deliberate misbehaviour in a private and controlled setting. It may well be, however, that its initiation ritual was influenced by traditions of the witches' sabbat, absorbed either directly from Scottish folklore or from the published accounts reprinted at intervals since the seventeenth century. It was this similarity, and those to Freemasonry, that caused some twentieth-century folklorists to speculate that The Horseman's Word, Masons and witchcraft were all ancient organizations descending from a prehistoric fertility religion (McPherson, 1929: 290; Davidson, 1956: 70–2; Evans, 1966: 228–36, 259; Evans, 1972: 225; Evans, 1975, 42–3). By the 1960s this idea had been taken up by members of The Horseman's Word itself, which still survives as a secret society of horse-lovers in northern Scotland (Evans, 1975: 36; Evans 1987: 56–63). It could only be supported by failing to consider any historical records. Now that Ian Carter has done this work for the Horsemen (Carter, 1979: 1545), just as David Stevenson has carried it out for early Freemasonry, it has been possible to put together the chronology outlined above.

All these were popular outgrowths from Freemasonry. It remains to consider some which derived from the same root in the late nineteenth century, but were of a very different kind; closed orders of working magicians. These were inspired directly by the revival of interest in learned magic, viewed partly as a branch of science and partly as an antidote to

the rationalist tendency of some thought of the age, which occurred in
Europe in the middle years of the century. Its epicentre was in France,
and its most famous exponent Alphonse Constant ('Eliphas Levi'). Working partly in response to the French example, but drawing upon older
esoteric traditions, a set of British Freemasons led by Kenneth Mackenzie
and Robert Wentworth Little set out to promote new study of the
Cabbala, the Hermetic texts, and other arcane wisdom of the ancient
world. The result was the Societas Rosicruciana in Anglia, founded in
1866 and restricted to men who held the top grade of Mason and
explicitly avowed Christianity. It had itself a hierarchy of three orders of
three grades each, and was governed by a Most Worthy Supreme Magus,
a structure copied from an eighteenth century German society of mystical
Freemasons, the Order of the Gold and Rosy Cross. Mackenzie claimed
to have been initiated into this order by a member of it still operating in
the Austrian Empire, which made his British organization a direct offshoot
(Regardie, 1937–40; i.19–20; iv.270; King, 1971: 17–18; Howe, 1972:
15–26; Gilbert, 1983: 16–20). In 1887 Hargrave Jennings provided it with
a pseudo-history of its own, to match those of Freemasonry proper and
the Friendly Societies, linking the eighteenth-century order directly to the
probably mythical early modern Rosicrucians, and through them with a
chain of succession coming down from the mystery religions and mystical
philosophers of pagan antiquity (Jennings, 1887).

It may be helpful at this point to address directly the question of why a
belief in (or at least an assertion of) a direct and unbroken descent from
the immemorial past, should have been such an important component of
all these secret societies. Any answers must of necessity be inferences, as
the members themselves were naturally not disposed to discuss something
which was taken to be unquestioned fact. The issue must none the less be
confronted, as it has equal relevance to the later development of modern
pagan witchcraft. One answer is a truism, that virtually all human societies,
at all times, have turned to the past to authenticate the present. Another is
functional, that a system of initiation in itself begets a sense of continuity
and a curiosity about origins, providing an incentive for the production of
foundation myths. Two others are more specific to the times and places
considered here. One is that a particular value of these secret societies is
that they provided safe spaces within which members could operate more
or less independently of the surrounding public culture; something all the
more important when that culture was suffering the strains of pronounced
social, economic or intellectual change. The sense of safety was much
enhanced if the space was believed to have existed from ancient days,
surviving all the stresses of the intervening ages. Furthermore, these bodies
usually attempted to provide services, skills and knowledge which would
make members more potent in that wider culture. As that culture was

dominated by political and religious institutions which themselves claimed authenticity, at least in part, from the past, and often did so by a system of succession, the ability of the societies to represent independent forces was greatly increased if they could claim a proportionately independent, and antique, origin.

It is also important to develop the comments made above, about the particular attraction of occult studies to some Europeans in the late nineteenth century. The challenge of scientific rationalism increased this attraction in two very different ways. It could drive people to whom a sense of divinity was instinctually important to seek a more direct contact with the superhuman, replacing that offered by orthodox religions. To such people the mediation of the established faiths had been badly compromised by the errors which the progress of knowledge had revealed in their teachings. At the same time, the impulse towards a revival of magic could itself be scientific, addressing precisely those areas which the new sciences had most neglected, and applying their techniques of empirical study and experimentation.

This is the context of Theosophy, the movement inspired by the much-travelled Russian noblewoman Helena Petrovna Blavatsky, which was founded in New York in 1875 and spread rapidly thereafter through North America, Europe and India. Like the bodies considered above, it was embodied in a society, organized in lodges. Unlike them, it had a much more public face, represented by open lectures and the publications of its leaders. The basic tenet of the latter was that behind all the world's major religions and philosophical systems had always lain a single, accurate, body of arcane wisdom, which could now be reconstituted. To Madame Blavatsky herself, and to her most important early associates, the purest traces of that wisdom were to be found in eastern teachings, and one major effect of the Theosophical Society was to make Buddhist and Hindu mystical literature relatively well known in the West for the first time. She did not merely promise theoretical knowledge, however, but practical powers of the sort generally reckoned to be supernatural. These she apparently manifested herself, causing voices to speak and objects to appear from empty air; although the authenticity of these displays has been disputed ever since her lifetime. Whereas previous European esoteric societies had claimed an impressive lineage, Blavatsky went further and taught that her instruction and authority derived directly from certain mighty sages, themselves long possessed of semi-divinity, who resided on the physical plane in the Himalayas. To her European contemporaries she offered both the comfort of teachings handed down from an antique golden age and the prospect of a future in which humans might evolve into divinities. Her most significant contribution was to popularize the notion of reincarnation in the West (Blavatsky, 1877; Cranston, 1933).

Neither the Societas Rosicruciana nor the Theosophical Society actually practised ritual magic; the most that the latter would do was establish an Esoteric Section in 1888, for the study of it. This was itself an indication of growing interest in the subject, which ran in tandem with a tendency among some British Theosophists to dislike the Society's emphasis upon Indian and Tibetan traditions and to call instead for a concentration upon ancient European and Near Eastern occult teaching. In 1884 some of them seceded to form the Hermetic Society, dedicated to this end. These concerns, and organizations, came together in the persons of the two men who led the Societas Rosicruciana at the time, its Magus, William Wynn Westcott, and his deputy (also a leading member of the Hermetic Society), Samuel Liddell Mathers. In 1888 they announced the existence of an organization which was to become known as the Hermetic Order of the Golden Dawn. Like the Societas Rosicruciana, it was a secret body with a hierarchy of grades entered through initiation rites, and rooted in Western esoteric traditions. Unlike it, but like the Theosophical Society, it had no restrictions of gender, religion or masonic membership. Unlike either, its main purpose was to study and to work ritual magic.

Westcott and Mathers initially represented the order as a long-existing organization. They rapidly modified this claim in favour of two other forms of legitimation; first, that the order had been based upon, and recognized by, an initiatory line of German Rosicrucians, and second, that Mathers had been contacted and supported by semi-divine magi of the same kind as Madame Blavatsky's Himalayan Mahatmas. Both assertions remain in the same historical category as Blavatsky's powers of psychokinesis. What is certain is that Westcott provided much of the theory behind the Golden Dawn, and Mathers worked out its training programme and developed its system of rituals. To do so he mixed ancient Greek, Hebrew, and medieval and early modern Christian magical traditions, to provide an interlocking series of ideas and images. The result was the most celebrated society of magicians in British history (Regardie, 1937–40; King, 1971; Howe, 1972; Torrens, 1973; Gilbert, 1983).

For the purposes of a history of pagan witchcraft, two aspects of the Golden Dawn are of especial interest. The first is the way in which it blended masonic forms with those of traditional ritual magic. Like Masons, its members had symbolic objects, but their nature and associations were different. Pre-eminent were the 'elemental weapons', the chalice (for water), pentacle (for earth), dagger (for air) and wand (for fire). Behind these ranked the sword, representing the mind. The medieval association of the pentagram, as a sign which controlled spirits, was developed by Mathers into an elaborate ritual whereby it was drawn in a different fashion at each cardinal point to invoke elemental powers, using the ritual dagger upon the air, and then reversed at the close of the ceremony to banish them. To purify the magician as well as the working space, he produced another known as the 'Qabbalistic' (i.e. Cabbalistic) Cross, in which the body was blessed using Hebrew forms, and the four Hebrew names of divinity invoked at the four quarters, followed by the names of the four archangels. The latter were for some purposes identified with the Lords of the Watchtowers, the mighty angels who guarded the quarters of the world in John Dee's Elizabethan system of Enochian magic (Regardie, 1937–40; Torrens, 1973).

The other important aspect of the order for present purposes was the way in which it handled the relationship between Christian and pagan elements in its material. To Westcott there should have been no problem in this, because like Theosophists he believed that a single mystical system lay behind all religions (Gilbert, 1983). The rituals incorporated pagan deities (especially Egyptian) promiscuously with Hebrew and Christian angels, as representatives of particular forces and qualities. As the 1890s progressed, however, members of the Golden Dawn began to diverge notably in their approach to these. In 1896 Mathers had a vision of the goddess Isis, commanding him to restore her worship, and thereafter he and his wife Moina worked rites representing a revival of the ancient Egyptian mysteries. A striking feature of Mathers's system of operation was that magicians did not merely call upon deities; they attempted to draw them into their own minds and bodies, and so to become one with them and partake in some measure of their divinity (Crowley, 1969: 1937; Howe, 1972: ix–xiv; Harper, 1974: 19). Similar interests characterized other sub-groups of the Golden Dawn, such as that which contained Florence Farr, who painted her sitting room walls with figures of Egyptian goddesses and gods (Yeats, 1926: 151). They contrasted with increasing clarity with those of colleagues in the order such as A.E. Waite, whose preoccupations remained firmly Christian, and the poet W.B. Yeats, who worked with the images of Irish pagan deities in particular, but whose fundamental religious aim was to develop an improved Christianity. To such people, the more starkly pagan loyalties of their fellows were a cause for anxiety (Ellmann, 1949: 42–129; Ellmann, 1954: 2975; Harper, 1974: 71). These differences combined with a clash of personalities to produce the quarrels which tore the Golden Dawn apart in 1900 and caused its progressive fragmentation into a series of successor groups, some of which survive to the present.

In an important sense, Wicca was to be the last of the secret societies to grow from the stalk of Freemasonry, conditioned by some of the ideas of the Golden Dawn. This was, however, only one of its points of origin, and not one which its practioners have generally recognized. They have tended instead to emphasize a quite different one, the traditional magic and witchcraft of the common people, and to this the present investigation must proceed.

POPULAR WITCHCRAFT AND MAGIC

Popular magic and witchcraft have been a major theme of this series, and their history in modern Europe is treated in another part of this volume; it is necessary here only to look at those few aspects of the subject in England which have a direct bearing upon the origins of modern pagan witchcraft. The first is the very large amount of data, most collected by folklorists between 1870 and 1930. Although none was gained from an actual practitioner, there is plenty to reflect the experience of clients, and as the process of collecting continued, the people who supplied the information were recorded increasingly in their own idiom. There can have been very few aspects of the activities of self-professed or suspected workers of magic which went wholly unobserved.

It must be emphasized at once how numerous those workers were. Nineteenth-century England and Wales abounded with cunning folk, conjurers and magical healers, occupying a hierarchy ascending from the village charmer who had power over specific human and animal ailments to the regional magician, usually resident in a town, who countered hostile magic, predicted the future, and traced stolen goods. In 1816 the small Yorkshire seaport of Whitby had no less than eight 'wise women' as permanent residents (Gutch, 1901: 208). This means that in England and Wales at the present day there must be thousands, if not tens of thousands, of people who are descended, relatively recently, from workers of traditional magic. This figure would in turn be greatly expanded if it incorporated the different, and also substantial, category of individuals who did not offer such services but had none the less acquired well-established reputations for being witches.

Another specially pertinent feature of the subject is the total lack of a dividing line between popular and learned magic. Most Victorian 'cunning folk' and many of the charmers possessed books relevant to their craft, and often very important to it. Many were printed, and some in manuscript. The fate of these works is seldom recorded. Doubtless many were discarded and destroyed upon the deaths of the owners, but there remains the possibility that many more passed down through families, and that a large number of such texts were still owned and valued by people in early twentieth-century England. They still regularly come into the possession of occult booksellers, and I am aware of several manuscript collections of spells preserved (and treasured) in private hands at the present day.

This situation was the more likely in that the world of English popular magic adapted rather than atrophied during the twentieth century. Charmers of human and animal diseases were still practising in large numbers, known only to neighbours, in Devon and Cornwall during the 1950s and 1960s (Thomas, 1953; Brown, 1970). They probably still do, and there is no reason to suppose that these two counties are exceptional. The higher-grade cunning folk did disappear, but only to the extent that they metamorphosed into modern astrologers, Tarotreaders, and providers of a range of healing therapies grouped loosely under the name of 'natural medicine'. Many of these self-consciously linked themselves to the old tradition of popular magic. It is possible that there was a period in the early and mid-twentieth century in which the number of practitioners of occult remedies did contract absolutely, before a later revival; but this has yet to be proved.

It is also important in this context to consider the organisation of the traditional English witches and magicians. Apart from the very rare phenomenon of the cunning-man-and-son, the avowed practitioners worked alone; indeed, they were mostly in direct competition for clients, save in the occasional case that one would be paid for taking off curses supposedly directed by another. Individuals who were locally suspected of being malevolent witches, without making any formal profession of a connection with magic, seem generally to have been unusually isolated and antisocial people. There is a slight difference between accounts of real people and popular perceptions of the activities of the nameless and amorphous witch-figures upon whom general misfortunes could be projected. Some Sussex people had a belief that evil witches were all secretly in league with each other, although they would pretend no acquaintance in public (Simpson, 1973: 75–6). In Essex it was said that those on opposite sides of the river Crouch would visit each other, individually, sailing across in wash tubs or flying on hurdles (*The Times*, 27 January 1959). South of the river lay the isolated village of Canewdon, notorious in local opinion for always being the residence of six evil witches, whose identities were concealed. They were supposed to work separately, but to be subject to a single male wizard, a Master of the Witches (Maple, 1960a, b); such an arrangement was not thought to exist anywhere else.

Witches were reputed to be more sociable in the Celtic fringe. All those in westernmost Cornwall were said to feast together in the Trewa district every Midsummer Eve, in a counterpart to the bonfire parties traditionally held that night by the western Cornish (Hunt, 1881: 328). In the same area witches were rumoured to gather more irregularly at rocking stones, and a legend told of a hunter who happened upon a meeting of them in one of the enigmatic local Iron Age tunnels called fogous, and was driven mad (Bottrell, 1870: i.245–7; Courtney, 1890: 145). The folklorist Marie Trevelyan likewise recorded that in Wales they were reported to revel at prehistoric and Roman monuments, on rocky islets, and (above all) on mountain peaks; although there is little trace of such stories in other Welsh collections, and her work lies generally under some suspicion of fabrication (Trevelyan, 1909: 207–9). Manx and Scottish lore, however, is famously full of accounts of sociable witches.

This all makes the contrast with England the more striking. There families which had a generally disreputable local reputation were sometimes suspected of witchcraft as well; a well-recorded example is the Harts at Latchingdon in eastern Essex (Maple, 1962: 178). The Shropshire folklorist Charlotte Burne thought that certain outcrops might have been regarded as meeting places for witches, but the stories might instead have referred to spirits (Burne, 1888: 157–8). A man at Willoughton, Lincolnshire, asserted that there were witch 'conventions' at certain local landmarks, but it is not clear how eccentric his opinion was (Rudkin, 1934: 250). Leigh Common, at the north end of Dorset, was pointed out as such a meeting-place (Udal, 1922: 212). Finally, a millwright in the Cambridgeshire Fens claimed that in his youth he had spied upon a meeting of six witches in a derelict cottage, and described their bizarre costumes in elaborate detail; but he may have been telling a tall story (Porter, 1969: 167). This seems to be all, among the enormous collections of Victorian and Edwardian witch-lore, and even in these few cases the supposition seems to be that the witches were solitary operators who met up for social reasons rather than to work rituals. The Scottish word 'coven' was utterly unknown in nineteenth-century English popular culture.

Likewise, there is no sign among these records that witches of any kind venerated, or were believed to venerate, ancient deities. Cunning folk were usually assumed to be Christians, and many obviously were, with an unusual intensity of devotion. Where bad witches were reputedly associated with supernatural beings (which was in the minority of cases), these were usually imps in animal form (especially in East Anglia and Essex), larger demons, or the Devil himself. The images of these entities were thoroughly Christian, and there is no sign that pagan gods were hidden behind them. The sole possible exception consists of an identical story told of two different Shropshire witches, Priss Morgan and Betty Chidley, who when forced to take off destructive spells by saying 'God bless . . .' allegedly tried to say 'My God bless . . .'. The narrators of the tales, however, plainly identified this other god as Satan (Burne, 1888: 151–3)

There existed some traditions that witches and cunning folk passed on their powers, although these were localized and inconsistent. To an extent they were supposed to be hereditary, most famously by seventh children of seventh children, but this genealogical phenomenon rarely occurred (which was of course the whole point), and a talent for magic seems to have passed in blood no more securely than any other. The Harries or

Harris family of Cwrt y Cadno, Carmarthenshire, was an exceptional case where it did, for two generations Davies, 1911: 232–58). The most famous of all Essex wizards, 'Cunning' Murrell, produced 20 children, not one of whom seems to have inherited or learned his skill (Maple, 1960a: 36-43). The second most famous, George Pickingill of Canewdon, did sire a younger George who manifested some of his powers, but did little to practise them (Maple, 1960b: 249). The greatest cunning man of nine-teenth-century County Durham, Wrightson of Stokesley, tried without success to transmit his craft to his own son, and eventually left his books to a nephew who seemed more promising but turned out to be a hopeless failure (Brockie, 1886: 21-7). It seems possible, however, that the lowest grade of arcane specialist, the village charmers, had more success in transmitting skills down through families (Thomas, 1953; 304–5; Tongue, 1965; 76; Brown, 1970: 38–42;).

In south-eastern England, between the Wash and the Channel, there existed a strong tradition of a different sort, that dying witches had to pass on their power before they could be released from this life. In Sussex it was believed to transfer in spirit form from the old to the new owner's body, and there were tales told of the desperate efforts of witches in their death agony to find somebody willing to take it (Simpson, 1973: 76). An outlying example of this idea is represented by the story of one at Burnley, Lancashire, who breathed it into the mouth of a friend (Hardwick, 1872: 122-3). Some in the Cambridgeshire chalklands were thought to pass on their familiars in the more tangible form of white mice (Porter, 1969: 161). A dying cunning woman in an unnamed part of East Anglia was rumoured to have given her successor a kind of regalia, consisting of a fox-pelt collar, worn next to the skin with another pelt hanging from it in front (Newman, 1940: 36). The only thing resembling any sort of initiation ceremony of a new witch by an existing one occurs in a cautionary tale from Crosby, at the north end of Lincolnshire, where the old witch made her apprentice bend over to touch her toes and recite 'All that I 'ave a-tween me finger-tips and me toes I give to thee'. The point of the tale was that the girl cunningly added 'God Almighty', and so saved her soul (Rudkin, 1934: 262).

On Britain's western fringe there are traces of a tradition by which a hereditary magical power was passed more formally. Anglesey witches were supposed to hand on their skills from mother to daughter (Owen, 1887: 222-3). In the Isle of Man during the late nineteenth century, the famous Celticist Sir John Rhys found that the knowledge of charming ailments supposed to pass alternately between genders down generations; thus, father–daughter–grandson (Rhys, 1900: i.300). The same custom obtained among charmers in Cornwall and Devon in the twentieth century, and may have been an old one there also; although it is not recorded before then, and could even have been inspired by Rhys's famous book (Thomas, 1953; Brown, 1970).

It will become obvious from all the above that in many major respects, modern pagan witchcraft would have very little in common with the traditional magic to which its practitioners often looked as a precursor. The two would, however, be linked in two important ways. First, the old-style magical craft would bequeath to the new pagan religion a mass of natural lore, spells and charms, which would be incorporated into its operative functions. Second, the personnel of the new religion sometimes themselves belonged to families which had practised these techniques, and so represented a human bridge between the two. They would unite this operative magic with a Masonic system of organization and initiation, and a language and structure of religious belief which derived from yet another source, and which must now be considered in turn.

THE THOUGHT-WORLD OF MODERN PAGANISM

There were four different languages employed when talking about paganism in nineteenth-century Europe. One assumed it to be a religion of savages, characterized by animal and human sacrifice and a superstitious dread of idols; it was used mainly to describe tribal beliefs and some Hindu traditions in the contemporary world, but these were commonly projected back onto prehistoric Europeans. In addition, it was often applied to the temple-based religions of the ancient Near East and North Africa. This language strengthened during the century, under the impact of reports generated by increasing European missionary work in the tropics, and evolutionary theory. The latter made it easy to portray this brutish paganism as the lowest form of religion, from which European humanity had ascended as part of a general progression of knowledge and manners, aided (for the pious) by divine revelation. The second language did not conflict with the first, but represented a different emphasis within the same picture, by concentrating instead upon the most developed form of European paganism before the triumph of Christianity. This was the religious world of classical Greece and Rome, with its Olympian deities which had been so firmly built into the familiar images of European culture. The traditional admiration of western Europeans for classical civilization only strengthened in the eighteenth and nineteenth centuries, and made it impossible to regard its deities and festivals with the contempt manifested towards other polytheist systems. Instead, they were treated as a religion which was inferior only to Christianity itself, and which had possessed virtues which had been incorporated into Christian culture, a mixture which represented the most perfect of all systems of belief.

These were attitudes held by the overwhelming majority of Europeans during the nineteenth century; but during that century they came to be accompanied by two others, which were essentially languages of disaffected intellectuals and which posed challenges to the first two. One was that of Theosophy, and embodied the principle that behind all the more sophisticated systems of religious belief recorded in the world lay an original body of common wisdom, more ancient than and superior to all. This, ran the argument of Theosophists, could now be recovered, by a process of comparative study enhanced by renewed contact with superhuman intelligences. The other radical language was one which was explicitly or implicitly hostile to Christianity. It characterized the religions of pagan Greece and Rome as inherently superior, at once more in touch with the natural world and with human nature; joyous, liberationist and life-affirming. This was to be the discourse of modern pagan witchcraft.

It appeared in Germany at the end of the eighteenth century, as one result of the fusion of that idealization of classical Greece and nostalgia for a vanished past which were hallmarks of the German literature of the time. In March 1788 it was given its first full expression, in Johann von Schiller's poem 'The Gods of Greece', an impassioned lament for a lost pagan fairyland, in which everyday sights had been invested with divinity, and happy and serene deities made objects of adoration. This theme was taken up, with equal feeling, by followers of Schiller such as Hölderlin. It did not, however, remain a major one in Continental Europe. In its German birthplace it suffered from the general waning of interest in Greek and Roman cultural models, while French dissident intellectuals preferred an all-out anti-clericalism and a scepticism which flirted with blasphemy and Satanism. Only occasionally did it resurface in these countries during the nineteenth century; but in England it found a new homeland, a reflection both of the greater secularity of English culture and of its increasing preoccupation with rural images.

It was taken up there at once by virtually all of the Romantic poets. Wordsworth, in 'The World Is Too Much With Us', and Byron, in 'Aristomenes' both wrote verse which echoed the sentiments of Schiller. More radical in its employment of them was the group which gathered in 1815–16 about the essayist Leigh Hunt, and included Keats and Shelley. All three writers felt that Christianity had proved inadequate to the spiritual needs of the age, and looked to a selective revival of classical paganism to provide a happier, more beautiful, and more positive form of religion, which celebrated the world. All three propagated this idea in their works. At times the activities of Hunt and his friends extended to practical gestures of worship, such as hanging up of garlands and other acts of consecration in places of natural loveliness. How literally any of them believed in the existence of the old deities is difficult to say – they retained a vague Platonic faith in a single Great Spirit and Creator – but they certainly treated them as potent symbolic forces (Barnard, 1937; Scott, 1943: 43–4; Scott, 1944: 61; Ryan, 1976).

Such sentiments continued to be expressed through the middle of the century. In 1844 Elizabeth Barrett Browning was sufficiently incensed by continuing admiration in England for Schiller's poem to write a Christian response, 'The Dead Pan', against the 'vain false gods of Hellas'. One of those who was deaf to her call was George Meredith, who between 1851 and 1901 wrote a long series of poems developing the idea that humanity needed to be reconciled with 'Great Nature' in order to be complete once again. He employed classical deities as aspects of this being. Another was Algernon Swinburne, who published two volumes of verse in the mid-1860s which renewed the arguments of the Hunt circle, assailing Christianity for its morbidity and praising the life-affirming qualities of the old religions. Such sentiments were expressed by lesser writers of the period such as James Thomson, Roden Noel and Lord de Tabley.

By the late Victorian period, the word 'pagan' had become laden with such associations. Thomas Hardy used it in passing three times in his novel *The Return of the Native*, in each case to evoke, without need of gloss or explanation, a sense of self-indulgent liberation and renewal of contact with an archaic life-force. The same language runs through other poems and novels of the 1870s and 1880s. As the century drew to a close it became more self-consciously aggressive. In 1889 the socialist mystic Edward Carpenter called for a return of the cosmic consciousness' of 'the old religions' to modern Man: 'on the high tops once more gathering he will celebrate with naked dances the glory of the human form and the great processions of the stars, or greet the bright horn of the young moon' (Carpenter, 1889: 44–7). The following year W. E. Henley founded *The National Observer*, a magazine which ran for half a decade and was designed to oppose 'Puritanism, Labour, and Humbug'. One antidote proposed by contributors was a restoration of the antique worship of nature and realization of the animal side of humanity; among them was the young Kenneth Grahame, who gathered his articles into a book brought out in 1893 under the title of *Pagan Papers*. The previous year William Sharp had launched a *Pagan Review*, writing the whole of the first issue himself, under the motto 'Sic Transit Gloria Grundi'. True to this, the contents were mainly dedicated to a celebration of eroticism, of various kinds, but Sharp gave the new connotation of paganism a further twist by declaring that it also stood for 'a true copartnership' between the sexes. More soberly, at the end of the decade the classicist Lowes Dickinson suggested in *The Independent Review* that ancient Greek religion had been 'the ideal of a full and satisfied humanity' and thus a revival of it was 'fitted for a new age'.

All this produced some hostile reactions, which themselves were evidence of how seriously observers could take these statements. In 1891 W.F. Barry coined the expression 'neopaganism', summing it up as a reputed wisdom which 'overcomes death with the exuberance of eternal nature, all rhythm and harmonious evolution, a great unceasing festival of flowers and lights and easy sensuous love.' He went on to assert traditional Christian teachings against it, and to try to expose it as a corrupting, negative, creed (Barry, 1891). His term was used in *Punch* in 1894 to attack the first issue of the magazine which was to be the most famous expression of Fin de Siècle British decadence, *The Yellow Book*. It was employed later by another Christian apologist, G.K. Chesterton, in reply to Dickinson's article. Chesterton drew a distinction between the more serious and formidable proponents of a new paganism, such as Dickinson himself, and the more common expression of it, as an evocation of a classical never-never land in which people 'were continually crowning themselves with flowers and dancing about in an irresponsible state . . . above all things inebriate and lawless'. The former, he suggested, had to be answered from theology and history, while the latter could be dismissed with ridicule (Chesterton, 1905: 153–70).

Much of the self-confidence of the 'pagan' writing of the early 1890s was destroyed, along with so much of the Aesthetic Movement to which it was linked, by the fall of Oscar Wilde whose poetry had itself been one expression of the genre. What followed, however, was not so much a decline as a more subdued and thoughtful continuation. Dickinson's work was an example, and in many ways the less provocative and flamboyant use of this language of paganism made it all the more effective and ingrained in British culture. During the first four decades of the twentieth century it is found in works as different as the novels of E. M. Forster and D. H. Lawrence, the popular short stories of Algernon Blackwood, H. J. Massingham's books about the English countryside, and the verse of minor poets such as Victor Neuburg, James Elroy Flecker, Geoffrey Sefton and Teresa Hooley. In most cases it functioned as a means of mere escapism, but employed so powerfully as to suggest a genuinely alternative way of looking at nature, divinity, gender roles and sexuality. Wicca was to represent a means of trying to put it into practice; and in doing so it adopted the particular deities which this literary 'neopaganism' had identified as especially important. It is time to consider these.

THE GODDESS AND GOD OF MODERN PAGANISM

The deities most commonly and fervently revered in the classical ancient world were those concerned with aspects of civilization and society; there were certainly others associated with aspects of wild nature, but these were represented by conspicuously fewer temples, shrines, dedications and literary references. The pattern obtains in early Celtic literature, and it holds good for most of the Christian period, when the old goddesses and gods had become allegorical or mythical figures. A systematic survey of English poetry written between 1300 and 1800 reveals that the favourite goddess was Venus, patroness of love, followed by Diana, representing female chastity and (much more rarely) hunting, then Minerva, for wisdom, and Juno, symbol of queenliness. The favourite male deity was Jupiter, the pattern for rulers, followed by Neptune, patron of sailors, Mercury, sponsor of education and communication, and Vulcan, for smiths and metalworkers (Smith, 1984). A more impressionistic look at intellectual works, between the twelfth and sixteenth centuries, shows Minerva (not suprisingly) to be apostrophized most often; she was hailed with equal dramatic eloquence by Pierre Abelard, Christine de Pisan and Giordano Bruno. Urban statuary in western Europe, from the Renaissance to the nineteenth century, seems most commonly to represent her, as a civic goddess, plus Jupiter, Mercury and Apollo.

There were slight traces of alternative traditions. In one classical text, the *Metamorphoses* of Apuleius which dates from near the end of the pagan period, the female deity was declared to be the embodiment of all other goddesses, and represented by the moon and the natural world. This, combined with Neo-Platonism, produced a concept in a few seventeenth-century hermetic works, of a female figure identified with the starry heaven, who stood between God and the earth, and acted as a world soul. This was, however, by definition a tradition limited to a handful of specialists, notably Robert Fludd and Athanasius Kircher. It is more relevant to our present interests that the ancient Greeks spoke of the earth as being feminine in gender and the sky as masculine. As most western science was based ultimately upon Greek thought, this language became embedded in it. It was developed further in early–modern Europe, where the scientists were virtually all male and easily adopted an imagery of male investigation and exploitation of a female natural world (Merchant, 1980). Conversely, from the high medieval period a few intellectuals and poets employed a female figure as an allegory of nature; the most famous was Geoffrey Chaucer, who cited as his source for the idea the twelfth-century scholar Alanus de Insulis. Like the 'world soul', however, she was a rarity compared with the more familiar, 'civilized', goddesses.

This pattern was completely reversed by the Romantic Movement, one aspect of which was a self-conscious reaction to the mindset of early modern scientific rationalism. It included an exaltation of the natural and irrational, those qualities which scientific language had come to identify as 'feminine'. This accompanied a recognition that humanity could at last be suffering from too much civilization. For the first time in European history, mountains were seen as beautiful instead of frightening, and wild nature began to be valued over farms and cities, the night over the day, and the moon over the sun. These impulses first strongly manifested themselves in the late eighteenth century, and intensified during the nineteenth, as urbanization and industrialization spread across Europe. They were especially powerful in Britain, where both processes began earlier, and advanced more rapidly, than elsewhere (Nicolson, 1959; Thomas, 1983; and sources cited in these).

The impact upon the poetic imagination is very clear. Between 1800 and 1940 Venus and Diana (or Artemis) were still the two favourites. Juno, however, almost vanished, and after 1830 so did Minerva. They were replaced by Proserpine, as goddess of the changing seasons, and Ceres or Demeter, the Corn Mother. A reading of the texts, moreover, discloses a more dramatic alteration. Venus is now often related to the woods or the sea, while Diana is no longer primarily a symbol of chastity or of hunting but (overwhelmingly) of the moon, the greenwood or wild animals. Furthermore, the importance of Venus depended upon incidental references and metaphors. When a goddess was made the major figure of a poem, it was Diana who ruled, or a nameless female deity of moonlight or of the natural world. Among the gods, likewise, the supremacy of Jupiter came to an end, and references to Neptune fell off even more strikingly; indeed, most of the classical male deities became less popular with poets, save for two dramatic exceptions. One was Apollo, the favourite god of the early Romantics, who saw him both as patron of poetry and male sovereign of nature in his capacity as solar deity. After 1830, however, his popularity also atrophied, to be overtaken by a god who had also been thrust to prominence by the Romantics and who continued to attract attention all through the nineteenth century until he became the most frequently cited male deity in the whole canon of English literature. He was the one most intimately associated with the wild, disturbing and exciting aspects of nature: Pan (Smith, 1984, and sources there; Merivale, 1969: 118–19).

The development of the two deity figures proceeded in parallel, and that of the goddess was more complex as it drew on no single classical character. Keats repeatedly apostrophized the moon as a female deity, and made her the subject of his first long and ambitious work, *Endymion*. Shelley preferred the image of Mother Earth, as in his 'Song of Proserpine.' The identification of the divine feminine with the moon became ever firmer in subsequent decades. In 1831 the librettist of the century's most famous drama about Druids, Vincenzo Bellini's opera *Norma*, has the heroine stand in sacred grove and invoke a goddess in that form, in preference to the sun traditionally venerated by Druids. More remarkable still is the case of Charlotte Bronte, who was intimately associated with Anglican Christianity in her upbringing, home life and marital partner. She made her own most famous heroine, Jane Eyre, contemplate going abroad as a missionary. Jane operates emotionally, however, within a cosmology by which a single supreme god has created Nature to be a divine mother to living things. It is to this mother (and not to Jesus) that Jane turns for comfort when in trouble, and who appears to her out of the moon in a dream-vision, to give her advice. It never seems to have occurred to Bronte that this view of divinity was not actually Christianity.

Jane Eyre came out in 1847, and in that decade another celebrated writer made the union of moon-goddess with nature-goddess, when Robert Browning wrote his poem 'Artemis Prologizes'. The next stage in the evolution of the image was to eliminate the creator god, leaving the composite goddess as the single mighty source of all being. Swinburne took this in 1867, giving resounding voice to this deity under the name of a Germanic earth-goddess, in his poem 'Hertha'. There the mighty creatrix of later feminist paganism appeared fully formed. The precise form which she was to take in Wicca, however, was yet to appear, and did so through a route which although profoundly influenced by creative literature was qualitatively different from it: academic history and archaeology.

The beginning of the process lay, once again, in Germany at the end of the eighteenth century, as one contribution to a debate over the nature of prehistoric religion. Put crudely, this took place between those who suggested that primitive religious belief was a superstitious compound of ignorance and fear, and those who viewed it as an embodiment of sublime truths, which had degenerated and been forgotten among modern tribal peoples. The former stance was taken most prominently by the French *philosophes*, the latter by the German Romantics, especially Herder, Tiecke and the Schlegels. Most important of those truths, according to this latter school, was a monotheism linked to an instinctual understanding of the rhythms of nature and of human life. Given the increasing power of the identification of nature with female divinity, it is not surprising to find that in 1849 a German classicist, Eduard Gerhard, advanced the novel suggestion that behind the various goddesses of classical Greece had stood a single great one, venerated before history began (Gerhard, 1849: 103).

In the second half of the century more and more scholars, in Germany, France and Britain, began to adopt this idea, although it remained (and remains) controversial for lack of any conclusive evidence (Ucko, 1968: 409–12). One difficulty with it was the need to incorporate within a single ancestral figure historical goddesses as different as those who represented virginity and those who stood for sexuality or motherhood. A solution was proposed in 1903 by a Cambridge classicist, Jane Ellen Harrison; that as goddess-forms in the historic period sometimes appeared in threes (such as the Fates and the Graces), the prehistoric Great Goddess had been venerated in three aspects, the first two being Maiden and Mother. She did not name the third (Harrison, 1903: 257–322). A parallel classification was suggested by Sir James Frazer, in the successive editions between 1890 and 1922 of his enormously popular work, *The Golden Bough*. This postulated the former existence of a single fertility goddess responsible for cereal agriculture, who was later personified, according to region, as a Maiden, a Mother or an Old Wife.

By the Edwardian period, therefore, English literary culture had long been used to a broad notion that the divine feminine should be related to the night sky and to the natural world. By then, also, this was being associated with another notion, that it should be conceived of as a single mighty, and very ancient, goddess. It would be easy, but unnecessary, to explore its history further in early twentieth-century literature; to examine, for example, George Russell's poetry about Mother Earth, or D. H. Lawrence's changing relationship with the concept of Woman as Magna Mater, symbolized by the moon, in his successive works. It would be almost as straightforward a task to document the growing consensus among professional prehistorians that Neolithic Europe had venerated a Great Goddess, which reached its apogee in the 1950s and caused psychologists, and especially Jungians, to declare such a figure to be an archetype of the collective unconscious. Within this broad concept, there was a more precise one, of a goddess in three aspects. This was to be given its final refinement in 1946 by Robert Graves's poetic reverie *The White Goddess*, which combined the deities of Harrison and Frazer, to produce a triple female divinity in the aspects of Maiden, Mother and Crone, each corresponding to a phase of the moon. For present purposes, however, it is enough to note that by the 1920s the female deity of Wicca was already formed in the English consciousness.

Unlike the goddess-image, that of Pan has already been the subject of a full-length academic study (Merivale, 1969). Its development was a simpler matter, in that the ancient world had bequeathed it to the modern imagination in an already complete form. Nonetheless, its reappearance was dramatic, and it did undergo certain alterations of emphasis. Between the time of Milton and that of Wordsworth, the goat-foot god did not feature in a single work of English literature by a major author. With Wordsworth, however, he resurfaced in a form reproduced by the other Romantic poets, and in which he was to be celebrated in verse and prose for the next 150 years; as the embodiment of an idealized past of rural tranquillity, suffused into the English landscape. As such, he was also hailed by Keats, Shelley, Hunt, Byron, William Hazlitt, Swinburne, Matthew Arnold, Roden Noel, Lord de Tabley, Wilde, Flecker, John Cowper Powys, Walter de la Mare, Gordon Bottomley, Geoffrey

Sephton, Eleanor Farjeon, and a host of poetasters whose verses never rose above magazine publication. Whereas to the early Romantics he was still one deity among several, between 1895 and 1914 he was, in Patricia Merivale's words, 'the one fashionable subject on which every minor poet thought that he could turn out a ditty' (Merivale, 1969: 118). This concept of the god was also expressed notably between 1880 and 1930 in the prose fiction of Robert Louis Stevenson, Kenneth Grahame, E. M. Forster, Maurice Hewlett and Lord Dunsany.

During this same period in which the benevolent, rural, Pan became such a cliche, other aspects of the god were expressed. Keats, Leigh Hunt and Hazlitt had already, in the 1810s, suggested that he was the fount of poetic inspiration (Hazlitt, 1931: vi.192; Merivale, 1969: 65–6;). In 1910 Richard le Gallienne powerfully restated this idea in his *Attitudes and Avowals*, with the gloss that as poets were beyond conventional morality and constraints, they required a deity who shared that characteristic. In asserting this, he was giving expression to that aggressively neo-pagan language which has been described as one product of the Fin de Siècle, and in which Pan was turned into a more exciting and disturbing deity than the embodiment of rural nostalgia. This dangerous, radical, Pan, the personification of the animal aspect of humanity, was given artistic form in the drawings of Aubrey Beardsley. As a cathartic force, shattering the prison of bourgeois conformity, he was celebrated in E.M. Forster's first publication, *The Story of a Panic* (1902), and then predictably, at several points in the work of D.H. Lawrence. He liberated an entire English village in Lord Dunsany's novel *The Blessing of Pan* (1927), while in the preface to Dion Fortune's *The Goat Foot God* (1936), he is destined to 'wake up the living dead' of contemporary Britain.

What he could awake most spectacularly, of course, was sexuality, and in particular those kinds of it which had been either repressed or proscribed. Into the former category could fall the female libido, and Somerset Maugham's short story *Cakes and Ale* (1930) could look back to the time around 1900 when 'literary ladies in Surrey, nymphs of an industrial age, mysteriously surrendered their virginity to his rough embrace.' One female writer who evoked this aspect of the god with especial fervour, and beauty, was Teresa Hooley, whose 'Prayer to Pan' may stand as an exemplar of the genre.

He was also, however, the deity of forbidden, which in this context meant gay, sex. Victor Neuburg and Aleister Crowley, themselves lovers, produced a pair of poems between 1910 and 1914, 'The Triumph of Pan' and 'Hymn to Pan', which remain literary monuments to homosexuality and bisexuality respectively. It is Pan who is invoked by a schoolboy in Forrest Reid's novel *The Garden God* (1905), as he struggles successfully to come to terms with his love for a male friend. The same decade witnessed a crueller and more subtle employment of Pan in a gay ideology, by Hector Munro ('Saki') in his short story 'The Music on the Hill'; the deity causes a stag to gore to death a forceful and Philistine woman who has persuaded a contented bachelor into marriage with her.

More subtle still, and more profoundly significant, was an expression of E. M. Forster's about his hero Maurice, in the novel of that name which he wrote in 1913–14 as a means of acknowledging his own homosexuality. Having committed himself firmly to living out the truth of his sexual orientation, Maurice feels detached from all the rest of the Londoners about him; instead he now realizes that he is at one with 'the forests and the night'. Those domains were the traditional Otherworlds of the civilized imagination; they were precisely the realms of the two pagan deity forms which had emerged most powerfully in the English literary imagination by the early twentieth century; the horned god of the countryside and the wild woods, and the goddess associated with the green earth and the white moon among the stars.

ROMANTIC FOLKLORE

By the early twentieth century, also, the language of paganism as a force for positive renewal, and the images of the two deities, were starting to combine with another cultural development: a set of attitudes to the English countryside and to rural folk customs. The intellectual framework for these was constructed as one of the products of Victorian rationalism, a particular response to the new sciences of geology and palaeontology and the new theory of the evolution of species which was associated with them. Applied to the development of human culture, the geological model suggested that the minds of all humans worked in essentially the same way, but had developed at different rates, according to culture and class, along the same orderly and linear track. If this were true, then it was possible to treat the customs of tribal peoples and of European peasants alike as cultural fossils, representing earlier stages in the evolution of civilized societies, and by a comparative study of them to construct a general theory of religious development for the human race.

This approach to the history of religion was first fully expounded in England in the 1870s and 1880s by Sir Edward Tylor. The most striking and influential early application of it, however, was made between 1860 and 1880 by the German scholar, Wilhelm Mannhardt, who was himself inspired by a new interest in folk culture which had been another hallmark of the Romantic movement in Germany and was sustained by the quest of nineteenth-century German intellectuals for a unifying Germanic iden- tity. Mannhardt made the first systematic collection of contemporary peasant customs, and concluded that they were survivals of pagan rites primarily intended to ensure the fertility of humans, livestockand fields and based upon the concept of animating vegetation spirits.

These approaches promised both to make possible the construction of a history of world religion, even for places and times which had left no written records, and to rescue the study of European folklore from mere antiquarianism and turn it into something like a scientific discipline. The latter was the avowed aim of Britain's Folk-Lore Society, founded in 1878, and of its leaders in the next two decades, such as Sir Lawrence Gomme, Andrew Lang, Edwin Sidney Hartland, Edward Clodd and Alfred Nutt. Its most ambitious and best-known expression, however, was to be the work of a Cambridge don who was only tangentially connected with the Society: Sir James Frazer's *The Golden Bough* which, as said above, went through successive editions between 1890 and 1922. Its basic thesis was that primitive religion had been based largely upon the veneration of Mannhardt's dying and returning spirit of vegetation, personified as a god and identified with human kings, who were killed either after a set term or when their powers waned. The result was not only an important theoretical structure, but a vast compendium of human ritual practices, often lurid. Frazer intended it from the first to reach the largest possible audience, writing in a vivid and accessible style and having it packaged in an attractive format.

These developments have been well studied, notably by John Burrow, Robert Ackerman and Gillian Bennett (Burrow, 1966; Ackerman, 1987; Bennett, 1994). The same scholars have noted that the impulse which drove Tylor and Frazer was a hostility to all forms of religious belief and practice, which they hoped to discredit as part of the development of a wiser and more rational society. Frazer's attempt to prove the former existence of a universal ancient pagan mythology of a dying and resurrecting god, in particular, struck deliberately at the central claims of Christianity. This recent research has also delineated very well the failure of the intellectual enterprise of which these writers had formed part. Between 1900 and 1930 both anthropologists and historians of religion lost faith in the notion of folk practices as authentic survivals and in the method of equating them with beliefs and customs in modern tribal societies, regardless of context. Folklore studies failed to establish themselves as an academic discipline, falling through a gap between the emerging sciences of anthropology and archaeology.

Gillian Bennett has also noted, however, that what the founders of the Folk-Lore Society had characterized as a rational and objective enterprise was coloured from the start by one of the most powerful cultural forces of the time: a romantic and nostalgic cult of rural England (Bennett, 1993). The origins of this may be expressed in a simple equation – in 1810 20 per cent of the English lived in towns, and by 1910 only 20 per cent did not. They had become the first modern nation to be predominantly urbanized and industrialized, the balance tipping in the 1850s. After then it seemed a real possibility that the whole land would turn into one vast smoking conurbation, and from the 1870s an almost hysterical celebration and veneration of the countryside began by way of reaction, gaining strength well into the twentieth century; a phenomenon now well studied, by Raymond Williams, Martin Wiener, Jan Marsh and Alun Howkins (Williams, 1973; Wiener, 1981; Marsh, 1982; Howkins, 1986). It was not simply that rural settings were regarded as being more beautiful and healthy than those of the town, but that their people were portrayed, for the first time, as having a superior wisdom, founded upon generations of living in close contact with nature and inheriting a cumulative hidden knowledge. Their culture was viewed as something static and immemorial, a comforting force of resistance to the dramatic and unsettling changes of the century.

This theme of continuity and timeless heritage was sounded with even greater strength by American visitors to England, seeking tap-roots for their own even more dynamic and novel civilization. It was already a central aspect of the work of Washington Irving, in the 1810s and 1820s. By the time that Nathaniel Hawthorne introduced an American readership to *Our Old Home* in 1890 it was long a commonplace, but no less potent for that: this England was 'fossilized in its greenest leaf' and 'hoary antiquity', a country in which

> the man who died yesterday or ever so long ago walks the village street today, and chooses the same wife that he married a hundred years ago since, and must be buried again tomorrow under the same kindred dust that has already covered him half a score of times.

Thomas Hardy, Rudyard Kipling and Kenneth Grahame were probably the most celebrated of scores of English counterparts to inoculate the reading public with the same sense, of the English countryside as an organic growth of experience and tradition, changing only in outward forms.

Deep in this humus lay the old religions, which some authors had come to view as having been possessed of virtues different in kind from, and perhaps superior to, those of Christianity. Those authors included prominent members of the early Folk-Lore Society. In 1894 its president, Lawrence Gomme, informed his colleagues that 'there is sometimes more humanity in a touch of genuine paganism than in some of the platitudes that at present do duty for higher things'. His successor, Edward Clodd, drew their attention to 'the pagan foundation which . . . upholds the structures of classical and Christian faiths'. Gomme was convinced that the latter structures were by comparison relatively fragile and recent creations, asserting that even as late as the seventeenth century English commoners had remained essentially pagan, Christianity being the religion of the elite (Gomme, 1892, 1894; Clodd, 1896). Like all the early folklorists, he undertook no actual research into social history; but then medieval popular religion barely began to be an area of systematic research until the 1970s. Earlier historians of the medieval English Church, such as the highly respected Geoffrey Coulton, writing in the 1920s, tended instead to confine their attention to bishops, councils and monasteries, and to adopt unquestioningly the model for society presented by the folklorists; of the old religion surviving among the populace beneath a veneer of Christianity (Coulton, 1923: i.179–83). The equally prestigious scholar of the medieval and Tudor English theatre, Sir Edmund Chambers, built the notion that rural customs were authentic survivals of pagan ritual into a succession of books between 1903 and 1933.

The same set of concepts was swallowed whole by the man who proved to be the principal influence behind the revival in English folk dances; the London music teacher, Cecil Sharp. His avowed mission was to rescue the urban working class from what he thought to be the vulgarity and tawdriness of their recently evolved culture, by restoring to it the ancestral songs and dances of the countryside. Following Frazer and Chambers, he firmly believed the latter to be descended directly from ancient fertility rites, and when collecting them in the 1900s and 1910s he added a new aspect to the evolving myth of rural England: that of the village 'tradition'. This was the assumption that certain distinctive forms of dance had descended within closed communities of English country people, from time immemorial to the present. He was wrong upon this last point, as he was upon the larger one of pagan origins for the dances concerned; but he made such beliefs integral to the work of the early twentieth-century English Folk Dance and Song Society (Sharp, 1912–24; Strangways, 1933; Hutton, 1996: 262–76, 295–303).

One of the better known ironies of the history of ideas is that just as professional enthusiasm for *The Golden Bough* collapsed, in the 1920s, the abridged edition made it a popular best-seller. Frazer's striking images influenced the work of T. S. Eliot, Ezra Pound, W. B. Yeats, Edith Sitwell, Robert Graves, E. M. Forster, D. H. Lawrence, and a host of lesser creative writers. They became part of the Western popular consciousness. Like Nietzsche and Freud, Frazer seemed to have revealed the savagery which lay beneath the surface of civilization and of reason (Fraser, 1990; Beard, 1992). Some found that apparent revelation disturbing, and some exhilarating.

The failure of folklore studies to establish themselves as a respectable academic discipline had a parallel effect, of releasing them into the hands of Frazer's devotees. From the 1920s until the 1970s the doctrine that modern customs were living fossils from pagan antiquity dominated the field. Its methodology consisted of collecting information upon such customs as they existed in the present or the recent past, and then collating it in order to reconstruct the primeval beliefs or activities from which they were derived. None of the people engaged in this work attempted to consult local historical records to trace the evolution of these activities over time; it was much more exciting to observe them in the field, or to talk to elderly people about their memories of them, and then to let the romantic imagination play over the data. The presumed wisdom of the common countryfolk counted for nothing when it came to interpretation, the folklorists cheerfully disregarding current contexts or explanations with the assumption that only their trained expertise could retrieve the original, and 'true', significance of customs.

Scholars now know that the character of Father Christmas arose out of disputes over the value of the festival in the 1610s, but to Lady Gomme, in 1929, he was 'obviously' a former pagan god. It now appears that the Hobby Horse dance at Padstow, in Cornwall, is an amalgam of different traditions put together since the late eighteenth century, but to Mary Macleod Banks, in 1931, it was 'obviously' descended from a pagan ritual of marriage between earth and sky. The late medieval foliate heads carved in churches are now known to have nothing to do with the foliage-covered figure dancing in May Day processions, who appeared in the nineteenth century; but to Lady Raglan, in 1939, they were 'obviously' representations of the same ancient vegetation spirit, 'The Green Man'. The northern English sword dance now appears to be another inheritance from the eighteenth century, but to Violet Alford, in 1962, it was 'obviously' a blend of a Neolithic rite to waken the sleeping earth with a Bronze Age one to confer manhood (Hutton, 1996: 70–94, 117–19, 241–3). The 1930s was an especially febrile decade for such interpretations; in 1937 another presidential address to the Folk-Lore Society, by S. H. Hooke, suggested that pancake-tossing had been a ceremony to make crops grow, that Shrovetide football had started as a ritual struggle between light and dark, and that Mother's Day was rooted in the worship of the prehistoric Corn Mother (Hooke, 1937). As all of these writers presented their interpretations as scientific deductions, the reason for their instinctual attraction to such associations can only be inferred, but it is clear that they found something inherently fascinating in the primeval fantasy-world which they were constructing under the guise of scholarship.

In a very real sense, Wicca was to come directly out of the Folk-Lore Society, the framework for it being laid out by one member of the society and then given life by another. That framework consisted of an apparently proven historical link between paganism and Witchcraft, which completed the cultulral context from which a new religion would arise.

THE MYTH OF PAGAN WITCHCRAFT

As the earlier contributions to this series have made clear, by the end of the eighteenth century educated opinion in Europe had virtually ceased to believe in the reality of acts of witchcraft. Such a change made the early modern trials and executions appear to have been a senseless series of atrocities, born of superstition and obscurantism, and that is how they were portrayed by the writers of the Enlightenment. As such, they represented a superb weapon with which to castigate the old order in Church and state. This liberal, rationalist, discourse became the dominant one in European and American academe until the 1960s; the ending of the trials for witchcraft was repeatedly cited as one of the supreme triumphs of reason and science over the ancient evils of humanity.

There was, however, an alternative scholarly tradition, which first appeared, like so many of the cultural currents in this story, in Germany. It was not, however, a product of the Romantic movement so much as of that period of reaction which followed the fall of the Napoleonic Empire. Two scholars working under authoritarian rulers, Karl-Ernst Jarcke at Berlin in 1828 and Franz-Josef Mone at Baden in 1839, proposed that the victims of the trials had in fact been practising a surviving pagan religion (Jarcke, 1828: 450; Mone, 1839: 271–5, 441–5). If this theory was correct, then it made witch persecution rational, and perhaps even excusable. Mone may have arrived at it independently of Jarcke, and indeed it seems to have been in the air of Germany at this time; in 1832 Felix Mendelssohn's choral work *Die Erste Walpurgisnacht* portrayed a group of medieval pagans who frighten off Christians trying to disrupt their traditional May Eve festivities by pretending to be witches. Jacob Grimm's *Teutonic Mythology*, written in 1844, incorporated a 'softer' version of it, by suggesting that behind the early modern stereotype of the witch lay memories of pagan beliefs and rites, and an ancient tradition of magic-wielding women (Grimm, 1883: iii.1044–93).

This idea had the potential to deprive liberalism of one of its favourite means of discrediting the confessional state, and invited a response. It was provided resoundingly by the Frenchman Jules Michelet, one of the century's great radical historians. He was a bitter enemy of the Roman Catholic Church and the aristocracy, an unqualified admirer of the Renaissance and the French Revolution, and an author of vivid and very popular books. He knew virtually nothing of medieval social history except romances and fairy tales, and almost all his information upon witch trials was taken from pamphlets. This did not inhibit him at all. In 1862 he brought out *La Sorcière*, a best-seller which asserted that the pagan religion of the witches had been the repository of popular liberties all through the tyranny of the Middle Ages. In his fantasy of it, it was feminist, always led by priestesses, and also nature-loving, joyful, democratic and pacifist. Michelet, indeed, went further than even the most uninhibited modern pagan writer, by claiming that the Renaissance had been produced by the natural wisdom of the witches working its way upward to artists and writers. After *La Sorcière* it might be said that Wicca was a religion waiting to be re-enacted, but the book appeared too early, and in the wrong country, to act as a direct inspiration. French intellectuals were both too irreligious and lacked an admiration of the rural world.

Michelet's influence in this respect, therefore, was to be more potent when filtered through writers in English. One of these was the American adventurer Charles Godfrey Leland who, after many travels, came to settle in Italy and publish a succession of works upon Tuscan folklore. Initially, these included wholly traditional tales of malefic witchcraft and of witches' revels, although apparently not without the habit of embroidery and rewriting which marred Leland's reputation in the eyes of more scholarly folklorists (Powell, 1903). In 1899, however, he published a work of quite a different, indeed unique, sort, *Aradia*, which purported to print the gospel of the Italian branch of the old pagan witch religion, given to him by one of its last representatives. Its debt to Michelet was explicit, as was its political purpose; to counter what Leland took to be the unhealthy contemporary nostalgia for the Middle Ages, and to expose them again as a time of repression in which the witches featured as freedom-fighters. In one major respect, his text was still more feminist than that of the Frenchman, for the deity of his vision of the religion was a goddess, Diana, who was both associated with witches by some medieval writers and with the ideal pagan female deity of the nineteenth century. No historian of medieval or early modern Italy has ever found a context for this 'gospel' or accepted it as genuine.

Leland was only the most colourful of a trio of writers in English who took up the idea of a witch religion during the 1890s. Another was the eminently respectable Sir Lawrence Gomme, whose presidency of the Folk-Lore Society has already been mentioned. In 1893 he mispresented Grimm as having demonstrated the pagan character of traditional European witchcraft, and soared off into the imaginative stratosphere to present readers with a picture of an initiatory faith which had carried on teaching the secrets of Druidry. To Gomme, the witch was the medieval and early modern successor of the Druid priestess (Gomme, 1893: 48–57). Five years later a professor of mathematics in London, Karl Pearson, took a similar intellectual holiday by opining that witches had been the adherents of a cult of the Great Mother Goddess surviving from prehistoric matriarchy. He suggested that the purpose of its rituals had been to promote fertility and that Joan of Arc had been one of its leaders. Although generally hostile to the religion which he portrayed, he concluded by proposing that a recognition of its former existence would be beneficial in improving the status of women in the modern world (Pearson, 1897: ii.1–50).

What all these portraits lacked was a systematic basis in research conducted into the early modern trial records, and this was apparently provided between 1917 and 1921, in a book and series of articles by Margaret Alice Murray. She was already distinguished as an Egyptologist, and that remained the mainstay of her career. For present purposes, however, it is important that she was a member of the Folk-lore Society and a devoted admirer of the ideas of Sir James Frazer. Her portrait of early modern witchcraft combined Michelet's idea of a pagan peasant cult mostly staffed by women but venerating a horned nature-god, Leland's characterization of it as 'The Old Religion', Gomme's notion of an initiatory succession of devotees, Pearson's belief that it had mainly been concerned with fertility rites, and Frazer's concept of the regular sacrifice of sacred kings. She supported each part of it with liberal quotation of evidence from the records of actual trials. Her first papers upon the subject were delivered to the Folk-Lore Society and published in its journal in 1917 and 1920. Encouraged by their reception, which included immediate praise from worthies of the society such as Charlotte Burne, she brought out a first book on the subject in 1921, *The Witch-Cult in Western Europe*, from Oxford University Press.

In the following three decades she produced three more works in the same field. By far the most influential in the academic world was an essay in *The Journal of the Royal Anthropological Institute* for 1934, which concerned the then enigmatic figures of naked women carved in medieval churches and known by the Irish name of sheela-na-gig. She proposed that they had represented pagan goddesses of fertility, still venerated by the bulk of the population, and exposing further the fragility of the covering of upper-class Christianity which overlay the enduring paganism of medieval Britain. This idea was the direct inspiration for Lady Raglan's theory about the 'Green Man', and remained an orthodoxy among archaeologists until the late 1970s (Hutton, 1991: 308–16).

In 1931 she had published a sequel to *The Witch Cult*, entitled *The God of the Witches*. It represented in a sense a culmination of the cult of Pan in modern England, for it asserted the doctrine that the horned god of the greenwood had been the oldest male deity known to humans, and traced his worship across Europe and the Near East, from the Old Stone Age up to the seventeenth century. This was achieved by seizing upon every representation of a horned god in European art or literature and identifying it with him, and reasserting the idea that he had been the focus of worship for the witches, and the origins of the figure of the Christian Devil. In doing so, she popularized some of the other names under which horned male deities had been known in the ancient world, notably the Gallic Cernunnos and the Arabic Dhu'l Karnain, applied to the ram-horned images of Alexander the Great.

The book was also notable for revising the picture of the 'Old Religion' given in *The Witch Cult* in order to make it much more attractive. The earlier work had been both more objective in tone and more inclined to credit witches with some of the more discreditable customs, such as child sacrifice, which had been alleged against them by demonologists. The new book went to some lengths to refute or extenuate these, and to emphasize the joyous and nature-loving aspects of the religion. Furthermore, it took up Pearson's suggestion that Joan of Arc had been a witch priestess, and extended it to include other notable figures such as William Rufus and Thomas Becket as victims representing a divinity of the Frazerian kind, killed according to the traditional faith. This idea was taken still further in a third book, *The Divine King in England* (1954), which claimed every violent royal death and almost every execution of a prominent politician in England until 1600 to have been a sacrifice of the same sort.

In these later years, also, her attitude to witchcraft seems to have shifted once more, meshing with her preoccupation with the theme of human sacrifice obvious in that last book. During the late 1940s she took an interest in a number of unsolved murders recorded in England during the previous 10 years, and came to the conclusion that they were evidence that witch groups were still operating in the country and despatching victims in rituals dedicated to devil-worship. She was particularly interested in an exceptionally brutal killing near Lower Quinton, Warwickshire, and when the villagers indignantly denied her claims, she responded with the traditional contempt of learned folklorists for popular opinion, by declaring that they were obviously concealing their true beliefs. She printed her views in *The Birmingham Post* (2 September 1951) and imparted them to a writer of popular works on crime, who made them the theme of a book which he wrote upon the two most sensational of the cases concerned (McCormick, 1968: 64–80).

In 1954, however, she was persuaded to act formally as the godmother of Wicca, in the sense that she contributed an approving forward to the first book which announced the existence of that religion to the world, Gerald Gardner's *Witchcraft Today*. The work concerned asserted that Wicca was no revival, but a genuine survival into modern times, of the historic witch faith described in her own publications. That the faith had survived should itself have been no difficult thing for Murray to believe, as she had so recently been suggesting the same thing; her problem was, rather, that she had been warning the public that it had been corrupted into something evil and dangerous, and now she had to cope with the suggestions that other lines of it had come down to the present in a benign form. Her response was to state that she took Gardner's word, both for the genuine nature of the survival and the postive nature of its activities, and then to inform readers that all good religious rituals must honour the same God. She suggested that Christianity did so 'more decorously although not more sincerely' than witchcraft.

Colleagues of Margaret Murray in the Folk-Lore Society were convinced that she herself was 'a whole-hearted sceptic and rationalist' in matters of religion (Simpson, 1994: 89), and she informed readers of *The Sunday Dispatch* (4 November 1951) that the power of witches resided only in the credulity of others. These attitudes were not wholly consistent. She was certainly not a Christian, and acquired a detestation of the more enthusiastic adherents of that faith because of the attacks which some made upon her portrait of the Old Religion (Murray, 1963: 103; Oxford University Press Archive, 881053). Towards the end of her life, however, she began to testify to her awareness of 'an Almighty Power' which rules the universe and of which she would obtain higher knowledge upon death (Murray, 1963: 197–204). In her preface to *Witchcraft Today* she gave this power a gender, flagrantly ignoring the duotheism of the religion actually described in the book to declare that all religious ritual was 'gratitude to the Creator and hope for the constance of His goodness'. She also believed herself to be a witch, and put curses upon people; the proof of this is contained in a letter preserved in the archive of Oxford University Press (881053). One example of a public demonstration of her techniques is recounted in the entry upon her in the *Dictionary of National Biography*, although its author assumed rather uneasily that she was joking.

Her influence was powerful, if complex and uneven. No academic seems to have taken seriously her theories about Joan of Arc, William Rufus, and other historical celebrities, although they were developed by 'pop' historians such as Hugh Ross Williamson and Michael Harrison. Her original work upon early modern witchcraft as a pagan religion, by contrast, convinced such distinguished scholars as Sir Steven Runciman, Christopher Hill and Sir George Clark. These were, admittedly, not experts in the field concerned. Those found fault with her suggestions from the very beginning (Thomas, 1971: 514–19), and eventually utterly disproved them in the period 1970–90. It is also true that she met with opposition even in her stronghold of the Folk-Lore Society, and *The Witch Cult* received a withering review in its journal (Simpson, 1994: 89–96). On the other hand, there were also regular demonstrations of support for her ideas in the same society (Hutton, 1996: 424), and as the case of Frazer has spectacularly illustrated, public acclaim and influence can actually flourish in inverse proportion to expert opinion.

In the 1920s her picture of the witch religion, no doubt reinforced by the older writings of Michelet, Leland, Gomme and Pearson, had already been taken up by occultists (as the contributions to *The Occult Review* make plain) and by the very popular novelist John Buchan, who built it into *Witch Wood* (1927). Her books on the subject, none the less, sold slowly until the 1940s, when *The God of the Witches* suddenly enjoyed a runaway success which continued for the next two decades, producing a reprinting of *The Witch Cult* and the appearance of *The Divine King* (Murray, 1963: 104–5; Oxford University Press Archive, 881053). In 1947–8 alone, her theories were endorsed by a serious study of folklore by Arne Runeberg, a scholarly survey of witchcraft beliefs by R. Trevor Davies, and a novel and a sensational work of amateur history by Hugh Ross Williamson. It will be argued that these years were also critical in the formation of Wicca, which in this respect was one, and the most important, aspect of the vogue for her writings at this time.

FORERUNNERS

The work of setting out the context from which modern pagan witchcraft arose must now be completed, by considering a set of groups and individuals who illustrate different ways in which notions of paganism and magic were put into practice in the early twentieth century. One of these ways, which has until recently been hardly studied in this context, was through the medium of woodcraft organizations. All of these, ultimately, took their inspiration from North America, and the work of the Canadian Ernest Thompson Seton. From the end of the nineteenth century, he popularized the idea that the new industrial and urbanized society would be redeemed both in body and spirit if its young people were given the ability to spend regular periods of time living in natural surroundings, learning skills and lore associated with that environment in the manner of tribal peoples. The first and most famous of the British organizations to spring from his example was Baden-Powell's Boy Scout Association, founded in 1908. During the First World War and its aftermath, the increasingly patriotic and militaristic tone of the Scouts produced a series of secessions among their more socialist and pacifist members, to set up alternative bodies which were designed to pursue Thompson Seton's orginal aims within a more radical political and social framework. These were the Order of Woodcraft Chivalry 1916) and the Kindred of the Kibbo Kift (1920), joined in 1924 by the Woodcraft Folk, founded by defectors from the Kibbo Kift who sought formal links with the Labour Movement.

What all these organisations had in common was an element of ritual, especially associated with the lighting of a communal camp fire, and a tendency to view the universe as animist, ingested by the importation of native American stories, chants and names through Seton's writings. These traits were weakest in the Boy Scouts, which strove most selfconsciously to preserve a Christian emphasis, although in 1920 the Commissioner for Wolf Cubs, herself a Roman Catholic, protested vehemently against the prevalence of 'heathen' and pantheist ideas in some troops, and especially at the use of an Omaha prayer (Evans, 1930: 160). The Woodcraft Folk made much more extensive use of native American material, basing their concept of religion upon a Great Spirit whom all faiths could revere in common (Evans, 1930: 165–73). This was also the profession of the Kibbo Kift, which employed a large range of prayers and chants drawn from tribal societies with animist beliefs in Australia and Africa, as well as the Americas (Hargrave, 1919, 1927).

For present purposes, by far the most significant of these groups was the Woodcraft Chivalry, which has recently been made the subject of a pioneering academic study (Edgell, 1992). Its most important formative influence was a naturalist called Ernest Westlake, who was a Quaker by upbringing but came in the course of the 1900s to argue for the need to revive ancient pagan values to redress the shortcomings of Christianity. Among his favourite authors were Frazer, Nietzsche, Harrison and Carpenter. His dream was an England revitalized by the liberation of the forces of creativity and sexuality, and he saw classical Greek religion in particular as the force which might achieve this. He coined the phrase 'one must be a good pagan before one can be a good Christian'. To him the 'trinity of woodcraft' were Pan, Artemis and Dionysos. From 1921 the Order camped annually on land which Westlake had bought in the New Forest, and he opened its first meeting there with an invocation to Pan; he had considered naming the organization 'the Bacchae'. During the 1920s it adopted a set ritual whereby a sacred fire was lit within a circle, consecrated by torchbearers arriving from the cardinal points of ritual magic and bearing the greetings of the guardians of the quarters, from east to north.

During the same decade, also, an acute tension developed within it, between members who had been attracted to it as a pacifist Christian alternative to the Scouts, to which to entrust their children, and those who saw it as a vehicle for libertarian social change. The latter increasingly advocated naturism and sexual freedom as well as paganism, and some of the adults, at least put these ideals into practice. The most colourful of them was a fiery young Londoner called Harry Bingham, who changed his first name to Dion, an abbreviation of his favourite deity Dionysos, whom he extolled as 'the virile son of the all-Mother'. He argued for both social and ritual nudity, and quoted lavishly from his friend, the poet of Pan, Victor Neuburg. This faction was supported by the Westlake family, led after the death of Ernest in 1922 by his son Aubrey who likewise believed in the need to balance the respective virtues of paganism and Christianity.

The constant wrangling between radicals and conservatives told heavily upon both. In the last four years of the decade membership of the Woodcraft Chivalry fell by two-thirds, and in 1928 the Society of Friends formally withdrew its support as it felt that the Christian identity of the order had been too severely compromised. This did not hand victory to the radicals, who themselves were getting worn out by argument. By 1930 Bingham had departed to join Vera Pragnell's mystical community in Sussex, the Sanctuary, where he continued to preach and practise paganism and naturism through the 1930s. Aubrey Westlake resigned the leadership in 1933 and withdrew the next year, leaving a smaller and calmer organization, dedicated to broad ideals of social and religious harmony, to continue and prosper until the present. For a few years it had almost become the vehicle for a modern pagan revival, but that period of its history was past.

The same kind of flirtation with paganism, ripening at times into a love affair, was found among members of the societies of magicians which sprang out of the disintegration of the Golden Dawn. Two in particular, a woman and a man, were to leave legacies of thought and action to Wicca. The former was Violet Firth, known better by her pen-name of Dion Fortune. After training which included membership of the Theosophical Society and the Alpha and Omega, a successor-group of the Golden Dawn, she founded her own society of occultists, the Inner Light, in 1928. Brought up a Christian Scientist, all through the 1910s and 1920s she remained attached to a devout, if unorthodox and non-denominational, Christianity. In her writings of those decades she repeatedly expressed her personal affection for Jesus as 'the Master of Masters' and 'the Great Initiator'. Her morality was of a piece, as she attacked promiscuity, homosexuality, abortion and racial impurity, while extolling a spiritualized sexuality within marriage. Towards the end of the 1920s she began to accept some merit in ancient Greek and Egyptian religion, but on a lower level to that of Christ.

Things started to change for her in the 1930s, under the influence of three different people. One was D.H. Lawrence, whose novels, especially *The Rainbow*, made a deep impression on her. The second was her husband, Thomas Penry Evans, whom she married in 1927. By 1933 he was teaching the Inner Light that the 'Pan within' was as important a component of spiritual growth as the 'Christ within'. The third was a recruit to her society, Charles Seymour, who argued like Westlake that the deficiencies of modern Christianity could be made good by a selective revival of classical paganism. To him the latter had contained vital truths which the faith of Christ lacked, and its deities were timeless forces with whom people could still work.

Under the impact of all three, Fortune's opinions began to buckle. In 1934, in *Avalon of the Heart*, she declared that both pagan and Christian mysteries had value, but still identified herself with the latter. The following year she published a novel, *The Winged Bull*, in which she suggested that Christ had presented only one facet of the truth of God. In 1936 there came another, *The Goat Foot God*, in which she changed sides decisively and repeated Seymour's argument that modern society had grown so stilted, artificial, hidebound and rationalist that it could only be redeemed by a reinfusion of paganism (which she termed 'Vitamin P'). 'P' could also stand for 'Pan', the divine hero of the story, but it was not the god who now seized her imagination but the moon-goddess, whom she identified primarily with Isis. It was this figure who dominated what became her two most famous novels, *The Sea Priestess* and *Moon Magic*, the first published at her own expense in 1938 and the second apparently written in 1939.

Even now she hedged her bets a little. She suggested that the Virgin Mary was also a face of the Great Goddess, that Nature herself was the self-expression of 'God', and that the Goddess was one aspect of a single 'Initiator'. Jesus, however, had vanished altogether, and Isis was treated in the plots very much as a divine personality in her own right. Fortune's earlier interest in the magical potential of the sexual polarity between woman and man was developed to the point at which the sublimated erotic current between the male and female protagonists is made the basis of most ritual. The invocations of the moon-goddess which she wrote for these books represented the finest and most celebrated of her poetry, and would be heavily used by Wiccans. There is no doubt that she enacted these or similar rites in real life at this period; Seymour noted the repeated performance in 1938–9 of a ceremony in which she personified Isis.

During 1939, however, the course of her life and thought was altered again, by three developments. First, she became estranged from Seymour, who ceased to work with her. Then her husband suddenly left her, for a younger and prettier woman. Soon after, the Second World War began, giving her an incentive to concentrate more upon patriotic and conventional themes. In one sense she never recovered from these events, for *Moon Magic* was abandoned, unfinished, and she did not publish another book. In another, she retreated to older and safer ground; her messages in the magazine of her society took on a fervently Christian tone again, and in the visualization which she prescribed to help defeat Nazi Germany, the Master Jesus was firmly back at the top. She died in 1946, leaving the Inner Light to function as a specifically Christian organization. There is reason to think that in her final year she was starting to turn back towards pagan images, for she approached Aleister Crowley for information about his way of working with them. How she might have used this, if her health had not collapsed, remains an open question (Richardson, 1987; Chapman, 1993).

The case of Dion Fortune shows how complex a matter the religious attitudes of a British occultist of that generation could be. The same point is made by a consideration of her most famous male counterpart, Crowley himself. Here, indeed the complexities are even worse. Not only did he live longer and harder than Fortune, and work with many more systems of magic and mysticism, but it is by no means obvious whether much of what he wrote should be taken as revealed truth, metaphor or joke, or a combination of those; Crowley himself may not always have been certain. There is a broad shift in his attitudes, from the years in which he was young, fit, confident, rich, iconoclastic, and eager to horrify and challenge conventional opinion, to those in which he was ageing, troubled by illness, poverty and the consequences of his appalling public reputation, and anxious to appear as a more serious and substantial figure. In both those phases, however, there were many cross-currents, as well as a consistent commitment to preach the reality and importance of ritual magic, to an associated use of sexual polarity much more physical and omnivorous than that of Dion Fortune, and to a sustained assault upon traditional morality.

In many ways his attitude to religion was very similar to his attitude to sexuality; enthusiastic, adventurous, and linked very firmly to magical ends. A single passage in his periodical *The Equinox* (1911) contains a typical pair of balancing statements. He begins by declaring that 'I hate Christianity as Socialists hate soap'. Then, however, he adds a qualification, that 'the best test of a religion is the manhood of its adherents, not its truth', and that he would rather be ranked with Christian heroes such as Livingstone and Gordon of Khartoum than with the mediocrities whom he found in the quasi-pagan world of occultists and Theosophists. The same sort of contrast can be extended across his life. In his younger days he enjoyed contrasting Christianity and Crowleyanity, and a large part of the point of his most cherished single text, *The Book of the Law* (written 1904) is that the religion of Christ belongs to a former aeon and is now obsolete. In 'The Paris Working' of 1914 Crowley was characterized by his partner Victor Neuburg as a 'fiery arrow', shot by the true gods in their struggle to regain the earth from the 'slave gods' such as Christ. On the other hand, in *Moonchild* (1929) Crowley called the cross 'the symbol of Him who gives life through his own death, of the Holy One appointed from the foundation of the world as its redeemer'. Later in the same book he stated that his real quarrel was with modern, bourgeois, Christianity.

It is very hard to tell whether Aleister Crowley truly believed in any deities. *The Book of the Law* reads like a genuine religious revelation, of a universe dominated by a star-goddess and two gods of the earth. All three, however, could be seen as symbols of cosmic principles. In his most famous public work, *Magick in Theory and Practice* (1929), he said that the object of all magical ritual is union with God. He repeated this in his (strictly private) instruction for the seventh degree of his order of magicians, the Ordo Templi Orientis; that the aim of the Order was to find the one true God (King, 1973: 180). In *Moonchild* he declared that God is a lie, but that behind it is the truth of a single Central Spirit, a single soul of the universe, a single Sire and Lord of all. The problem here is that a world soul, to which all beings belong, and a divine master and lord of all, are actually two different concepts; but Crowley takes no heed of the difficulty.

In the preface to *Liber Oz* (1941), he states firmly that 'there is no God but man'. This could be linked to his earlier suggestion in *Magick*, that the ultimate end of the magician is union with God, being a process by which he gradually replaces the human part of himself with a divine equivalent. A similar achievement is one of the ends of *Liber Samekh*. This does not, however, get us any closer to understanding who or what God or divinity was to Crowley. In magical rites such as 'The Paris Workings', he invoked specific classical pagan deities as if they were real entities, with individual identities. At such times he was operating as a polytheist, just as at others he talked like an atheist and at yet others like a monotheist. It seems that either he did not make his beliefs clear, or that they were not clear to him.

All this precludes any easy answer to the apparently simple question of whether Crowley was a pagan. In his 'autohagiography', he declared that his mission was 'to bring oriental wisdom to Europe and to restore paganism in a purer form' (Crowley, 1969: 839). He did not say, however, what he meant by the latter expression. Perhaps the most revealing statement upon the matter comes in a letter which he wrote to a friend in about 1914 (Symonds, 1971: 194–5):

The time is just right for a natural religion. People like rites and ceremonies, and they are tired of hypothetical gods. Insist on the real benefits of the Sun, the Mother-Force, the Father-Force, and so on, and show that by celebrating these benefits worthily the worshippers unite themselves more fully with the current of life. Let the religion be Joy, but with a worthy and dignified sorrow in death itself, and treat death as an ordeal, an initiation. . . . In short, be the founder of a new and greater Pagan cult.

This was an almost perfect prophecy of the modern pagan revival in general, and of Wicca in particular, but it is noteworthy that Crowley was urging somebody else to undertake the work; in this specific case, a follower called George Cecil Jones, who never showed any inclination to do so. In essence, the master himself was interested in magic, by any effective means and by any effective system, and not in religion. He wanted to make things work, and why they worked was of secondary importance, if that. To say this is not to suggest that he was a dilettante or a lightweight, for as a theorist and practictioner of ritual magic he was absolutely the reverse of those. Nor is it to deny the importance of his contribution to Wicca, for the latter's use of his invocations and other liturgical forms was to be so heavy that if Margaret Murray can be called its godmother, then Aleister Crowley was its godfather. In both cases, however, the role was unwitting.

What the thought of Fortune and Crowley reveals on the grand scale appears in miniature in the records of lesser figures in the same world of ritual magic. Two examples may suffice to illustrate the point, from the same month (of June) in 1938. One appears in the record of meditations kept by that Charles Seymour who has been cited above. At the summer solstice he 'got the idea of linking the old symbolism of indigenous women's mysteries with the pagan mysteries of England right down to the present day, and through the witchcraft period.' A week later his working partner Christine Campbell Thomson (later better known as Christine Hartley), entered in her own diary a vision of

> little pictures of Ishtar worship through the ages, the most common being one of silhouetted witches in pointed hats and ragged skirts dancing round a fire. Then it seemed to focus a little more steadily and I was aware of the goddess standing before us mistily veiled . . . she stressed again the necessity for Joy in worship and that she was the goddess of Love of Life. (Richardson, 1985: 173–5)

Once again, these were exactly the sort of images from which Wicca was to arise, but it does not seem as if either writer did anything to take them out of dreamland. The question of how they finally did break out of the world of the imagination, into that of action, must now at last be addressed.

SECTION 2

The History of Pagan Witchcraft

GERALD GARDNER

The foundation legend of Wicca was first publicized to the world in 1960, in the biography of the person most prominently associated with its appearance, Gerald Gardner (Bracelin, 1960). As Gardner himself was the source of virtually all of the information in the book, it is effectively autobiography. It told the story of a long and relatively uneventful working life, spent first as the owner or manager of tea and rubber plantations in Ceylon, North Borneo and Malaya, and then as an inspector in the Malay customs service. Two traits marked him off as unusual in colonial society. One was a keen and active interest in the supernatural, which led him to read widely upon religion and the occult, to discuss them regularly with like-minded people, and to gain first-hand experience of Freemasonry, Spiritualism, Buddhism and tribal magical practices. The other was an equally active antiquarianism, which propelled him into becoming a pioneer of Malay archaeology, numismatics, maritime history, and folklore, and an author of respected monographs in these fields.

In 1936, aged 52, he retired to England, and immediately became involved in archaeology there and in the Near East. He also joined the Folk-Lore Society, collaborating with Margaret Murray to present a paper upon a set of apparent relics of witchcraft in 1939. Witchcraft was also a theme in his first novel, *A Goddess Arrives*, published in 1940. During the following decade he also became a prominent member of the Ancient Order of Druids. For present purposes, his most significant move came in 1938, when he settled at Highcliffe on the Hampshire coast and joined the Rosicrucian Fellowship of Crotona which staged plays at its own theatre in neighbouring Christchurch. This represented a mystical branch of the movement of Co-Masonry, itself an outgrowth of Freemasonry which admitted women. Gardner became especially attached to a set of fellow members who revealed to him in 1939 that they had become part of an old coven of witches, a survival from a pagan fertility religion, which met in the New Forest. He was initiated into this himself in September, at the house of 'Old Dorothy' a wealthy lady who functioned as its leader. When France fell in 1940 she 'called up covens right and left' for a ceremony in the forest to hold back the threatened German invasion.

In 1946, related Gardner, he visited Crowley, and found him a charming charlatan, who admitted that he had encountered the witch religion but disliked both its feminism and its lack of financial potential. Crowley initiated Gardner into his own Ordo Templi Orientis, but the latter did not want to develop his part in it after Crowley himself died in 1947. Also in 1946, however, the witches allowed Gardner to represent some of their practices in the disguise of a novel, *High Magic's Aid*, which was published in 1949. In 1950 the first museum and study centre for British witchcraft was opened in the Isle of Man (and soon passed into Gardner's management), and in 1951 the 1736 Witchcraft Act was repealed, allowing witches to advertise their practices without fear of prosecution. These developments made it possible for Gerald Gardner to proclaim the survival of the religion to the world in 1954, with the book *Witchcraft Today*, in which he posed as a disinterested anthropologist who had been lucky enough to discover its continued existence as a secret and initiatory system.

The religion portrayed in *Witchcraft Today* was called 'Wica', from the standard Anglo-Saxon term for a male witch (the name was amended after Gardner's death to the more accurate Old English form of 'Wicca', although the pronunciation remained with a hard 'c', whereas the Anglo-Saxon was a 'ch'). Its rites were alleged to consist mainly of dances intended to promote fertility, and of feasting upon consecrated food and drink. The performers were naked, in the belief that this more easily released magical power from the body. They venerated a god and goddess, whose names were secret, the former predominant in winter and the latter in summer. They worked within a circle, formed with a consecrated sword or knife and carefully purified, to contain the energy which they raised. They held the north to be the most sacred of the four cardinal points, believed in reincarnation, and trained to develop latent psychic powers. The religion was organized in covens, led by a high priestess supported by a high priest, which subdivided into couples for training purposes. Training, like initiation, was always between the sexes. As part of this polarity they revered the life-force within the world and regarded acts of worldly love and pleasure as sacred. They had eight sacred tools, of which the most important were the knife, the censer and the cord. Their seasonal festivals were the four traditional quarter days which opened the seasons, described as the great witches' sabbats by Margaret Murray. Trance and ecstasy were important components within their rites, and they aimed not merely to address their deities, but to feel as though they had become them.

No academic historian has ever taken seriously Gardner's claim to have discovered a genuine survival of ancient religion, and it was dismissed in the review given to it by the journal of his own Folk-Lore Society, in

1955. The complete collapse of the credibility of the Murray thesis, since 1970, has removed the historical context upon which it was based. These considerations make Wicca very firmly a part of modern history, but until now the only research into its 'genuine' origins has been carried on within the Pagan community. In particular, four writers have carried out work for which any subsequent scholar must be profoundly grateful. Janet and Stewart Farrar collaborated with Doreen Valiente between 1979 and 1984 to make the first textual analysis of the different versions of the standard Wiccan collection of rituals, the 'Book of Shadows'. Aidan Kelly took this work further in a series of investigations into Gardner's own papers, which culminated in 1991. Valiente has also conducted some research of her own, and is an important source of evidence in herself, as a major personality in the early development of the religion. Her testimony can at times be checked against that of another survivor from the first known Wiccan coven, the witch well known in the modern Pagan community under the name of 'Robert'.

It should be said immediately that there is nothing inherently implausible in Gardner's claim to have been initiated into an existing religion. The account which he provides of his earlier life in the biography is sober and understated, and carefully leaves out the more dubious claims which he sometimes made for himself verbally, such as his possession of two university degrees (Valiente, 1989: 41–2). It is striking also that he describes a coven composed partly of Rosicrucians and led by a wealthy lady, instead of announcing that he had discovered a group of witches hidden in a rural working-class community, presided over by a more conventional cunning woman. In view of the cultural patterns outlined above, it is precisely from this more educated esoteric milieu that one would expect a modern pagan revival to commence.

The problem lies in substantiating any of Gardner's story. He privately identified 'Old Dorothy' to his followers in the 1950s as Dorothy Clutterbuck, and in an exemplary piece of investigative research during the 1980s Doreen Valiente established beyond doubt that this was a woman better known by her married name of Dorothy Fordham, who had lived at Highcliffe in the 1930s and 1940s, and died in 1951 aged 70 years (Farrar, 1984: 282–93). From her family documents at Somerset House, the family graves in Highcliffe churchyard, and the local newspapers, it is possible to piece together a great deal of information about her. What it presents is a picture of a fanatically Tory and Anglican matron, ostensibly a personally devout Christian and friend and patron of the local vicar, who lent her energy and money to conventional causes such as the British Legion, the Girl Guides and the Seamen's Mission. She was a leader of respectable local society, an eager proselytizer for the Conservative Party, and married for most of the 1930s to a Tory JP and landed gentleman. He died suddenly in May 1939, leaving her not only prostrate with grief but locked in a legal battle with his relatives for his estate, which she finally lost in 1941. Diaries of hers from the 1940s surfaced in the mid-1980s and went on display; there was nothing in them about witchcraft.

This portrait leaves us with a stark choice; either Dorothy Fordham lived one of the most amazing double lives in history, or else Gardner has played a cruelly funny trick on posterity by making it imagine the local epitome of respectability standing stark naked in the New Forest and summoning up covens. If the first is true, then it was a deception which extended even to private diaries and beyond the grave, as manifested in her will, which initially either included or was abetted by her husband, and which would threaten at any moment to destroy the whole of the rest of the life upon which she lavished such affection and expense. It would probably be impossible to prove that Dorothy Fordham was *not* a witch, but a closer consideration of her so far provides doubt concerning Gardner's story rather than support for it.

There was, by contrast, a different woman who certainly links the Rosicrucian Theatre and Fellowship of Crotona in 1938 to the Wicca which appeared at the end of the 1940s: the one who was Gardner's high priestess in 1950 and is known in published sources as 'Dafo'. She was a very different sort of person from Dorothy, a music teacher with long-established interests in occultism and mysticism. Doreen Valiente met her in 1952 (Valiente, 1989: 38–9, 66), and two other members of Gardner's coven did so in 1958 ('Robert', pers. comm.). Her real name was known to them, and has been given to me, but by late 1952 she had already retired from Wicca and was very anxious to conceal her former role in it from her own family. As she is now long deceased, this precludes me from approaching her heirs in the hope of discovering personal papers, and indeed makes it most unlikely that she would have left any of relevance to this enquiry. Furthermore, when dealing with both Valiente and her two other visitors, she carefully avoided providing an answer to the question of whether Gardner's story about his discovery of Wicca was true (Kelly, 1991: 137–9; 'Robert', pers. comm.). Indeed, she seems to have said nothing about what actually went on before 1950 except to confirm that like Gardner she had been a Co-Mason and involved in the Rosicrucian Theatre.

Independent testimony as to the existence of the coven in the New Forest seemed to have been provided in a history of ritual magic by Francis King (King, 1970: 176–81). The author recounted a conversation with the occultist Louis Wilkinson in 1953, who told him that in the late 1930s or early 1940s he was friendly with some of its members. He then confirmed Gardner's story about the ritual to ward off Hitler in 1940, and added the details that the witches rubbed bear fat on their naked bodies to ward off the cold and used the fly agaric mushroom to achieve visions. He also repeated the story of Crowley's comments about Wicca, which King heard from two additional sources.

This is not, unfortunately, impeccable evidence. It is a second-hand account, recalled almost 20 years later. Wilkinson's dating of his acquaintance with the coven seems curiously vague, and bear fat has never, at any time in recorded history, been a readily accessible commodity in England. The anecdote about Crowley is the least credible, for at no point in his vast legacy of published and unpublished work, which draws or comments upon the widest possible range of magical and religious systems, did that magician mention anything like Wicca; including those documents of his which concern Gardner (of which more below). Possible reactions to Wilkinson's (alleged) words, therefore, range from a literal acceptance of their import, to a suggestion that some of it may be distorted or fictitious, to one that the actual source of all of Wilkinson's information, directly or indirectly, was Gardner himself.

Was the 'New Forest coven' actually the pagan section of the Order of Woodcraft Chivalry, which was active in the right area at approximately the right time, and with some of which (according to an eye-witness, the witch famed as a harper and commonly known as 'Bran') Gardner was friendly? An answer is at present precluded by the closure of its archive to non-members, but at first sight it is likely, again, to be negative. By the late 1930s, as shown above, the pagans had apparently all left the Order, and there is no evidence that it met in the New Forest between 1935 and 1945. The chronology seems wrong, and the earlier paganism of the Woodcraft Chivalry and the later paganism of Wicca do not seem very alike.

All this discussion, therefore, has led neither to a positive proof nor a positive disproof of the existence of Gardner's putative 'New Forest coven', let alone any solid information concerning its membership or practices. Instead we are left with the outline of his own career, extending between two of his books. *A Goddess Arrives*, published in 1940 and so therefore probably written in 1939, is certainly a pre-Wiccan text. It includes a witch, but the reader is not encouraged to identify with her practices, which include human sacrifice. They are represented as dedicated to the service of illusory deities while actually using a force which resides within all humans; the hero, by contrast, calls upon 'the Higher Powers' who abominate sacrifice. *High Magic's Aid*, published in 1949 and so presumably at latest a work dating from 1948, is clearly Wiccan. Although its hero is a ceremonial magician in the medieval tradition, the heroine is a pagan witch priestess of the Margaret Murray kind, working initiation rituals which are the basis for those used later in Wicca. The historian thus has a maximum of nine years through which to track Gardner in quest for the source of his ideas.

Not much seems to be available for the first half of the period, in which he seems to be, as he told his biographer, preoccupied with local measures for wartime defence; first writing to *The Daily Telegraph* to advocate the establishment of a Home Guard and then busy leading an ARP unit when deemed too frail for entry to the Guard himself (Bracelin, 1960: ch. 13). With the end of the war he drops out of sight again, to reappear in May 1947 (not in 1946 as he said) as a visitor on several occasions to Aleister Crowley. Crowley's diary, now in the Warburg Institute Gerald Yorke Collection (MS 23) shows that he introduced himself as a (bogus) Ph.D. Singapore and a holder of the Masonic Royal Arch degree; not as a witch. He was initiated into the Ordo Templi Orientis and chartered to found his own division of it, departing loaded with copies of the master's works. A letter from him in the same collection, dated 14 June (MS E.21), shows him enthusiastically trying to initiate new members. Then something altered dramatically; by the time that Crowley died at the end of the year, Gardner was living in Tennessee, and when members of the OTO contacted him about the possibility that he might take over as head of the Order in Europe, he was apparently unwilling to do so; these events are proved by a set of letters to and from Frieda Harris, printed in the modern Thelemite (i.e. Crowleyite) magazine *TLC* in November 1992. He still had friendly exchanges with members, and published the novel *High Magic's Aid* under his OTO. magical name; but when he returned to England in March 1948 he seems to have done so as a person committed to Wicca.

Nothing seems to be known about why he went to America or what he did there. It is possible that his change of course occurred as a result of experiences at that time, or that his holiday represented an opportunity to reflect upon his options which led to a decision to pursue the Wiccan one. When the Folklore Centre of Superstition and Witchcraft opened in the Isle of Man in June 1951, he performed the opening ceremony as a member of the Southern Coven of British Witches' (a Northern Coven was never identified) (Valiente, 1989: 13). Thereafter he functioned as the sole authority upon, and publicist for, the witch religion. It seems, therefore, as if the years 1947–8 were crucial to the development of Wicca, but an absence of information for the preceding period leaves any such suggestion insecure.

One further, very important, body of source material remains to be considered; the private papers which Gardner left behind him. Aidan Kelly carried out the pioneering work upon these, and although many of his arguments have been controversial (at least among Wiccans), the present writer cannot fault his textual analysis of individual documents. In particular he deserves credit for recognizing the nature, and significance, of a manuscript which Gardner called 'Ye Bok of ye Art Magical'. Copies of this were made and have been circulated by the Wiccan Church of Canada (the Gardner papers having been preserved at Toronto) against which Kelly's transcript can be checked. It commenced as a repository for notes which Gardner took from various systems, such as Cabbala and Tarot, and then became the repository for the first known Wiccan rituals, initiation rites for three progressive degrees. These were written in large and fair hand, as if to be read and used in actual ceremonies, but were subsequently amended to provide the form which two of them took in *High Magic's Aid*. They were subequently corrected again, and other rituals added in more careless fashion as if the book was again being used for rough drafts. At some point a set of ceremonies were copied into the first Wiccan 'Book of Shadows', which had been retired from use by 1953. Some further drafts were added which later appear in the second such book, which was employed during that year (Kelly, 1991: 37–94). The second set of revisions, and the later ceremonies, can therefore be located in the period 1949–51, but there is no way of dating the earlier work, save that the quantity of quotation from Crowley's work in it probably places it after Gardner's visits to him in 1947.

The earliest rites, the initiations and the ritual blessing of cakes and wine, assume that only two people, a man and a woman, are present. The intermediate set consists of ceremonies for the four main seasonal 'Sabbats' and for the consecration of tools, and the first of those are plainly designed for a group. The later additions, which were to go into the second 'Book of Shadows', are far more concerned to set the rites in a historical background by relating explanations and advice to the needs of a secret religion operating under persecution in previous centuries. Over the period in which these first known Wiccan rites were being written up and then rewritten by Gardner, therefore, their context seems to have developed steadily in his mind from a working couple to a working coven, to a religion with its own historical claims. This does not, of course, preclude the possibility that he was aware of the whole context from the beginning, while only slowly manifesting it in his work.

Aidan Kelly has built upon the previous research by the Farrars and Valiente to analyse the literary components of these first known rituals, and found that they include largescale direct quotations from Crowley, Leland and the famous grimoire called *The Greater Key of Solomon* (in Mathers's Victorian translation), with one borrowing from Kipling, and use of the practices of Margaret Murray's putative 'witch cult' for the Sabbats and of Freemasonry and the Golden Dawn for the initiations. The obvious question for a textual analyst is what is left when these are deducted, and Kelly has suggested that the remaining component was a set of observances designed to induce sexual excitement by flagellation, and that this was in fact the distinctive personal contribution by Gardner to what was otherwise a pastiche.

The process at work seems to be rather more complex than that. Kelly is absolutely correct to emphasize the techniques of binding and scourging which are the principal practical link between all the initiatory and seasonal rituals. Gardner's novels, however, are not works of flagellant fiction, and the operations involved are not standard acts of sado-masochism. What they define instead is a highly idiosyncratic and thoroughly unusual way of attaining an ecstatic trance, which is explained in detail in two of the sections added to the second 'Book of Shadows' (Kelly, 1991: 80–2, 91–3). The cords are used to apply a gentle restriction of the blood circulation to produce dizziness, and the scourge is employed very lightly and steadily to induce a rhythmical tingling sensation. It is one of eight methods for the achievement of trance described in another additional document (Kelly, 1991: 88–90) , and there is no doubt that it was the one which Gardner himself preferred; the same document expresses his distrust of drugs, and 'Robert' informs me that his asthma prevented the old man from engaging in more active techniques such as dancing. A very personal set of circumstances therefore lies behind this major motif in the rites.

Had this been the only, or even the most important, aspect of the whole sequence, however, then Wicca would never have appealed to more than a small number of asthmatic mystics. What they outlined as well was a very radical system of religious belief and practice which distilled the import of the cultural developments described earlier, in an extreme form. By uniting paganism with the figure of the witch in the Leland and Murray tradition, it automatically pre-empted any easy reconciliation of the result with Christianity or with conventional social mores. This was supercharged by the fact that it paid no reverence to any Great Spirit, Prime Mover or World Soul, who might be equated with Jehovah, but to the nature-goddess and the horned god who had arisen in the nineteenth century as the favourite deities of romantic counter-culture. Their Wiccan names were a secret of initiates, and Gardner drew a blind over them in *High Magic's Aid* by making his witches in that venerate Janicot, the witchgod named by Pierre de Lancre, the famous demonologist; in *Witchcraft Today*, however, he revealed the divine couple as the foci of the religion. Although both were invoked at different times in the various rituals, with equal honours, it was only the goddess who ever made a set reply, speaking through a worshipper. She did so in the text which was headed 'Leviter Veslis' in 'Ye Bok of ye Art Magical' (Kelly, 1991: 52–4, where it is translated as 'Lift Up The Veil'); in the mid-1950s Gardner altered this to the Masonic expression of 'The Charge'. From its calligraphy it was contemporary with the initiation rituals and thus one of the first Wiccan rites to be entered in the book. It revealed her to be a combination of the liberty-giving goddess of Leland and the ecstasy-giving goddess of Crowley, inciting her followers to treat wordly pleasures, if given and taken with love, as sacred, and to enter into an eventual mystical union with her.

Like Freemasonry and Co-Masonry, the ceremonies taught knowledge and skills through three progressive degrees of initiation, and included 'working tools'. Like Co-Masonry and the Golden Dawn, they admitted women members upon an equal basis, and like the Golden Dawn they operated magic, at times by techniques to draw divinity into, or from, human beings. Unlike all of these, they were conducted by groups led by a high priestess and a high priest, whose relationship mirrored that of the two deities, in that the priestess was slightly more important. Freemasonry, following long-established Christian tradition, shunned the north as the place of darkness; Wicca made its main invocations to that direction. By forcing its members to confront and recognize the merit in the dark, as in its feminism, its unqualified paganism, its counter-cultural deities, and its insistence upon complete nudity for its devotees during their rites, it was challenging a whole series of norms in the most dramatic possible way. The self-image of the witch performed a crucial function here again, as a means of nerving people up to do so. Like all the magical or quasi-magical secret societies which had flourished since the seventeenth century, it concealed innovation under a language of continuity or of restitution; except that it went one better than the lot, by claiming to descend from the Palaeolithic. Beneath Leland's label of 'the Old Religion' was an extraordinarily novel one. In its own way, it was seeking to drive a battering ram against the boundaries of the present, and of the possible.

Who, then, was responsible for it? There seems to be little doubt that Gerald Gardner might have been. The man who had pioneered so many enquiries into the Malaysian past, who was versed in so many different occult traditions, who certainly designed the rituals of the religion in the form in which they emerged into history, and who dedicated the last 15 years of his life to propagating it, was certainly capable of its conception. There is equally small doubt that he was perfectly capable of the cunning and duplicity involved in making false statements about its origins; both Doreen Valiente (Valiente, 1989: 41–72) and 'Robert' (pers. comm.) agree that he was a loveable rogue, whom they caught out in various attempted deceptions. The analysis of his papers has destroyed his key claim to have copied the first 'Book of Shadows' from one belonging to Dorothy Fordham. Whether he actually was responsible for the whole framework of Wicca, however, and if so whether any other people, such as 'Dafo', actively assisted him in its creation, remains uncertain. In the last analysis, old Gerald is still in control of the early history of his movement.

THE GARDNERIANS

Throughout the 1950s, Gardner continued to revise the Wiccan rituals. At the beginning of the process, between 1948 and 1953, he was taking ideas from a remarkable range of printed sources. The sudden appearance of a stanza of Kipling in the May Eve ceremony is characteristic. Doreen Valiente discovered that the wonderfully evocative term, 'Book of Shadows', used to replace the traditional and tarnished one of 'grimoire', was snatched from the totally different context of an article on a Sanskrit manual concerning the art of divination by the observation of a person's shadow, published in *The Occult Observer* in 1949 (Valiente, 1989: 51–2). She also found the distinctive name 'athame', employed by Gardner for the black-handled ritual knife otherwise described from the *Key of Solomon*, in a short story by Clark Aston Smith, published in the American magazine *Weird Tales* in 1947 (Valiente, 1978: 78). It seems to have been taken by Smith in turn from an eighteenth-century recension of the *Key* kept in the Bibliothèque de l'Arsenal and reproduced in Grillot de Givry's *Pictorial Anthology of Witchcraft, Magic and Alchemy* (1931), a book which Gardner himself possessed; the spelling in both those earlier texts was 'arthame', and the derivation of the word is unknown. From Givry, also, Gardner probably took the rhyme beginning 'Bagabi lacha bachabe', a piece of apparent gibberish which features as an invocation to Satan in the thirteenth-century play *Le Miracle de Theophile*; it reappears in the seasonal rite for Hallowe'en, as an opening chant. The numinous term which he used as an alternative to Wicca, 'the Craft of the Wise', had been employed for Margaret Murray's witch religion by Hugh Ross Williamson, in a novel, *The Silver Bowl*, which came out in 1948. His discussion of witches' chants, added to the second version of the 'Book of Shadows', is based on Graves's *The White Goddess*.

A particularly important addition to the Book was 'The Legend of the Goddess', a psychodrama telling the story of the Goddess's descent to the Underworld to confront the God, as Lord of the Dead. It was published in *Witchcraft Today*, and added to the second degree initiation rite. Gardner himself noted that it seemed to derive from Indian and Babylonian myths about Shiva and Ishtar, but that the resemblance was very loose. Indeed, these stories had been heavily and effectively reworked to expound the Wiccan version of the of reincarnation, and to this day the responsibility for the passage remains unknown, although the central place given to the technique of gentle scourging would argue for some input, at least, from Gardner himself.

After 1953 his revisions, although persistent, ceased to take in material from external and literary sources and consisted instead of responses to the practical needs of working the rites, training initiates, and regulating relationships among coven members, between covens, and between Wicca and the wider world. He also began to act on suggestions from his own witches. A clear case of this is in the matter of seasonal festivals. The first two Books of Shadows had provided ceremonies only for the quarter days identified with witches' gatherings by Murray at the opening of February, May, August and November. By December 1953 Gardner was already celebrating the winter solstice as well, at least informally (Farrar and Farrar, 1981: 148). In 1958 his principal coven asked him if the solstices and equinoxes could be fully incorporated into the Wiccan ritual calendar, the former at least being famed ancient festivals and also celebrated in modern Druidry ('Robert', pers. comm.). He readily agreed, and so was created the eight-fold pattern of the ritual year which became standard in Wicca and passed from it into virtually all of modern Paganism.

The most significant single source of additions to the Books of Shadows, however, was Doreen Valiente, who was initiated at mid-summer 1953 when she was at the end of her twenties. She provided Wicca with a prolific gift for poetry, which Gardner first exploited six months later when he instructed her to compose an invocation, at a few hours' notice, for a winter solstice celebration for which no set one yet existed. The result, suggested by a carol in the famous Hebridean folklore collection *Carmina Gadelica*, was the poem 'Queen of the Moon, Queen of the Stars', which was immediately published with the accompanying ritual in *Witchcraft Today*, as a traditional witches' seasonal liturgy; and that is just what it became (Farrar and Farrar, 1981: 148). Valiente and Gardner wrote together what became the standard rhyme used in round dances, 'The Witches' Rune' (the last word an Anglicization of the Hebridean *rann*, again from *Carmina Gadelica*). In the mid-1950s she urged upon him the need to shed the material taken from Crowley in the Book of Shadows, as it threatened to tar Wicca with the brush of the dead magician's bad reputation (Valiente, 1989: 60–2). He agreed to let her rewrite The Charge, and she duly produced a new verse version, and then a prose one which became standard. The second part of it is given here, even though it has been published many times before, as it embodies so neatly the spirit of Wicca:

I who am the beauty of the green earth, and the white moon among the stars, and the mystery of the waters, and the desire of the heart of man, call unto thy soul, arise and come unto me; for I am the soul of nature, who giveth life to the universe. From me all things proceed, and unto me all things must return; and before my face, beloved of gods and men, thine inmost divine self shall be enfolded in the rapture of the infinite. Let my worship be in the heart that rejoiceth; for behold, all acts of love and pleasure are my rituals and therefore let there be beauty and strength, power and compassion, honour and humility; mirth and reverence, within you. And thou who thinkest to seek for me, know thy seeking and yearning shall avail thee not, unless thou knowest the mystery; that if that which thou seekest thou findest not within thee, thou shall never find it without thee, for behold I have been with thee from the beginning and I am that which is attained at the end of desire.

From the outset, Gardner's witches faced the dilemma that if they were to multiply (or, as Gardner put it, to save the Old Religion from extinction), then they needed publicity; but that negative publicity might destroy them. Having taken on themselves both the glamour and the fear which were associated with witchcraft, they needed to capitalize on the first without provoking the latter. Gardner's initial airings in newspapers, arising from the interest created by the Isle of Man museum during 1951–2, had brought him Valiente. She joined his coven, which was currently meeting in the London area and recruited mainly from his naturist club, at the time when Dafo's retirement had left it without a high priestess. This place she rapidly supplied, making the impact which has been described above, and remained in it until she hived off to found a sister coven in 1957. This was made possible by the influx of new initiates consequent upon the publication of *Witchcraft Today* and growing general interest in Wicca.

The latter, however, was also responsible for a proportionately increasing tendency for the popular press to run features attacking witchcraft as Satanism, which commenced in 1955 and continued until the end of the decade. In 1957 and 1959 the original London coven was denounced sensationally and unscrupulously, putting a considerable strain upon its members and fracturing relations between Valiente's group and Gerald Gardner. The latter, from the relative security of his museum in the Isle of Man, continued to feed the interest of the mass media in Wicca at a time when the former were anxious to see it diminished. The result was not merely a total breach between the two, but the addition to Gardner's Book of Shadows of a new document called 'The Craft Laws'. Purporting to be traditional, and studded with archaisms which looked odd within a thoroughly modern syntax, they represented something like a constitution for Wiccans, regulating relationships between them and providing for common rules of action within a framework of autonomous covens. They also, as Valiente noted with particular anger, attempted to limit the power of the high priestess and set a term to her office (Valiente, 1989: 65–74; Kelly, 1991: 145–62).

Gardner himself generally profited from his own regular appearances in the press, which attracted a growing number of would-be witches to contact him at his base in the Isle of Man. Coupled with introductions made through existing friends, this process meant that during the last five years of his life, from 1959 to 1964, he initiated a set of new high priestesses who were between them to be responsible for the foundation of most of the subsequent lineages of Gardnerian Wicca. Patricia Crowther established covens in the north of England, and became well known during the early 1960s as a spokeswoman for witchcraft on radio and television. Monique Wilson produced the main line of American Gardnerian covens, and most fertile of all was Ray Bone, whose initiates spread through Britain to generate most of its present-day Gardnerians. Gerald also crowned his literary work with a last book, *The Meaning of Witchcraft*, answering the press attacks and attempting to establish the historical credentials of his religion more firmly by relating it to a string of ancient religious texts and images, and later magical groups. When he died, aged 79, its existence was secure.

OTHER TRADITIONS

The reality of Gardner's claim to have discovered an existing religion is only one of two large problems which confront a historian concerned with the origins of Wicca. The other, closely related, is whether any other groups of pagan witches existed at the time when he was forming his own. It was crucial to his portrayal of this process that he was believed to be reviving an old and secret faith that had almost died out; built into that portrayal, therefore, was the suggestion that other adherents of that faith might have survived in the manner of the 'New Forest coven', and could surface to claim their rightful place in history now that Gardner had initiated the process of emergence. In order to do so credibly, however, such groups would either have to approximate to the Gardnerian model of what traditional pagan witches ought to be like, or else to challenge that model directly as fraudulent or inadequate. For anybody who wanted to follow the former course, an adequate blueprint was available at any time from 1954 in *Witchcraft Today*, reinforced by *High Magic's Aid*. The whole Gardnerian Book of Shadows was published in 1964, in a pirated edition issued by Charles Cardell.

At the beginning of the 1960s a New Forest witch, Sybil Leek, became well known as a media personality, and ran a group of her own according to what she asserted to be ways learned in an international network of old covens into which she had been initiated long before; Doreen Valiente thought that her rites sounded similar to those of Gardner (Alderman,

1973: 169–72; Valiente, 1989: 145–7). From 1958 to 1964 the aforementioned Charles Cardell mounted a campaign to descredit Gardner and to substitute himself as the true fount of knowledge concerning traditional pagan witchcraft. There is no doubt now that he was a charlatan (Kelly, 1991: 137–43; 'Robert', pers. comm.; 'Bran', pers, comm.). Since that time the number of pagan covens using the labels of 'hereditary', 'traditional' or simply 'old' has grown fairly steadily.

There seem to have been a number of different processes at work to produce this phenomenon. In several cases known to the present writer, it has been the result of the desire of groups, or founders of groups, to practise pagan witchcraft in ways different from those of mainstream Wicca and without any sense of accountability to the national Wiccan network. In three more, also in personal experience, people genuinely trained in the old-fashioned popular witchcraft described earlier, founded covens in the 1960s which followed the Wiccan model but in which they practised a lot of the older operative magic. As said above, most modern pagan witches employ techniques gained, directly or through reading, from this tradition.

When these phenomena are taken into account, however, there remain a number of claims for the continuous existence of certain covens from before 1950. In some cases these are made at second hand, people repeating what they were told since the 1950s by elders of the group concerned; into this category would fall the accounts of a nationwide network of traditional covens made by Bill Liddell (Liddell and Howard, 1994), of one which met near Chanctonbury, Sussex (127–36; Valiente, 1989: 139; Jones and Matthews, 1990) and of one in Lincolnshire, described to me by a man trained in it. There are also, however, memoirs by two people who were themselves allegedly initiated into long-established covens in the 1940s; Rhiannon Ryall, who set her experiences in the Devon–Somerset borderland (Ryall, 1989), and a recent contributor to the Pagan magazine, *The Cauldron*, who told of his inception into a group in north-western England. The only positive proof of these assertions would be either completely independent testimony or evidence (diaries, letters, photographs) from the period in question or earlier. Neither would, in the nature of things, be easy to produce, and the absence of it does not automatically invalidate the claims concerned; although Liddell's testimony can be faulted in specific points of fact and Ryall describes a religion so widespread and rooted in local society that it seems bizarre that nobody else would have recorded or testified to it. There is nothing inherently improbable in the idea that pagan witch groups could have evolved independently from Gardnerian Wicca, drawing upon the same common cultural pool of images and impulses. In the present state of the evidence, this is probably all that can be said.

This being so, it is ironic and may be significant that the most important developments in pagan witchcraft during the 1960s were produced by two individuals who are now generally considered to have masked considerable creative talent behind an insistence that they were following inherited teachings; the whole image of 'the Old Religion' at that time would hardly have allowed them to be taken seriously had they stated anything else. The first was Robert Cochrane, who flourished between 1963 and 1966, and inspired a small network of groups which worked between the Cotswolds and Sussex. He laid great emphasis upon witchcraft as a mystery religion, with an elaborate symbolism which he expounded with considerable skill, and an ingrained sense of the age, majesty and fearsome power of its pagan deities. He rejected the Gardnerian use of nudity and the scourge, laid a much greater emphasis upon a close relationship with the natural world, had a different system of correspondences between the cardinal points and the elements, and worked a quite distinctive set of rituals. His groups were termed 'clans' and were centred upon a male 'magister' rather than upon the high priestess.

In 1964 he gained the support of Doreen Valiente, who had spent the years since her breach with Gardner working with pagan witches in Sussex. She had also become a writer upon witchcraft herself, although posing (as Gardner at first had done) as a scholar observing others (Valiente, 1962). Delighted to find a tradition which was apaprently both old and independent of Gardner, she lent Cochrane her considerable skills as a priestess and a poet. Near the end of the year he and his friends established the first national body for pagan witches, the Witchcraft Research Association, with the first national periodical for them, *Pentagram*. At the same time, he drew the interest of a journalist, Justine Glass, who duly produced a book in 1965, *Witchcraft*, giving a sympathetic account of his tradition as if it were the normative one.

This was the fundamental weakness of his strategy; that he and some of his friends aimed not merely to become the guiding forces in British witchcraft, but to guide it firmly into their own ways. The opening of a full-scale attack by them upon the Gardnerians led to the collapse of both the organization and the magazine during 1965, and the alienation of Valiente. The latter had also caught out Cochrane in a deceit and an inconsistency concerning the alleged antiquity of his tradition, and begun to suspect that he had devised the latter himself. His personal life collapsed at the same time as his ambitions, and he committed suicide in 1966, leaving some devoted followers behind to continue his practices and teachings (Valiente, 1989: 117–36). He was still young when he died; had he survived this period of crisis to practise as a witch until the present, then it is likely that 'Cochranian Wicca' would have taken its place alongside Gardnerian as one of the great formal divisions of modern pagan witchcraft. Instead, his successors have continued to use the labels 'Traditional' or 'Old' Craft, which create some confusion and invite discussion.

His tragic demise cleared the way for the rise to pre-eminence of a different personality, and variety of Wicca. Until this point the centre of gravity of the religion had remained firmly in the south of England, its chief representative in the north being the Gardnerian high priestess Patricia Crowther, who had founded covens in Yorkshire, Lancashire and Nottinghamshire, and come out in public as a witch, giving numerous lectures and media interviews, and producing a book with her husband Arnold (Crowther and Crowther, 1965). In November 1961 she received a letter from a man in his mid-thirties and living in Manchester, signing himself Alex Sanders. He told her that he had been gifted since childhood with clairvoyance, that his grandmother had informed him that they were descended from a witch, and that he had always wanted to be one himself. He went on to say that he had never been able to contact anybody who could help him, until he saw her and Arnold on television. Pat Crowther subsequently took a look at him and rejected him for initiation, a slight which he never forgave (Johns, 1969: 58–60; Valiente, 1989: 165–6). Instead he got himself accepted into her daughter coven in Nottinghamshire, the high priestess of which was Pat Kopinski. He may also have visited Gardner; by either or both means he obtained a copy of the Gardnerian Book of Shadows (Valiente, 1989: 166; Kelly, 1991: xiii). In September 1962 he launched himself into the world of media relations in which the Crowthers had established themselves so effectively, staging a ritual for the *Manchester Evening Chronicle*. As a result he was dismissed from his job, and Kopinski tired of her role as high priestess and abandoned him at some point soon after that (Johns, 1969: 61–7; Valiente, 1989: 166–8).

This sequence of events would have deterred many another person from a career in witchcraft. Instead, Sanders set to work to build up covens of his own in and around Manchester, and by 1965 he seems to have founded three. He had also acquired as a high priestess a stupendously beautiful and strong-minded woman called Maxine Morris, who was aged 18 in that year. The two of them were handfasted to each other then, in what was probably the first Wiccan wedding service to be featured in the press. Sanders had, indeed, begun to play the media field again, and now with conspicuous success. In March 1966, infuriated by reports that he had been engaged as adviser on a film about contemporary witchcraft, two Gardnerian grandees, Patricia Crowther and Ray Bone, made the fatal mistake of informing a newspaper that he was a charlatan who knew nothing of genuine Wicca. They provided him with the perfect opportunity for revenge, for he blithely replied, to a media community which had come to regard him as good copy, that they represented a phoney modern cult, whereas he worked the true and ancient witchcraft, taught to him by his grandmother (Valiente, 1989 : 168–71). From that moment onward he stuck to the tale that this grandmother had initiated him at the age of seven, and that the Gardnerian Book of Shadows which he used for his rites had in fact been copied from hers. When these additions are pared away from his biography, what emerges instead is a story of a Manchester upbringing marked by poverty, and a career in Spiritualism in which he demonstrated gifts as a psychic healer (Johns, 1969: 10–60).

In 1967 Alex and Maxine moved to the capital, with the titles of King and Queen of the Witches, and held court together there for six years. They became the principal beneficiaries of the decade's powerful rein-forcement of those same impulses in modern culture which had created Wicca in the first place; nostalgia for the natural and rural world, feminism, sexual liberation, dissatisfaction with established religious institutions and social norms, and a desire for a greater individual self-expression and self-fulfilment. To the radical counter-culture of London around 1970, there were two basement flats which really mattered: the one from which Oz magazine was edited and the one from which the Sanders operated. They worked indefatigably, lecturing, training and initiating, and also providing spiritual healing and counselling; their home became an un-official out-patient clinic for drug addicts. They also maintained their status as the favourite witches of the mass media. By the early 1970s their initiates outnumbered those of any other pagan witch tradition in Britain.

Alex Sanders's one deficiency was as an author, and here he compen-sated with Robert Cochrane's trick of finding a tame journalist; in his case June Johns, who produced an admiring biography of him in 1969. He then found another, Stewart Farrar, to write an account of the actual workings of his Wicca which was published in 1971 as *What Witches Do*. Farrar provided a double reward, because he was initiated himself and he and his wife Janet became two of the Sanders's most distinguished pupils. In 1976 Maxine brought out an autobiography, and the following year another sympathetic study of her was produced by a journalist, Richard Deutch. Gardner's ghosted autobiography had been low-key and objec-tive; the Sanders, by contrast, told their life stories as medieval hagiogra-phies, full of miracles and portraying the protagonists as warriors in a constant battle of good magic against bad. This was further gall for the Gardnerians and other witches, but it was also a reply to continuing attacks in the popular press which sought to equate all witchcraft with evil.

There was more to 'Alexandrian' Wicca, however, than outrageous flamboyance. In part the name was, of course, self-referential ('Sandersian

Wicca' did not have the same ring), but it was formally represented as an allusion to the great city of the ancient world in which the religious and magical traditions of so many cultures had met. Alex brought into Wicca much of the traditional learned magic of Cabbala, the Tarot and the Golden Dawn, which other branches of it had deliberately kept out. The importation of much from Judaeo-Christian sources was made easier by the manner in which the Sanders blurred the boundaries of their paganism. Alex asserted that Christians were welcome in his covens if they recognized that his god was also theirs (Johns, 1969: 121), while Maxine claimed that her astral body had visited the Christian heaven and found it 'useful and beautiful' (Sanders, 1976: 144–5).

Their joint reign lasted until 1973, when they separated and Alex moved from London to Sussex. Maxine continued to preach and practise Wicca at the same rate from the same address until the end of the decade, when she too began to withdraw. In 1982 she joined the Liberal Catholic Church, an eclectic esoteric organization sprung from Theosophy. Alex's geographical retreat had been accompanied by a retirement from public availability and public attention, but he was neither idle nor any less a Wiccan. Instead, he was quietly developing forms of pagan witchcraft which were more accessible to gay and bisexual men, breaking down the overt hostility to homosexuals which Gardner had embedded in it together with the stress on gender polarity. He was also training initiates from Continental Europe, so that Alexandrian Wicca had become planted in several of its countries by the time that he died, in 1988.

It was not to be in Europe that the most significant expansion of pagan witchcraft was to take place, however, but in the USA; and this was in turn to rebound upon British paganism and alter its character. In this sense, the history of Wicca and its relations in the 1970s and 1980s was to be one aspect of the Special Relationship between Britain and America.

AMERICAN FEMINIST WITCHCRAFT

There is no doubt that the USA had its own indigenous pagan revival; indeed, it produced the first self-conscious modern pagan religion, the Church of Aphrodite, established in Long Island in 1938 (Adler, 1986: 233–6). From the 1930s at latest, also, it contained groups of witches working initiatory traditions, although their beliefs and rites are now very hard to reconstruct because they were later heavily overlaid by those of Wicca, coming in from England (Adler, 1986: 67–9; Kelly, 1991: 23–6). All the English branches of the religion arrived there in the 1960s and 1970s, but more important still were the books of Murray and Gardner, which were read by people trained in folk magic imported into America by the vast range of peasant cultures represented by its immigrants. These then imposed a pagan and ceremonial structure upon it to develop a very rich variety of 'family traditions' of witch religion (Alder, 1986: 70–8).

A different sort of current in American witchcraft arose in the late 1960s, and derived from the simple fact that the figure of the witch is one of the very few images of independent female power which Western civilization has offered to modernity. As such it had to be exploited by feminism, and was from 1968, when an organization called WITCH (Women's International Conspiracy From Hell) was formed in New York, with a manifesto which stated that witchcraft had been the religion of all Europe before Christianity and of European peasants for centuries after. Its persecution in the early modern period had therefore been the suppression of an alternative culture by the ruling elite, but also a war against feminism, for the religion had been served by the most courageous, aggressive, independent and sexually liberated women in the populace. Nine million of these had been put to death. To gain freedom, modern women needed, therefore, to become witches again, and could be so simply 'by being female, untamed, angry, joyous and immortal' (Adler, 1986: 179).

This was a full-blooded restatement of the nineteenth-century liberal myth of the medieval witch religion, and during the 1970s it became embedded in American radical feminism. A Hungarian refugee who had settled in California, Zsuzsanna Budapest, enunciated the principle that witchcraft was closed to men, and founded a tradition of covens which became called 'Dianic', after the man-shunning classical goddess (Adler, 1986: 178). More generally, the increasing American feminist concern with domestic and sexual violence compounded the preoccupation with historical witch persecution as the torture and murder of women. Gardner's dramatic expression for the early modern trials, 'The Burning Times', was widely used by radicals in the USA by the end of the 1970s, as part of an image of witchcraft as a religion conceived in rebellion, with the greatest toll of martyrs in the history of any faith, and which could only be true to its nature when fighting oppression (Adler, 1986: 178; Purkiss, 1996: 8–26). This theme combined with another which had also appeared in the late 1960s, in the writings of Tim ('Otter') Zell, then based in Missouri. He portrayed the planet as a single living being, whom he identified with the Earth Mother believed to have been a deity venerated throughout ancient Europe. He suggested that only a revived paganism, imbued with a mission to transform Western attitudes, could save that planet, and deity, from destruction by modern technology (Adler, 1986: 293–308). In America during the 1970s Mother Earth became conflated with the goddess of the witches and with a general feminist yearning for a recognition of female divinity, to produce an entity called The Goddess, whose devotees were pitted against patriarchy, militarism and ecological destruction.

There was a natural tension between a concept of witchcraft as something inherent in women and released in them by consciousness-raising, and one of it as a closed, hierarchical and initiatory mystery religion, which balanced the genders in creative polarity. This was brilliantly resolved in 1979, with the publication of *The Spiral Dance* by Starhawk, a Californian feminist writer who had been trained by Gardner-ians and initiated into one of the home-grown American witch traditions influenced by Wicca, the Faerie. She showed how the coven could be turned into a training group in which women could be liberated, men re-educated, and alternative human relationships explored. She reinterpreted magic in terms of psychology, as a set of techniques for self-fulfillment and the realization of human potential, linking witchcraft to poetry and creative play. And she suggested that, once developed, a network of covens could be a potent mechanism for campaigning for radical reform. In the 1980s, as Reaganism further polarized and embittered American attitudes, her writing became more obviously devoted to the specific ends of left-wing politics, but still soaked in the language, and the historical mythology, of feminist witchcraft (Starhawk, 1979, 1982, 1987).

America in the 1970s and 1980s was the nursery of feminist thought in general, and radical feminist thought in particular, for the whole Western world, and the impact of its new view of pagan witchcraft upon European counter-cultures was proportionately profound. *The Spiral Dance* became the best-selling book on modern witchcraft yet written, and all over Europe and America in the 1980s feminists began thinking of themselves as witches, and starting covens, simply because of reading it; it had replaced *Witchcraft Today* as the model text. As well as equipping them with books, America also gave these new-style pagan witches songs and chants, the product of another development of the 1970s: the growth in numbers of American pagans to the point at which large conventions of them became possible. Cost and convenience meant that these took the form of summer camps, a phenomenon with which Americans of the time were commonly familiarized in youth. A feature of such camps had always been fireside singing and chanting, and pagan musicians swiftly responded to the need for these. It was at the Pan-Pagan Festival held in Indiana in 1980 that the chant 'We All Come From The Goddess' first became widely known (Adler, 1986: 346–7, 424). In that year, also, Charlie Murphy wrote a folk song, 'The Burning Times', which both summed up and augmented the radical feminist notion of the early modern trials. These and several others spread across North America and then to Britain, giving witches and the growing pagan community in which they were now embedded an enhanced sense of solidarity as an international resistance movement. This was further increased when another Californian, a Wiccan high priestess called Marion Zimmer Bradley, published a historical novel in 1982 which interwove the feminist myth of the Old Religion with the traditional Arthurian cycle. It was called *The Mists of Avalon* and became an international bestseller.

Even in its English homeland, Wicca had to adapt in response to these developments. It was indeed already changing during the 1970s as a result of internal dynamics. Doreen Valiente at last went public as a witch, and being now outside the established system of coven leaders, attempted to circumvent it. She wrote three books during the decade which taught readers how to initiate themselves, work their own rituals and magic, and start their own groups (Valiente, 1973, 1975, 1978). Reinforced by *The Spiral Dance*, they produced a crop of 'Do It Yourself' covens in the 1980s, most loosely employing the label of Wiccan. Towards the end of this next decade a further phenomenon became prominent in both America and Britain, of pagan witches who preferred to work alone, and a set of books were published as manuals to assist them in doing so (Beth, 1990; Cuningham, 1990; Green, 1991). These in turn naturally encouraged the appearance of such people, to whom the author of the most famous, Rae Beth, gave the engaging term of 'hedge witches', inculcating a sense of them as examplars of a rural and traditional England.

British Wicca had been altering in other ways as well. It had always been linked to other strands of thought in the esoteric fringe, and its most influential figures had always been autodidacts; some (including Gardner and Valiente) openly contemptuous of formal education. Now they often swallowed whole the new 'alternative' beliefs in energy-bearing lines running across the earth's surface ('leys') and the feminist interpretation of British prehistory made by Michael Dames; notable subscribers to these included Valiente, again, and Alex Sanders (Valiente, 1978: 56; and 1989: 214–15; 'The Sussex Workings', *The Cauldron*, Hallowe'en 1979).

The American ideas none the less still made a dramatic impact. Valiente was fully converted to an indignant feminism after reading them (Valiente, 1989: 180–90). Alex Sanders, who in the 1960s had talked mostly about the god of the witches, brought out in the 1980s a tape dedicated to celebrating The Goddess, with 'The Burning Times' sung behind his words near the end. In a series of books produced during that latter decade, Janet and Stewart Farrar accepted the American radical feminist belief in the literal existence of prehistoric matriarchy, and stressed the identity of Wicca as a goddess-centred faith. More generally, whereas Wiccans had tended until the mid-1970s to represent their tradition primarily as a means of expressing psychic powers, in the 1980s they emphasized it instead as the feminist religion par excellence. In so doing they were certainly meeting a challenge, from the number of essentially feminist covens springing up on the Starhawk model. In the middle of the decade a Dianic witch inspired by Z. Budapest, Shan Jayran, established The House of the Goddess in London, a temple dedicated primarily to feminist witchcraft and very firmly outside the Wiccan networks. She went on to develop a national contact service ('Paganlink') and held Britain's first national Pagan festival at Hallowe'en 1987, a tremendous success which attracted about 1350 participants (Valiente, 1989: 193–4; Jayran, 1987).

The whole process had brought considerable gains to modern pagan witchcraft. The latter had been given a much larger and well-defined constituency of support, had been brought out of the occult fringe into the mainstream of international cultural politics, and had been greatly enhanced in its obvious relevance to contemporary issues and needs. Its identification with the cause of female liberation had made it respectable among radical intellectuals, and scholars involved in religious studies were starting during the 1980s to recognize it as a valid contribution to the quest for a feminist spirituality – at least in North America (Spretnak, 1982). By the end of the decade the American mass media, also, was starting to distinguish between witchcraft and Satanism and to regard the feminist credentials of the former as giving it the status of a genuine, if eccentric, religion (Rowe and Cavender, 1991).

There were also, however, some disadvantages to the new situation, at least in the eyes of many Wiccans. There was a real danger that by being identified so firmly with a particular counter-culture, their faith would be boxed into a corner, and left there as society moved on. In particular it troubled some that the composite American myth of the Old Religion and the Burning Times was so seriously at variance with recent developments in professional history and archaeology, including the final abandonment of the Murray thesis. The incorporation of that myth into a radical creed made a questioning of it among its devotees very difficult without attracting charges of defending patriarchy or betraying the great struggle to save the planet. Starhawk's glorification of the imagination as the finest human faculty had led in many of her readers to a disparagement of reason and the intellect which cut them off from dialogue with the wider society.

By the late 1980s, therefore, it seemed possible that Wicca and its relations would be marginalized in a new way, as a cluster of fundamentalist sects. It was also especially disturbing to some British Wiccans that they had apparently lost the initiative to a rhetoric sprung from a foreign culture, which although it had some relevance to humanity in general, and a lot more to Western civilization in particular, was also fashioned according to the circumstances of a very different society, undergoing a different process of change. Ironically, although there was indeed to be a way out of the trap into which pagan witchcraft appeared to be falling, it was itself to be pioneered in the USA.

A COMING OF AGE

One of the most impressive qualities of modern American culture is that it is so self-critical; it is quite hard to find an ideological position taken up by one citizen of the USA which is not ably contested by another. This pattern holds good for its Pagan community. Only a few years after Wiccan beliefs had arrived in the USA, they were questioned and investigated by other members of that community; a process launched by two individuals above all. During the first half of the 1970s Isaac Bonewits ruthlessly and accurately exposed the shortcomings of the authors upon whom Wiccans most relied, notably Margaret Murray and Robert Graves. He argued against the notion of a Europe-wide pagan witch religion, and suggested that the reality had been a scatter of different survivals from a pre-Christian ancient world (Bonewits, 1972). During the second half of the decade he contributed a series of articles to the pagan journal *Green Egg*, which divided witchcraft into several different categories specific to time and place. Between 1971 and 1975 Aidan Kelly conducted the first textual research into the Books of Shadows, revealing the long process of revision which they had undergone even since 1950 (Kelly, 1991: xiv–xvii).

It is significant that both men were intellectuals who had allegiances to alternative modern pagan traditions, a reflection of the much greater early diversity of modern paganism in the USA, which itself reflected a much more heterogenous society. Bonewits was a magician with an interest in Celtic literatures, who subsequently became a Druid. Kelly was the author of the liturgy of a witch religion founded in California in the late 1960s, the New Reformed Orthodox Order of the Golden Dawn, which openly and honestly took its material from literary sources and creative experimentation and did not claim to be a continuous tradition. Their impact, although in the case of Bonewits initially acrimonious, was profound; by the mid-1970s it could already be claimed that most American witches were starting to accept the Old Religion more as metaphor than reality (Adler, 1986: 86–7). This was, at the least apparently, not true of the new-style feminist witches who multiplied from that time onward, but it remained so of many Wiccans in the USA. One of them was a high priestess called Margot Adler.

In 1979, just as *The Spiral Dance* was published in San Francisco, a Boston press brought out Adler's book, *Drawing Down the Moon*. The contrast between the two was in many ways the stereotypical one between the more poetic and visionary radicalism of the West Coast and the more rational and intellectual kind of the East. Whereas Starhawk's book was a celebration and a prospectus, Adler's was a history and an analysis. It explained the development of the many different varieties of paganism which existed in the USA by that time and portrayed their nature. In the process it constantly displayed a sophisticated sense of the special character of specific times and places, and of the considerable differences between individual spiritual needs. It at once celebrated the power and utility of myth and drew a firm distinction between mythology and reality. It recognized that Wicca had probably been built upon a pseudo-history, and then suggested that this was hardly unusual in the development of religious tradition, and that Wiccans deserved credit for the fact that they were increasingly conscious of this without losing a sense of the viability of their actual experience of the divine. What emerged from *Drawing Down the Moon* was an argument for paganisms as ideal religions for a pluralist culture, and for witchcraft as one of these.

Nothing as intellectually rigorous and powerful as this had emerged from a modern pagan pen before, but as it was more demanding, more expensive, and less intoxicating than *The Spiral Dance*, its impact was proportionately more muted, and especially so in Britain where its readership was long mostly confined to Wiccan intellectuals. There was, indeed, a parallel development, which might have produced a more objective sense of historical context among British witches. It took its origin in a quarrel between Alex Sanders and the Farrars, as a result of which he revoked their authority in his tradition. This was the worst mistake that Sanders ever made, for it alienated his most talented and respected early initiates and freed them to develop a reformed Alexandrian Wicca.

As part of this work they formed an alliance with Doreen Valiente to compare the Gardnerian and Alexandrian Books of Shadows, an enterprise which proved conclusively that the latter had derived from the former, in the version current around 1960. This destroyed the Alexandrian foundation legend, but also increased the interest of the three Wiccan grandees in the textual history of the Book before that date. In unison between 1980 and 1984 they identified many of the revisions made in the 1950s and the sources for some of the passages found in the earliest recension. Further than that, however they could not go, partly because they lacked the necessary knowledge of the wider cultural context of the earlier period and partly because the vital documents were all hidden from them, in North American collections.

It was also the case, however, that their venture was not only, or perhaps even primarily, antiquarian, but linked to the process commenced earlier by Valiente, of setting would-be Wiccans free of the established coven structure by giving them books from which they could learn if a suitable coven was not available. The text of the Book of Shadows was not merely analysed by this exercise, but established, and every part published in a 'definitive' form, and to its rituals the Farrars added others, for augmented seasonal festivities, and for naming of children, marriages and funerals, in which the Book had been deficient. Not only was a growing Wiccan community thus properly served at all points, but a self-constructed coven could operate in wholly 'orthodox' fashion (Farrar and Farrar, 1948, 1981).

As said above, also, all three writers heavily subscribed to newly arrived ideas which made British witchcraft less, and not more, sophisticated than that of Margot Adler and her like in the USA; nor was there any writer within it who could match the poetic rhetoric of Starhawk. By the mid-1980s it was trailing behind its American equivalent in every respect, and to a great extent being dragged behind it. Nevertheless, forces which were to restore a balance were already at work, springing from roots which lay now over a decade in the past. In 1968 a small group of Gardnerians had started an informal newsletter to keep in touch with each other, which took the title *The Wiccan*. Two years later this became the official communication of the Pagan Front, a Wiccan committee set up to present the case for paganism to the public. The latter continued to function at a low level for the rest of the decade, acting mainly as a contact service and as a defence mechanism for witches who were suffering from local victimization (Leonora James, pers. comm.). In 1977 a second 'Craft' newsletter was founded, *The Cauldron*, which catered more for those traditions which lay outside the Gardnerian and Alexandrian mainstream.

In 1979 the editorship of *The Wiccan*, and the co-ordination of the Front, was taken over by a Gardnerian high priestess, Leonora James, who was an Oxbridge-trained classicist. In 1981 the name of the organization was changed to The Pagan Federation, an alteration provoked partly by the way in which the term 'Front' had been appropriated by neo-Nazis, and partly by the sense that the body itself would function best in the future as a network of local groups. For the first half of that decade, however, its work depended almost wholly upon James's own family of covens, while the two magazines continued to consist in practice of home-produced sheets of type (Leonara James, pers. comm.)

At the same time the ground was being prepared for expansion, in the form of a multiplication of varieties of paganism equivalent to that which had taken place much earlier in the USA. From the 1970s small groups were practising versions of the religions of the ancient Norse and Anglo-Saxons, and the Fellowship of Isis was founded to provide a common framework for celebrating goddess-focused traditions. The second half of the 1980s saw a dramatic expansion in pagan Druidry and the burgeoning of the fashion for solitary pagan witchcraft. In large part these movements were encouraged by the example of Wicca, and to some extent they sprang from it; the founders of two of the four new Druid orders of the period had been Wiccan high priests, and the two most celebrated writers upon the pagan Celtic mysteries had been members, respectively, of a Gardnerian and a Traditional coven. It is also true that many of these people were reacting against Wicca and striving for a different way of working rather than inspired by it, but the common experience was important. By the last years of the decade, the potential existed for a national alliance of Pagan traditions (the capital letter now indicating a self-conscious modern application of the term).

The catalyst for one came, again, from the USA, this time in the shape of a panic over alleged ritual abuse of children by Satanist networks conflated with Pagans, conceived and propagated by fundamentalist Christian organizations. It arrived in Britain in 1988 with the agitation of the Reachout Trust, and rapidly made an impression upon social workers and police In the event, the tragedies which resulted afflicted families which were not Pagan, but this was partly due to the speed and vigour with which Wiccans responded to the threat, and fought it during the five years until a government report disproved the assertions of the Reachout Trust and its allies. On May Eve 1988 the Pagan Federation was refounded with a leadership of five officers, a treasury, and an extended framework for dealing with correpondence and for production of *The Wiccan*. The president was Leonora James, the secretary another high priestess, Vivianne Crowley.

The latter had been trained in both the Alexandrian and the Gardnerian traditions in the 1970s, and come to prominence in the 1980s. She was also an accomplished poetess, a natural speaker, with a gentle, musical voice, and a very proficient Jungian psychologist. In 1989 she brought out a first book, *Wicca: the Old Religion in the New Age*, which provided British witchcraft at last with a writer to match Starhawk. In Crowley's pages Wicca was portrayed as an elevated Neo-Platonist mystery religion, in which each stage of training and initiation corresponded to parts of the human psyche, and led eventually to a personal completion. If her elegant prose pleased the intellect, the senses were nourished by the power of her verse, and the whole exuded a profound spirituality. She was representing a mature religion, capable of taking its place alongside the more established varities; symbolically, in that same year she led a Pagan ceremony as part of a Festival of Faith held at Canterbury Cathedral.

Simultaneously, she and her colleagues on the committee of the Federation were pushing forward their work under the forceful leadership of Leonora James, bombarding national and local politicians, the mass media, and educational institutions, with objective information about

British Paganism. A structure of regional groups rapidly developed to underpin it, and made possible the adoption of an elective system for the ruling committee from 1991. The same process drew in representatives from the range of other Pagan traditions which had now developed, and the Wiccan dominance of the Federation gave way naturally and painlessly to an equality of representation. Membership swelled from hundreds to thousands, annual conferences were held from 1989, and over the same period an annual Pan-European Wiccan Convention was established in parallel, involving witches from all over the Continent; in drawing closer to a European family of nations and away from a transatlantic axis, Wicca was of course following a general shift in British attitudes. Both *The Wiccan* and *The Cauldron* changed to a full magazine format, and in 1994 the former went glossy, with the significant change of title to *Pagan Dawn*.

The system of elections had brought with it a regular change of presidency, releasing Leonora James to foster the intellectual life of British Paganism. Her academic training had made her impatient of the increasingly emotional, anti-rational and counter-cultural drift of British witchcraft in the 1980s, and determined to realize more of the potential of Paganism to become a stable and imposing complex of religions drawing upon a tremendous inheritance of ancient civilization. At the end of the 1980s, therefore, she began to make her mark upon television and radio. Witches had of course been doing this since the 1950s, but almost invariably as a branch of the entertainment industry, in the format of the interview or the chat show. James now weighed in as a participant in serious religious affairs programmes, and the columns of the highbrow press, representing the merits of Wicca and a broader Paganism successfully against theological pugilists such as the Archdeacon of Durham. At the same time she fostered links between the Pagan Federation and academic scholars; the work of the present writer, growing out of his earlier interest in ancient paganisms and folklore, is partly due to her initiatives.

American academics had taken some notice of Wicca in the early 1970s, but subsumed this in general considerations of the burgeoning interest in the occult. Only in 1981 did a sustained study commence, carried out by an American postgraduate student based at Cambridge University, Tanya Luhrmann. This was concerned with the practise of magic in English society, and so dealt with only one aspect of Wicca and devoted more of its time and space to groups of ritual magicians who were not necessarily Pagan. Nonetheless, it was assisted by James, and by a famous Gardnerian coven into which Luhrmann was actually initiated, and represented the most serious and informed academic appraisal of modern witchcraft which had yet been made. Published as *Persuasions of the Witch's Craft*, in 1989, it made a considerable impact upon both the academic and the Pagan worlds.

The relationship between the two, indeed, was now changing fast. This was partly because the new size, sophistication and public profile of the Pagan community inevitably drew scholarly attention. It was partly because the panic which had been manufactured over alleged satanic ritual abuse of children, and the damage that this had done, had revealed the persisting ignorance of Pagan and other new or revived religions in public bodies of all kinds. It was also, however, because young academics who had themselves acquired Pagan beliefs were starting to make their mark; and in this process Britain had become the crucible. A seminar was convened at King's College London in December 1990 to discuss the relationships between Paganism and other traditions of religion. It was attended by several notable Wiccans, including Leonora James and Vivianne Crowley, and a number of academics from different disciplines, including myself. One of the most significant aspects of the occasion was the spectacle of one Wiccan after another speaking of the Murray thesis as foundation myth, and of the Old Religion as metaphor, in the manner of Margot Adler; but now with a yet greater sensitivity and erudition. Until the end of the 1980s, probably the overwhelming majority of British witches had believed in both as objective truths; now that barrier between Wicca and scholarship (which was one major gateway for it to the wider national community) was dissolving.

Events now tumbled like dominoes. In 1991 a further impetus to them was provided from America, when Aidan Kelly at last published his study of Gerald Gardner's papers, *Crafting the Art of Magic*. It was a gift to any future researcher, for not only did it print vital source material for the first time, and launch a determined assault upon the weakening notion that Gardner had revealed an old religion, but it did so with such intemperance that it would make any subsequent scholarly treatment of the same issues look moderate, and therefore be more welcome to the Wiccan communities, by comparison. In 1994 the first full-scale academic conference on Paganism in contemporary Britain was held at Newcastle University, and two years later it was followed by another at Lancaster, this time a huge and truly international event concerned with 'Nature Religion Today'. From 1994, also Pagan chaplains began to appear in British universities, and Paganism was recognized as a valid complex of religions by the hospital and prison services. In 1995 the British Pagan community produced its own revised version of its history, briefly in Vivianne Crowley's *Phoenix from the Flame*, and extensively in the *History of Pagan Europe* by Prudence Jones and Nigel Pennick, the latter another project directly inspired by Leonora James. Based upon original research rather than inherited or second-hand belief, this portrait celebrated the extraordinary richness of pagan traditions in old Europe, and the ways in which paganisms's images and ideas had persisted in Western cultures ever since.

In the process the figure of the witch herself was starting to recede, to be replaced by those of the priestess and priest. Wiccans were ceasing to identify primarily with the victims of the early modern trials and starting to look over and around them, to reclaim the heritage of classical antiquity, and of the Celtic and northern literatures. They were less and less the representatives of an age-old peasant resistance movement and more and more a trained group of religious and magical practitioners, answering a growing call from mainstream society and appropriating some of its oldest and most familiar images. They were no longer so much the inheritors of an archaic faith as members of the earliest, and foremost, of an important constellation of modern successors. These changes were symbolized neatly by the increasingly rare usage of the word 'witch', at least in public discourse, and the substitution of 'Pagan'. For all this, however, the challenge which Wicca's forms still pose to established notions of religion is not the less radical because it has become more familiar; and at the heart of its mysteries lies a particular notion, and experience, of the transformative power of something which is called magic. In those senses, its initiates will always be witches.

THE NATURE OF MODERN PAGAN WITCHCRAFT

The pleasing rhythms and rhetorical flourishes of narrative history, even narrative in which sections of analysis are embedded, can always neglect a great deal; it should be obvious that the one above is limited by being, at least until the very end, a view from the outside looking in, and from the top looking down. Other perspectives would produce very different emphases, though perhaps not a different story. What the treatment most obviously fails to convey, however, is more than a hint of the qualitative nature of modern pagan witchcraft, and this is an important enough aspect to deserve consideration now, in conclusion. I have to date worked with 20 British covens, almost three times the number observed by Tanya Luhrmann, the only other academic to publish in the field hitherto. They represent between them Gardnerian, Alexandrian and Traditional varieties (the tradition in some of the latter certainly being the old and honourable one of DIY). To most of these I was an occasional, often a one-time, visitor, but I have observed five of them simultaneously, over a period of half a decade (effectively the early 1990s). My analysis below may well neglect some kinds of backwoods Traditional or Hereditary coven, and it does not treat of the large number of solitary pagan witches; but my acquaintance with a score of the latter suggests that their beliefs and practices are substantially the same, within the bounds of individual operation.

The Pagan Federation has issued, since 1989, a set of three principles which define a Pagan: love of, reverence for, and kinship with, the natural world; a positive morality based upon the discovery and development of each person's true nature, providing that this is done without harming others; and an active acceptance of both female and male divinity. These principles were drafted by Wiccans and so are certainly true of them; but at a glance it must be obvious that they can easily characterize not only every other variety of modern Western Paganism, but Hinduism, Shinto and many tribal animist beliefs as well. Furthermore, there is nothing here that could not be endorsed by liberal Christians, even the last being no obstacle to a theology which views 'God' as a being beyond gender, incorporating both female and male. Conversely, the same principles leave room for a very wide range of inclusive beliefs, let alone practices. An unspoken definition is therefore crucial; that in practice modern Pagans are people who hold those tenets and turn for symbolism, kinship and inspiration to the pre-Christian religions of Europe and the Near East.

Furthermore, other characteristics of modern pagan witchcraft seem to be as important and definitive as those above, if left implicit. One is that the aim of religious ritual is not to honour or supplicate the divine alone, but to bring out the divinity in human beings; this is a large part of the point of the modern Craft. A literal faith in its deities is not necessary. Some witches view them as archetypes, representing fundamental truths of the cosmos; others as entities which have been given life by projection from human beliefs and desires; others as symbols of perceived aspects of the world; and yet others as genuine beings, with their own personalities, consciousness and wills. As Luhrmann has shown, modern witchcraft can be *par excellence* the religion of the romantic atheist.

The central purpose of it is not to pay reverence to divinities but to cultivate personal powers of self-control and self-knowledge, and perhaps of clairvoyance, prophecy, psychokinesis and psychic healing. Whether or not the witches whom I have met have ever obtained power over anything or anybody else, the elders among them have certainly acquired it over themselves; which is quite an achievement in itself. It is not, however, merely a secular system of technical training, but a mystical one which is interwoven with notions of an active supernatural and divine world, whether or not the existence of this is taken literally. Some witches identify the acquisition of magical ability as being the discovery of a 'true self', and with it to release, develop and utilize normally latent mental abilities. Others view it more as a discovery of the inner workings of the cosmos, providing a greater opportunity to operate in harmony with it oneself, and thus far more effectively. Both notions, of course, are rooted deep in the Western tradtion of learned magic. They mean that modern pagan witchcraft is a religion which can have no passive participants; it is a system which must be 'worked'.

This involves an abolition of the normal distinction between religion and magic. In saying this I am aware that I appear to be opening a large can of semantic worms, in that professional sociologists and anthropologists have failed to arrive at any universally agreed definition of either, or means of distinguishing them, after 100 years of debate (cf. Hamilton, 1995: 1–120). My task here is simplified in that I use the definitions employed by witches themselves, taken in turn from those established long ago by Sir Edward Tylor and Sir James Frazer. Whether or not they apply to the thoughts and activities of any other peoples, they do fit those of historic Europeans: both religion and magic are means by which humans negotiate with supernatural beings, but in the former, humans are dealing with forces which are outside their control, in the latter they are seeking to control and compel them.

One aspect of this collapsing of categories is eclecticism; that modern witches, like ritual magicians, will often address classical goddesses and gods, and Hebrew angels and demons, in the same sequence of operation. Another is that all of them have the notion that human abilities can be magnified by causing a supernatural being to combine with the spirit of the person concerned. A third is that modern witchcraft has wholly lost the concept of sacrifice, as divinities do not require propitiation; rather, they are to be attracted to the witch by ritual and then enticed into cooperation. They are certainly reverenced, but are expected to find pleasure and reward enough in participation in a magical or religious act performed with sufficient shill. The combination of religion and magic is embodied in the Wiccan initiate's designation as 'priestess (or priest) and witch'. A priestess can be a passive agent, merely serving and praising the divine; not so a witch.

Pagan witchcraft is also distinguished by being a mystery religion, without public places and acts of worship. It is almost always the preserve of closed groups or solitary individuals, operating a process of training and initiation which usually takes some considerable time. Much of the joy, and effectiveness, of it lies in its identity as a tradition of secrets, associated with the night and with wild or hidden places. It is usually recognized as requiring considerable dedication and hard work, and as being unsuitable for the faint-hearted, lazy or flippant. It is accordingly highly selective and exclusive, and is mandated to care only for those who seek its aid. It lacks any sense of a missionary duty, or of a redemptive purpose, and depends instinctively upon the existence of other religions alongside it, which cater for other needs and would suit other sorts of people.

It is a highly eclectic and protean system of operation, in which the basic format of the consecrated circle with potent cardinal points, in which deities are invoked and magic worked, is filled with images and systems taken from a huge span of sources. These include the cultures of ancient Greece, Egypt, Rome, Mesopotamia, Ireland and Wales, and of the Anglo-Saxons and the Vikings, the folklores of the British Isles, the structure of prehistoric monuments, Hinduism, Buddhism, eighteenth and nineteenth-century Celtic romanticism, native America, and the modern earth mysteries and radical feminism. Nonetheless, the existence of the Book of Shadows does result in a stronger common structure to activity than obtains in other varieties of present-day Paganism. This structure includes the duotheism of the divine couple (the god sometimes being eliminated in Dianic witchcraft), the careful consecration of the sacred space for each rite, the blessing and sharing of food and drink, the personification of divine beings by celebrants, 'magical' work of healing and consecration, a system of training and initiation (usually through three degrees) and the observation of ceremonies at the full moons and the eight major seasonal festivals.

Both of the two most famous Wiccan traditions have in some respects evolved away from the tastes of their founders; few Alexandrian covens work Alex Sanders's full panoply of Cabbalistic and other ritual magic, while Gerald Gardner's technique for entrancement by binding and scourging has virtually died out. Most covens retain the scourge as symbol, and for (token) use at initiation; it provides the traditional component of the ordeal for the initiate, but also forces the latter to confront the problem that life contains an almost inevitable element of suffering, and the need to come to terms with this.

A final major characteristic of modern pagan witchcraft, which it shares with other contemporary Paganisms, is the absolute centrality of creative ritual. It is a religion with a minimal theoretical structure, and its only holy writings are a book of ceremonies, which are not regarded as canonical but as a starting-point for the development of further rites. Its sacred words are not employed to hand down law but to invoke or evoke divinity. The most important function of modern witchcraft is to provide a means by which humans can experience the divine directly and power-fully; the meaning of that experience is to be rationalized later, if at all. A single coven can contain as many different interpretations of divinity as there are members. Established religions have commonly been there to tell people how they should feel *about* the divine; pagan witchcraft is there to tell people how they can *feel* the divine, using one particular system to do so. If ancient paganisms were characterized primarily by propitiation, modern pagan witchcraft is characterized primarily by consecration, of people, places and objects. Its most powerful effect is to enhance the sanctity, mystery and enchantment of modern living.

There are other aspects of Wicca, in particular, which are unusual among religions of any period. One is the tradition, firmly observed by most covens, of alternating reverence and mirth in the circle, in such a way as to balance the solemnity of some rites with others which are designed to provoke joy and merriment. A second is the celebrated practice of ritual nudity, which is maintained by most Gardnerians and Alexandrians, although not by Traditionals. Wiccan authors have provided a range of mystical justifications for this, but observation would lead me to suggest two practical reasons for its persistence. One is that it demands a high degree of trust between members of the group, and so is an excellent test for the existence of harmony and unity, without which the rituals cannot be effectively worked. The second is that, in combination with other components normally present, such as candlelight, incense and music, it conveys a very powerful sense that something abnormal is going on; that the participants in the circle have cast off their everyday selves and limitations and have entered into a space in which the extraordinary can be achieved. This is why, of course, although nudity is a great rarity in the history of religion, it is an important theme in that of magic, worldwide.

It is time to turn to more straightforward sociological aspects of the subject, the first one being the number of adherents to modern pagan witchcraft. In this respect its stronghold is certainly now the USA; Aidan Kelly suggested in 1991 that America contained about 200,000 Pagans, and the majority of those would be witches (Kelly, 1991: ix). In Canada and Australia they can be counted, at the least, in thousands, while most European countries have populations ranging from a few hundred to a few thousand; these estimates are suggested by the representatives at recent Pan-European Wiccan Conventions. My own calculation for Britain is based upon the Pagan Druid orders, who keep track of their membership in a way that other varieties of Pagan do not. Their combined totals yielded a figure of about 6,000 Pagan Druids in the nation in 1996. In the local Pagan festivals, gatherings, moots and networks, Druids are generally outnumbered by witches, with a ratio which causes me to believe that about 6,000 Druids indicates the present existence of about 10,000 witches, in initiatory traditions.

This figure, however, conceals the existence of an important and growing phenomenon, of non-initiated Pagans who are starting to treat initiates as clergy. This is illustrated by the case of a Wiccan coven in a Midland city, which I have been observing consistently for some years. In early 1995 it had five members, and took to holding rituals at the big seasonal festivals for members of the local Pagan community who wished to celebrate them but did not themselves belong to working groups. It immediately attracted an average of 30 of these on each occasion, joined after the ceremonies by an average 20 more, who participated in the feasting and merry-making; these were still wary of being involved in ritual, but wanted nonetheless to be present in a sacred space on a sacred night, and have fellowship with those who were involved. A year later, the coven had swelled to a dozen members, and the average number of guests at its ceremonies had grown to 80, and would have been still larger had a ceiling not been imposed; I had ceased to count the numbers of those who came after the rites.

This is part of a general development in present-day Paganism, so that at those varieties of local assembly mentioned above, initiates are always now considerably outnumbered by non-initiates who look to the former as the foci of traditions. If, therefore, I add to about 10,000 initiated witches and about 6,000 Pagan Druids the approximate number of members of other kinds of initiatory Paganism (those in groups inspired by ancient Germany and Scandinavia, or by shamanism, or working explicitly pagan magic, like the Ordo Templi Orientis), the resulting figure comes to a probable maximum of 20,000 initiated British Pagans. The ratios of the local gatherings mean that it is necessary to add to that about 100,000 people who follow Pagan beliefs and practices without initiation into traditions. That, in turn, ignores the leakage of Pagan images and customs into subcultures such as New Age Travellers and rave music devotees. Interestingly, David Burnett, an evangelical Christian scholar who has made an objective if unsympathetic study of modern British Paganism, has reached identical conclusions by quite independent means (aired in a discussion with the present writer on Radio Four, 18 December 1994).

Modern British witches are, as Tanya Luhrmann found in the 1980s, drawn from a wide range of backgrounds and occupations (Luhrmann, 1989: 99–111). There are, however, some patterns to that range. My close acquaintance with 20 covens has yielded biographical information for a total of 192 individuals (the average number of the covens was eight, but some have had a turnover of membership over the time in which I have known them). They proved to belong overwhelmingly to the upper levels of the working class and the lower levels of the middle class. None had considerable wealth or political importance, or held inherited titles of honour. None directed large companies, and they included only two doctors (both in general practice), two lawyers (both solicitors) and no tenured academics. On the other hand, only 13 were seeking employment at the time when we met, and only 10 were unskilled labourers. None were factory workers, miners or farmhands. Instead they were artisans (carpenters, blacksmiths, painters and decorators, skilled gardeners, builders, and plumbers), shopkeepers, artists, service engineers (notably concerned with computers or sound systems), owners of small businesses, employees of local government (especially in the library service) and financial advisers. The professional element was provided by the eight psychologists. The common theme to most of these occupations was a higher than usual amount of independence and self-organization. All these people showed an unusual enthusiasm for reading and self-education. Thirty-four were taking courses in colleges or universities when I met them, but fully 30 of these were mature students who had gone back into the educational system. All the covens concerned held firmly to the Wiccan rule of initiating nobody under the age of 18, but otherwise the span of age was fairly even overall although varying between groups; 46 members were senior citizens.

One striking fact which became apparent was the very marked sociological similarity between British Wicca and the fastest-growing sector of British Christianity, the house church movement. The basic unit of both is a small gathered group of enthusiasts, meeting in private homes. Both show a remarkable diversity of practice within a common framework, and a tendency for groups to dissolve or to splinter easily, and then to reform. Both draw inspiration from ancient literature, in the house church case, the Bible. Both place heavy emphasis upon irrational qualities in religion, and upon magic, the house churches describing this in terms of faith-healing, speaking in tongues, or possession by demons or the Holy Spirit. Both are suspicious of public or formal authority and instinctually feel that the future is likely to be especially favourable to them. Both draw upon similar social groups; both, overall, are aspects of the important contemporary phenomenon of the privatization of religion. In terms of belief, of course, they could hardly be more different, and it is important in this context that witches tend to be pluralist, tolerant and quietist, whereas members of house churches are frequently very intolerant of other faiths and hold evangelical attitudes. It is therefore also important, and ironic, that house church members generally benefit from the generally positive public value still placed upon the word 'Christian', while witches still suffer from the traditionally negative connotations of their name

A couple of final semantic points need to be made before wrapping up. Academics specializing in Religious Studies have increasingly followed American usage in talking of pagan witchcraft, along with most new or revived religions, as a 'cult'. This is not the precise meaning of the term, as still employed by many historians and archaeologists. According to this, a cult is the veneration of a specific deity, fictional work, person or object (e.g., Bacchus, *Star Trek*, brown rice or Sir Cliff Richard). Pagan witchcraft is now a more complex system of belief than that.

Likewise, it no longer resembles a New Religious Movement, defined and portrayed by Eileen Barker and her colleagues (e.g. Barker, 1994). It does not depend heavily upon one or a few charismatic leaders. It does not appeal overwhelmingly to a particular age group or cultural group. It does not offer a radical break with existing family and social relationships; and it does not challenge the wider culture as a whole. If it ever fulfilled some of these criteria (and Wicca once fitted the first, at least), then it has long outgrown them.

In the last analysis, pagan witchcraft can only be judged by the same standards as any other religion in a predominantly secular modern society; by the benefits which it seems to give to its members, and by its achievements in literature, art and philanthropy, and its general enhancement of the quality of life. I shall end by drawing aside for a moment the veil which lies over its activities, choosing an illustration which is representative rather than extraordinary, and which I have seen paralleled on numerous other occasions when I have worked with witches. The setting was a sloping meadow upon the side of an escarpment, close to the time of the autumn equinox. It commanded a panorama of a broad river valley below, bounded by a range of other hills which made a blue wall against the further horizon. Woods of beech and oak closed it in upon three sides, and clothed the slope below, affording privacy. The grass of the meadow was refreshed by September rains, the leaves of the woods just starting to yellow in places. The sun was melting into the trees further along the escarpment, in shades of honey and tangerine; the sky opposite was the hue of cornflowers, and it would not be long before the Harvest Moon rose there, reaching its fullness that night. This place was to be the setting, between sunset and moonrise, of the handfasting (nuptial rites) of an Alexandrian Wiccan high priestess.

She and her partner, and their guests (who would include many non-Wiccans), were still on their way, and the business of that moment was for the coven which was hosting the ceremony to consecrate the space in which it was to take place. The careful and elaborate rituals by which this is customarily done had been carried out, and now the high priest was about to call the power of the divine feminine into the high priestess, his wife. He knelt before her in the grass, the last rays of the sun tinting his fair hair copper and splashing his white robe with buttery hues. As he spoke the words of invocation, she flung her arms wide, a sword held in one hand, a wand in the other, and her face became radiant with joy. She seemed to gain a couple of inches in height, her own snowy robe and golden ornaments shining against the deep green of the meadow, while that gilded western sky made an iconic setting for her head, lighting the edges of her own streaming blonde locks. Then she spoke the Charge of the Goddess, and her coven came forth one by one, to address her and to receive responses from her in return. These are part of the mysteries of the tradition, and so I drop the veil upon the picture again. I shall only say, with pure personal subjectivity, that at that moment I thought the scene to be in its way as magnificent a manifestation of religion as a sung mass in a Gothic cathedral, the call to prayer in a blue-tiled mosque, or the conclusion to a seven-fold puja in a Buddhist temple.

With that closing reflection, perhaps, I have kept faith with two very different groups of people. First, with readers who may have been wondering, throughout the many pages of analysis and commentary above, about the actual quality of the religion which is being described. Second, with the witches who have taken me into their confidence and have been of such consistent help to me in my researches as a historian, believing that however inconvenient my conclusions might be in some respects, I would still come to understand something of the essence of their faith.

PART 2

Satanism and Satanic Mythology

Jean La Fontaine

Satanism, also referred to as devil-worship, describes both a set of ideas about evil that are part of the theology of already established religious systems, particularly Christianity, and also some reactions against them. The concept of Satan, that is, of a force representing evil that may sometimes be represented as a personified being, is not unique to Christianity, being found in both the other religions that originated in the Middle East: Judaism and Islam. However, the idea has been most powerful within Christianity and, after falling into abeyance in the early years of the twentieth century, has come into prominence again as the end of the second millennium approaches. Religious developments in the second half of the century have also included the formation of groups of people calling themselves satanists. While they cannot be understood apart from the Christian culture that provided the context for their foundation, they must be distinguished from the devil-worshippers that some Christians believe exist. One aim of this article is to demonstrate the difference between these two fundamentally opposed meanings of the term satanism; the other is to describe the international mythology concerning satanism in the first sense.

The history of the idea of Satan and Satanism[1]

The idea of Satan was little developed in early Judaism, although it has been pointed out that the Old Testament did contain references that might be taken to refer to evil mystical beings. Suffering and misery was attributed merely to the inscrutability of God's will. Then the Hebrew term *satanas* originally meant adversary or opponent and referred not to a being, but to the act or function of opposing. In afflicting human beings, a satan's role as a servant of God was to test the strength and sincerity of the commitment of human beings to God. However, during the persecution of the Jews and particularly during their Exodus into Persia, Judaic thought, under the influence of Zoroastrianism, began to express a sense of dualism, of forces of good and evil in opposition. On their return, the misery of their situation developed an apocalyptic notion of the world's being dominated by independent forces of evil which could not be changed but would one day be destroyed by God. The animal epithets, particularly that of 'beast', that were applied to these external forces of evil and contrasted with humanity and with good, were later to be applied to a Christian Satan. But the evil of Satan and his associated lesser satans and demons lay not so much in opposition to, or rebellion against, goodness but in the ability to disrupt the relationship between humanity and God. Moreover, it was believed that the Great Satan could be combatted by the exercise of human will. Demonic power was limited by this human self-control.

The dualism of good and evil and the apocalyptic tradition was transmitted to Christianity at its inception and, later, Islam showed a similar concept of evil spirits. Within its original home the idea of Satan faded into insignificance with the passage of time and of the three religions, the idea of the Devil is now least important in Judaism. In the Muslim world there are many who believe in evil spirits (*jinns*) or demons that possess human beings and may be exorcised and controlled in healing rituals. 'Shaitan', the Arabic equivalent of 'Satanas' in early Hebrew, may be used in the plural to refer to demons as *satanas* also was; it does not denote a single embodiment of evil dominating the rest. Moreover, not all the possessing spirits are clearly representations of evil; they may reflect many forces that are believed to cause human misfortunes but are not evil in themselves. However, belief in demons and possession by spirits is not doctrinally orthodox; the 'good Muslim' has no truck with such matters. Indeed, the conviction that such beliefs and actions are not proper to Islam is so strong that it has even been transmitted to some Western writers about Islam. Many of them claim that these ideas are survivals of pre-Islamic 'animistic' religions. However, if the previous religions were 'animistic', by which is meant they were based on a belief in spirits, one would expect to find some of these religions existing outside, but adjacent to, areas where Islam had spread. Alternatively one could expect to find them within similar areas that had been converted by Christian rather than Muslim missionaries. But although possession by spirits can be found in nominally Christian areas, neither of the situations that might lay claim to the indigenous nature of possession by spirits can be firmly established. On the contrary, there is counter evidence. One anthropologist of the East African coast, David Parkin, states that the ideas of the Muslim Swahili resemble those of the West, whether Christian or not, much more than they do those of the pagan Mijikenda among whom they live (Parkin, 1985b:231–2). One is led to the conclusion that, however unorthodox belief in devils is, the ideas are, in fact, indissolubly linked to the religious tradition of Islam. Nevertheless, concepts of evil beings in Islam are different from Christian ideas of Satan; one of the most important is that Muslims who take part in rituals designed to exorcise and control evil spirits (usually in order to heal their unfortunate human hosts) are not deemed to be worshipping Satan or any devil figure; they are merely failing to be good Muslims in having to do with evil spirits.

Early Christian doctrine did not reject the post-Exodus dualism of the Jews when it broke away from the Judaic religion. Having developed an idea of an all-powerful and beneficent God, the essence of pure goodness, the existence of suffering and evil was left as an unexplained problem. Either God was unable to prevent evil and was therefore not omnipotent, or did not wish to do so, and was thus responsible for the existence of evil. The figure of Satan as adversary of God and representing the sum of all evil, seemed to offer a solution to this problem. His attempt to achieve dominion over the earth and over human kind and his defeat by God's Son developed the Judaic dualism into a series of opposed powers, good and evil, that stretched between mankind and God. A complex hierarchy was gradually developed consisting of a multiplicity of figures of good (angels) and evil (demons). The idea of Satan became linked to the idea of a revolt against God among the angels led by Lucifer. God punished the rebels by perpetual banishment from heaven to the world, where they continued their battle against good, through seducing human beings into evil.

Protestantism swept away the hierarchy of spiritual powers, both good and evil, leaving the battle between Satan and Christ in stark isolation.

Moreover, as historians have pointed out, the apocalyptic vision which Christianity had taken over from Judaism allowed the temporary triumph of Satan before his final vanquishing by Jesus. But Christian faith provides human beings with the power, through faith, to resist Satan and expel the demons he sends to torment the righteous. Nevertheless, he is cunning and human beings must be constantly on their guard against his wiles. In particular, he lures his victims step by step onto the downward path and it is only when it is too late that they perceive their danger. In the late twentieth century it has been the Protestant ideas of satanism that have been the more significant, although it is on the human servants of Satan, rather than on subordinate devils or on the figure of Satan himself, that the myth of modern satanism focuses.

THE SERVANTS OF SATAN

While Christian theology portrayed the Devil as interested in drawing souls away from God and, ultimately in imposing his rule on the world, there were other images of evil that were incorporated into Christian demonology. As well as being the source of evil in the world, Satan and his demons were believed to have human allies and servants. According to Cohn (1970) it is this that distinguishes Christian beliefs in evil from those of other religions. The elaboration of this idea into the notion of the Witches Sabbath that let loose the witchcraze in the sixteenth and seventeenth centuries took time. It took up even older ideas and blended them into a single terrifying image (Cohn, 1975). Later versions of it remained a part of Western culture after the authorities had stopped the witch-hunts.

One of the ways in which devils, or the Devil, were believed to associate with human beings was in lending them extra-human powers to perform acts that were beyond the range of human beings. These demons were versions of the pagan gods from whom pagans had been believed to draw the powers of magic. By the Middle Ages, learned magicians were suspected of summoning and using demons by their magic in order to exchange their souls for magical powers in Faustian contracts. The practice of magic came to be associated with demons and hence with extremes of evil. Its practice in the twentieth century has been given similar connotations.

However, demonic magic was the pursuit of educated men, many of them clerics. Among the peasants magic consisted of the powers to heal sickness, pursue thieves and make charms to protect the wearer or bring good fortune. Those who possessed such powers, or witchcraft, the 'wise men' or 'wise women', might also be suspected of causing harm by evil magic but the term witchcraft was initially neutral. When, during the fifteenth century, the belief spread among the clergy and the elite that all such powers were derived from a contract with the devil, the idea of witches as servants of the devil came into existence.

The idea of Satan's servants had been developed earlier in the Church's fight against heretics. It came to be believed that there were regular gatherings to celebrate and worship their diabolic master. What was thought to happen at these gatherings drew on folk beliefs that had been used first against Christians by Romans. These were then used by Christians in their turn: against heretics, the Jews, Templars and all others who were considered enemies of the Church. The folklore referred to secret meetings in which demons and Satan himself participated and at which slaughtered babies were consumed in a feast and there were orgies of sex in which all normal restraints, including those prohibiting incest, were abandoned. Variations on the central themes of murder, cannibalism and orgiastic sex took into account particular practices or beliefs with which the accused were associated. Thus the Templars, who were sworn to celibacy, were accused of sodomy, and the Jews, whose food taboos set them off from Christians, of using the blood of Gentile babies to bake their ritual bread. The evidence that these gatherings actually took place was drawn almost entirely from the accused's confessions. Most of these were extracted under persistent questioning or torture, like those of the witches; Levack has pointed out that 'once torture was applied, then charges of diabolism arose' (1987:12). Details from the confessions of the tortured were widely circulated and might form the basis of other allegations and of some of the allegedly 'spontaneous' confessions.

In some early cases, however, like that of the heretic Canons of Orleans who were burned for heresy in 1022, stories of diabolism were invented after the execution of the accused and further elaborated three-quarters of a century later (Cohn, 1970:8). Such legends attached to enemies of the Church ensure that they are remembered as infamous and cannot form the focus of a rebel sect. They have become a folk mythology that may be quoted as evidence that satanism has existed all through the centuries, despite the fact that historical research has shown how unreliable the evidence has been, how partisan the arguments, and how and why the fabrications were made.

MODERN IDEAS OF SATANISM

Two strands can be identified in twentieth-century Christian concepts of Satan and satanism, neither of which is of recent origin. The first, which derives from the earlier ideas that have just been outlined, is a belief in a secret organisation dedicated to the worship of its head and master, Satan and to working for the overthrow of the Christian Church and Christian civilization. Its rituals of worship are believed to be characterized by all that is most evil and depraved; they include human sacrifice, cannibalism and depraved sexual orgies where all the rules of incest and social custom are ignored. Versions of this belief are held by many twentieth-century Christians all over the world, more particularly in the Protestant denominations, and most of all in the fundamentalist and charismatic sects. Some people who do not see themselves as Christian at all may also hold variants of this belief.

Many of these ideas are paralleled in the second source of satanic images, various folk beliefs concerning witches. The most widespread of these popular notions links witchcraft and magic with satanism, so closely that the two may be believed to be the same. Witches are thought to form covens that are sometimes said to consist of 13 witches, the unlucky or evil number. They hold meetings at night to worship the devil; these are referred to, with persisting anti-semitism, as the Witches' Sabbath and Satan himself may appear at them. These ideas were probably inculcated in the population by the witch-hunts in the sixteenth and seventeenth centuries because they do not seem to have existed prior to the early modern period. There are other subsidiary beliefs, in ghosts or vampires for example, that are also sometimes incorporated into the modern idea of satanism. In addition, the notion of the Black Mass, a diabolical rite that is a parody or an inversion of the Christian Mass and is believed to have been celebrated by worshippers of the devil, may also be incorporated. Some accounts confuse it with the ritual of the Witches Sabbath.[2] Since notions of what constitutes the greatest evil do change over time, modern ideas of satan-worship also incorporate the notions of supreme evil that are widespread in contemporary society, acts such as abortion and the sexual abuse of children.

All these beliefs are ideas held by outsiders *about* satanists, whether the holders are Christians or non-believing members of societies with fundamentally Christian cultures; they are not the beliefs *of* any recorded members of such cults. In fact, as later sections will show, satanic abuse mythology has grown up, in exactly the way the information about the Witches Sabbath grew up, from the questioning of individuals, adults and children, about their experiences. However, in the twentieth century it is the victims who are questioned, not the alleged satanists.

The generalization just made about beliefs in satanists may appear not to hold any longer in the twentieth century, when the existence of individuals and groups of self-styled satanists is fully substantiated. They form part of the occult revival of the second half of the century, although a few individuals from an earlier period, such as the notorious Aleister

Crowley, may be accorded the status of satanist retrospectively. Satanism can be said to be parasitic on Christianity, in that satanists consciously define themselves in opposition to Christians and characterize their practices by contrasting them with Christian practices. There also appears to be an element of conscious pleasure in shocking Christians by creating at least the appearance of what Christians fear. However, their main purpose is the study and practice of magic, not worship of any deity, although even their involvement with magic still makes them suspect in the eyes of some Christians for reasons which, as has already been noted, reach back into the past.

As Ronald Hutton has shown elsewhere in this volume, other occult groups have reacted against Christianity by attempting to recreate pagan religions that were believed to have existed before Europe's conversion to Christianity. They do not believe in Satan or devils, pointing out that these are elements in Christian cosmology not in theirs. Any or all of these occult groups may be labelled satanists by Christians but, as the next section will show, actual satanists are rather few in number and can easily be distinguished from the satanists of Christian mythology or folk-lore. In order to prevent confusion between the two types of satanists I shall distinguish them where necessary by referring to self-styled (the occultists) and alleged (the mythical) satanists. Finally, it is worth noting that some far-right political groups have adopted symbols and clothing that resemble those of satanists, just as the political ideas of some occult groups tend towards neo-Nazism, making it difficult to decide how, on the fringes, the religious and the political can be distinguished.

SATANISM AND THE OCCULT

The figure of Satan in romantic literature, particularly in the nineteenth century, has been used to represent the rebellion of the individual against the powerful, whether these are secular monarchs, Church leaders or the impersonal bureaucrats of the state. His fall from Heaven was portrayed as the result of his daring to opppose the all-powerful, rather than in the more orthodox manner as the triumph of good over evil, and he became, by this strange twist, a symbol of human liberty (Russell, 1991). Self-styled satanists perceive themselves as aligned with this idealistic Satan, as iconoclasts and rebels, fighting to free individuals from the respression imposed by a Christian society. There are two main tenets to their opposition: first, they claim that Christianity denies and suppresses the physical nature of human beings, stigmatizing the body and its pleasures as evil. They therefore take the opposite view. Secondly they deny the Christian moral evaluation of self-seeking as wrong, assserting that the only honest way is for each individual to pursue his or her own goals. Charity to others may be self-seeking or gratifying to the individual and should be undertaken only for these reasons and not because it is designated as morally righteous or because a group dictates such behaviour. The modern satanists could thus be described as both hedonist and individualist, although they might themselves refer instead to anti-puritan-ism and anti-authoritarianism, all authority being perceived as equally evil.

Interest in Satan waned towards the end of the nineteenth century and until the middle of the twentieth there was little further interest in Satan or what he represented. As this volume shows, beliefs in witches did not disappear completely and isolated incidents of 'swimming' witches or attacking those suspected of witchcraft occurred right into the twentieth century. Any connection with the devil was largely ignored, however, although the idea of the Witches Sabbath, which had originally centred on the worship of the Devil, had long been well-established in folk-lore. Conservative Christians continued to believe in the evil opponent of Christ and His Father and fear his intervention in human affairs and his seduction of humans into sin, but more liberal Christians and the growing number of non-Christians ceased to believe in the existence of such a figure. The imagery of Satan might still be used and (presumably) evoked public response: for example, the Kaiser was portrayed as a devil-figure in World War I British cartoons. Nevertheless, it was possible for an authority on the subject of the Devil to write that, by the end of World War II, most people regarded the idea of the devil as 'a silly superstition' (Russell, 1991:49).

An interest in the occult that had also developed during the second half of the nineteenth century did continue into the twentieth. The establish-ment, in the 1880s, of various occult organizations, modelled on Freema-sonry and Rosicrucianism, had brought together people interested in learned magic and the ancient sources of such knowledge, such as the Kabbala. Few of the original organizations survive today, although some have been revived. Others, like the Society of the Inner Light, have been founded in the intervening years and an interest in ceremonial magic is widespread among more recently established groups. This form of magic is quite distinct from charms, love potions, wax figures or other forms of folk magic, whether of the black or white variety. Instead, it harks back to the magic of the alchemists. The explosion of writing on the subject has also allowed the establishment of groups of ritual magicians that have not been trained by any of those in the mainstream of this tradition, but who are self-taught. Modern satanists are magicians in this sense.

The figure of Aleister Crowley, who today may be seen as the father of modern satanism, properly belongs in this section concerned with the occult and learned magic, since it was here that his influence was greatest, although it has been claimed that his religion was 'diabolism' (Rose, 1989 (1962):11; cf. Hutton in this volume). Born in 1875, Crowley's independent means allowed him to follow his own whims while the money lasted, although he died in 1947 poor as well as discredited. In the early years of this century he joined the Hermetic Order of the Golden Dawn and like the other members was deeply influenced by what was becoming known of the religion of ancient Egypt, to which they claimed to trace the origins of their order. When he quarrelled with the leader of the Golden Dawn, allegedly over differences of opinion about the morality of homosexuality, Crowley founded his own Order, the Astrum Argentinium[3] or Silver Star. He also joined the Ordo Templo Orientalis (OTO) and later became its head. He led the latter until his death but the Astrum Argentinium did not survive his move to America in 1914.

However, Crowley is also known for his temple, the Abbey of Thelema (a name taken from Rabelais' novel *Gargantua and Pantagruel*) that he established in Sicily to provide a place where he could pursue his interest in Tantrism and sex magic. His sexual activities and drug-taking with his disciples caused scandal which he appears to have enjoyed, since throughout his life he courted publicity for his iconoclasm, referring to himself with pride as 'the wickedest man in the world'. His upbringing among the Plymouth Brethren was said to have inspired in him a passionate hatred of Christianity which he aimed to destroy, identifying himself with the Egyptian God Seth,[4] with the Greek Pan and with Satan, and also calling himself 'The Great Beast'. This last title comes from Revelations, from which he also took the number 666 to be his personal number. Rather than being a satanist in the sense of worshipping the Devil, Crowley identified himself with the arch-antagonist in the Christian cosmos, as Satan himself; although he influenced some people to participate in his rituals and established a magical tradition that is still called 'Thelemic', he cannot be said to have founded a satanist religion. His books are widely read by many people who are not at all interested in satanism, but read him for his knowledge of magic. Nevertheless, he is popularly credited both with being a satanist and with being the founder of modern satanism.

The direct legacy of Crowley's example and writing is not devil-worship but certain forms of ceremonial magic, many of them performed by individuals rather than as a group (Sutcliffe, 1996). Crowley combined an interest in Tantrism,[5] from which he drew a distinction between self-directed (black) and other-directed (white) magic, with elements of Gnosticism.[6] His occult scholarship and his writing on 'magick' still earn him the respect of serious magicians, who distinguish these achievements from his personal way of life, particularly his drug-taking, which they deplore. Crowleyan magick (he spelled it with a 'k' to distinguish it from mere conjuring) continues to be practised by various groups, most of which cannot be called satanist. The OTO now has two branches, one in Britain and another in the USA and a National Symposium of Thelemic Magick has been organized by a group called the Oxford Golden Dawn Society. A form of magick called Chaos magick is the most recent development of his approach; described as 'the latest attempt to make magic more scientific' it was started in the late 1970s. Like all Crowleyan magick it aims to break down the inhibitions and fears inculcated in the individual by society and, particularly, by Christian precepts, and takes belief to be a tool of magick rather than its framework. The practice of magic throughout the neopagan movement shows Crowley's influence, even among those who explicitly reject many of his beliefs.

Crowley divided magick into Greater and Lesser forms: the Greater is aimed at transforming the subjective world and through that, by the imposition of human will, the objective universe. This may be expressed as unifying the microcosm of the individual self with the macrocosm of the entire universe but its purpose is unification not merely as an end in itself, but as the creation of a tool to secure change in the real universe. 'Magick', he claimed, 'is the science and art of causing change to occur in conformity with Will' (Crowley, 1973:131). Greater magick is the focus of ritual or ceremonial and requires esoteric knowledge and skills; lesser magick is 'wile and guile obtained through various devices and contrived situations which, when utilized, can create change, in accordance with one's will' (LaVey, 1969:111).

Crowleyan magick, together with some other subsequent forms, constitute what magicians refer to as Left-Hand Path Magick (Sutcliffe, 1996). According to Harvey this term is derived from the Tantric tradition and cannot be translated as 'black' or 'evil' because the moral distinction is irrelevant to it (Harvey, 1997:97). Magick is held to be neutral, neither good nor evil. Left-Hand Path Magick is self-directed and distinguished by the use of sexual energies as a power to energize magick, a practice derived from tantrism, but one which does not necessarily mean that sexual acts are part of the ritual employed by satanists, at least not in the public rituals. More important than this is the idea that magick should 'decondition' the individual, stripping away the inhibitions and conventions instilled by society in order to enable the individual to realize his/her true self. This 'self' includes the bodily or 'animal' dimension as well as the spiritual or mental, and sexuality symbolizes the complete self rather than aspects of the body's functioning that must be denied or hidden. Magicians of other persuasions may not use sex magick but would concur with the aims of self-realization expressed in the Crowleyan legacy.

Crowley is also influential today for his iconoclasm and for providing a way of shocking people that may be found attractive, even by people who know little or nothing of satanism or Crowley's ideas. The number 666 is displayed as a symbol by rock groups and is written on walls by young rebels, while the emblem of the Baphomet, which was designed by the nineteenth-century magician Eliphas Levi and popularized by Crowley, is widely used and recognized. Members of satanist churches claim to follow Crowleyian precepts. These come from his Book of Laws which he claimed was dictated to him by his Holy Guardian Angel. The three that have most currency today are:

1. Do what thou wilt shall be the whole of the law. This precept also comes from Rabelais, in whose novel the Abbey of Thelema is entered through a doorway over which is inscribed 'Fay ce que voudras' (do what you will/want). This Law has been interpreted by anti-satanists as a licence for total self-indulgence without any concern for others, but was used by Crowley to emphasize self-realization as much as self-indulgence. It is cited by the anti-satanists as evidence of the evil encouraged by Satan but, in fact, it reflects the sense in which it was used by Nietzsche who also expressed it in the words he put in Zarathustra's mouth: 'become who you are'. The term 'Will' (the translation of the Classical Greek, *Thelema*) refers to the essence of the self, its true being. Crowley explicated the aphorism in the following terms: ' "Do what thou wilt" is to will the Stars to shine, Vines to bear grapes, Water to seek its level; man is the only being in Nature that has striven to set himself at odds with himself' (Crowley, 1973: 352).
2. Love is the law, love under will. This aphorism is rarely glossed, perhaps because its meaning seems obvious. One can take it to mean total engagement (in body and spirit) with others, subject to the expression of the true self of each.
3. Every man and woman is a star, that is, is a unique self that has its unique existence and its own laws of being which must be respected. This is glossed by Harvey as: 'No individuals have the right to impose their beliefs or values on any other person, not even if they think themselves more aware of the nature of reality' (Harvey, 1997: 99).

Satanists may say that they do not believe in Satan as a personified force, but they are also inclined to refer to him as a person in such remarks as 'Satan will punish', or 'Satan doesn't like', etc. In this respect satanists resemble Christians, who vary widely in the degree to which they perceive God or his Son as personified beings, rather than 'persons' in the theological sense. It is doubtful whether the philosophical background and the full meaning of Crowley's precepts or the developments from them are understood by all of those who quote them, whether in approval or in denigration, but the attitude of concentration on the self they appear to encourage is one that is wholly consistent with other self-realization and therapeutic movements that have developed in the twentieth century. Indeed, 20 years ago it was argued that membership of the Church of Satan performed 'magical therapy' that encouraged self-confidence in young men who were too shy or inhibited to enjoy social gatherings or approach the opposite sex (Moody, 1974). The self-development aspect of Crowley's philosophy is strong in modern satanism but receives different emphases in the different groups, being more sensual and aesthetic in the Church of Satan and more intellectual in the Temple of Set. Other groups can be identified according to the special emphases they place on different readings of the works of Crowley or LaVey.

SECTION 2

Satanist and pseudo-satanist groups

There are only two long-standing, well-established groups of satanists and each is largely the creation of one man. The Church of Satan and the Temple of Set were founded 30 and 20 years ago respectively. The founder of the Church of Satan died only in October 1997 and the founder of the Temple of Set is still its leader. Both men have been public figures in California, although they should probably be described as notorious rather than famous for their activities, since their publicity has been, probably intentionally in the case of the Church of Satan, the cause of public scandal. These founders have published a good deal of material from which the observer can learn about the two organizations' ideas and rituals, but there have been no recent estimates of their membership, whether by themselves or observers. Their active membership, however, is probably a good deal smaller than the numbers who buy their magazines or show a short-term interest. Both organizations have an international membership but it is not clear whether all the groups outside the USA are affiliated to the original organizations, have been founded with their agreement as independent off-shoots, or are simply imitations.

Another organization that has been called satanist no longer survives, although dissident sections of it continued to exist for some time as different types of organization under other names; one for example is an independent branch of Jews for Jesus (Bainbridge, 1991:301). The Process Church of the Final Judgement was once well known, partly because for a period its members wore dramatic costumes in their public activities and also because their leader met Charles Manson, the murderer of the film actress Sharon Tate, while Manson was in prison. There have been persistent attempts, despite contrary evidence, to argue that Manson was a member of the Process and that the killings he perpetrated were ritual murders. More is also known about this group than about most satanist groups because it was studied in depth by the sociologist William Bainbridge, who published a detailed history and analysis of the Church and its activities. Since by this time it had already collapsed, his study covers the whole course of its foundation, development and decline (Bainbridge, 1978).

The founders of the Process had been members of the Scientology Movement, and it has been alleged that L. Ron Hubbard, the founder of

Scientology, spent some time as a member of the Church of Satan. This is one example of the links between the various groups in the world of new religious movements. Satanists write for each others' publications, review each others' books and publish interviews with each other in magazines; theirs is a small world. The Process differed from the other two groups mentioned above in that it was founded in England and its core members were English, although its development as a religious movement and its final disintegration took place in the USA. In its heyday, the Process revered four gods, two of which were Lucifer and Satan. It was therefore nominally satanist, but not exclusively so, because Satan was considered the equal of the other three, who included Jehovah and Jesus. When the movement began, only the first three were considered gods; Jesus was added at a later stage. Even at its height The Process never had more than a few hundred members and, despite periodic rumours to the contrary, it has never been revived.

In addition, there are other much smaller groups in many countries, with a handful of members, that are self-styled satanist organizations, although none has become well known or reached beyond its particular locality within one nation state. Like the larger groups they are explicitly anti-Christian and many are modelled on the Church of Satan, but they vary in the extent to which they consciously attempt to embody folk images of satanism. There has been little systematic research on them even in Britain and the USA (though for exceptions see the bibliography) and where there is press coverage it is liable to be sensationalist. The revolution in publishing technology has made it possible for even tiny groups to publish their own magazines, which may give a false impression of their size, but these give some indication of the general spread of satanism as a movement. In one of its issues, *The Black Flame*, the Church of Satan's magazine published in New York, reviewed 25 American magazines, two each from Sweden, Canada and New Zealand (though the last two have the same address) and one each from Finland, Norway, Scotland and France (1994, vol 5, nos 1 and 2). Translations of *The Satanic Bible* by Anton LaVey, founder of the Church of Satan (see below), are another indication of international interest; there are translations into Danish, Swedish and Spanish. *The Satanic Bible* and its companion *The Satanic Rituals* were published in 1969 and 1972, respectively, and were still in print in 1997, which indicates their status as foundation texts for the whole movement as well as for the Church of Satan.

Groups which aim to revive the pagan religion of north-west Europe, variously referred to as Heathens, Odinists or as the Norse or Anglo-Saxonic tradition may be mistaken for satanists as their clothing and general appearance as well as their anti-Christian stance encourages this. They are probably more numerous than satanists in Scandinavia and

Germany and seem to be growing in importance in Britain. As it is important to clarify their position, they will also be discussed in the section below.

THE CHURCH OF SATAN

The Church of Satan was founded in California in 1966 by Anton Szandor LaVey, a colourful figure of considerable personal magnetism, with a varied and unusual life already behind him. He had earned his living from music as a teenager, then worked in a circus as a lion tamer, calliope player, fortuneteller and hypnotist, was once employed as photographer in a police crime-laboratory and in an insurance company, and had been an organist and a clinical hypnotist. He was widely read in magic and the occult, on which he gave public lectures. His published rituals are in a variety of languages including Enochian. This is a magical language attributed to the magician John Dee, translated by the Order of the Golden Dawn and believed to be older than Sanskrit and possibly to derive from Ancient Egypt. LaVey's taste in music, at least as far as his choice of music for ritual is concerned, seems to be very different from the heavy-metal rock music associated in the popular imagination with satanists. His status as a celebrity has been enhanced by the publicity attendant on his conducting a satanic funeral for an American serviceman and a wedding for the daughter of a prominent New York lawyer. Added to this, his dramatic appearance, with shaven head, slanting eyes and the black circle of his moustache and beard enhancing his devilish looks, attracted wide publicity at the foundation of his Church. They must have helped to earn him his part in the horror film *Rosemary's Baby;* he had been appointed consultant to the director for his knowledge of magic and satanic symbolism. LaVey wrote several books expounding the Church of Satan's philosophy and describing its rituals. The best-known are *The Satanic Bible* (1969) and *The Satanic Rituals* (1972), both of which have an influence far beyond the membership of the Church of Satan.

The Church of Satan's philosophy is close to that of Aleister Crowley and contains both elitist and anarchist elements. One well-known owner of an occult bookshop, who is not a satanist himself, has described it as 'anarchistic hedonism'. First of all it is a rebellion against the authority of the Christian Church and a denial of its principles and theology, in particular what is seen as its rejection of the animal side of human beings. The Church of Satan proclaims that the physical nature of human beings is not something to deny but to indulge and celebrate. In labelling it 'evil' and 'dirty' the Christian Church has denied human beings part of their identity. *The Satanic Bible* contains an impassioned attack on the hypocrisy of Christianity and the wrongs done in the name of this religion. Using the figure of Satan is a symbol of this revolt against authority as it was in the romantic tradition, but LaVey denied that the organization worshipped Satan. On the contrary all that there is to worship is deemed to be within the individual. The rebel stance relates to all authority. LaVey wrote that 'He who saith "thou shalt" to me is my mortal foe' (1969: 30, 1:5), and according to one writer in the magazine *The Black Flame* who quotes this same dictum, 'A true Satanic society means a population of free-spirited, well-armed, fully-conscious, self-disciplined individuals, who will neither need nor tolerate any external entity "protecting" them or telling them what they can and cannot do'. On the other hand, LaVey was a firm believer in order and observing the rule of law, which appears somewhat inconsistent with rebellion against authority.

Like that of other satanist groups the Church of Satan's philosophy is also social Darwinist. In the article just quoted there is also a reference to 'human garbage' and to survival of the fittest as a natural law with which governments should not interfere. It is only the elite who are envisaged as free and disciplined only by themselves. In the preface to his book *The Satanic Rituals* LaVey envisages a time when 'it is the higher man's role to produce the children of the future' (1972:12). The former workers will produce fewer children because their work will be done by machines: 'One cherished child who can *create* will be more important than ten who can produce – or fifty who can *believe*' (LaVey, 1972; italics in original).

The rituals described in *The Satanic Rituals* are dramatic performances, in which the clothing worn by the participants, the actions and music (all light classical pieces whose titles or 'spookiness' link them to satanism) are all specified. The language to be used in the ritual is laid down, though translations are also provided where this is not English. However, LaVey specifies that only one language should be actually used in a ritual; if the prescribed language is not understood by participants, then they must study the translations beforehand to ensure they understand everything that will be said. The attention to detail of the provisions is entirely intentional, for the performance is created to engage the participants' feelings and aesthetic senses and to be appreciated at several levels, like a theatrical performance. In some rituals a naked woman acts as the altar (her body constitutes the altar and does not merely lie on it), but there is no place for sexual orgies, even in the ritual that is entitled 'Das Tierdrama' (the Beast Play). Alfred, who witnessed 52 rituals, writes that they included on occasion, 'stunning visual and vocal effects' and were appreciated as 'powerful psychodrama' (Alfred, 1976:188). There is no sacrifice, either animal or human, and the only ritual in which a child may be present is the Satanic Baptism for children. In this ritual, care is taken to express everything simply and ensure that the child understands; the parallel baptism for adults uses archaic and complex language.

In *The Satanic Bible* LaVey described three types of satanic ritual: sex ritual by which he meant love magic, the magic to attract the desired partner; compassionate ritual, which is magic to help people, including oneself; and finally, destructive magic which is motivated by negative emotions. LaVey described the last as a curse or hex, but hex also has the sense of black magic or witchcraft, so the Christian idea of a connection between witchcraft and satanism survives in this anti-Christian religion, if only minimally.

The equipment required is set out in detail. Black hooded robes should be worn by the male participants; younger women should dress attractively but older women wear black. Black is symbolic of the Powers of Darkness and the sexually suggestive clothing of the young women will stimulate feeling in the men. All participants should wear amulets of either the pentagram or the Baphomet. The latter is the god whom the Templars were accused of worshipping; the nineteenth-century French magician Eliphas Levi identified it with the Devil from the pack of Tarot cards, as did Aleister Crowley. The head of a goat can also be fitted into the reversed five-point star, the pentagram, which is the symbol of magicians, and this is how the Church of Satan represents it. The symbol of Baphomet is also placed behind the altar. The objects required are: candles, all black except for one white one, which is associated with destructive magic and is placed to the right of the altar to represent right-hand path magicians; a bell, which is rung nine times to mark the beginning and end of the ritual; a chalice, which may be of any material except gold; an alcoholic drink, to represent the Elixir of Life that will be drunk from the chalice (LaVey was reputed to use whisky); a sword, representing aggressive force; a model phallus, to be used as a sprinkler for water asperged in benediction; a gong 'with a full rich tone'; and parchment (or failing that, paper), on which requests to Satan are written before being burnt in the flame of a candle. In private rituals not all the paraphernalia is necessary.

LaVey emphasized that the rituals are not acts of worship but serve particular purposes or celebrate particular occasions. The Satanic rituals are magical acts and 'are not designed to hold the celebrant in thrall, but rather to serve his goals', that is to enhance his magickal powers. Because they aim to provide an occasion for entertaining unspoken ideas and impulses, and of invoking the opposite, inversions and blasphemies may be used for effect. They also have a liberating effect. Observers' accounts stress the theatricality of the performances they witnessed and this is deliberate. Pageantry is considered a necessary means for enhancing will and supporting participants in their desires. This enhancement of the Will enables satanists to improve their magical techniques. In fact, much of the

Church's ritual is expected to be performed by a satanist on his/her own. This is because concentration is essential and the larger the group the more likely it is that one or other person is not fully engaged in the ritual and thereby prevents it attaining its object.

The Satanic Rituals contains scripts for the more complex and public rituals using the equipment described in *The Satanic Bible*. The spoken word predominates and while there is music and drama there are no sacrifices or sexual orgies. A further gloss was put on LaVey's instructions 20 years later by Blanche Barton, who is described as an administrator of the Church of Satan and LaVey's authorized biographer.[7] In it LaVey is quoted at length. Her book about the Church of Satan attempts to correct public misapprehensions about the rituals. The chapter on 'How to perform Satanic Rituals' also stresses the aims of the rituals, of which the first and most important is to suspend the kind of thought used critically in everyday life, in favour of emotion, which is important in magick. Emotion is enhanced by rituals that are described as 'Intellectual Decompression Chambers' and which strengthen the power of the satanist. It is emphasized that the experience of magickal ritual is as important as knowledge about it, a view which is consistent with the general importance placed on feeling.

Organization

At first, the Church was centralized and hierarchical in structure and the local groups or 'Grottoes' were subordinate to the Central Grotto headed by LaVey. There was a hierarchical system of degrees, with tests and required tasks to be performed before passing from one to the next. Medallions with different coloured backgrounds indicated the different degrees. Public rituals were performed and group activities organized. In 1975 a different, more decentralized system was introduced, dissolving the formal hierarchy and giving independence to local groups. Public rituals ceased as did the organized activities and members were advised to demonstrate their independence by ceasing to rely on any structure for their satanism. Seniority in the organization was to be demonstrated by as much withdrawal from 'the common herd' as possible, into self-employment in the creative fields or similar forms of employment. Satanism is described by Barton as 'intended to be an alignment, a lifestyle' (1990:125) rather than an organization mirroring the Christian Church.

The Church of Satan was, from the outset, law-abiding; LaVey was firmly against acts that broke state laws, enacted for the communal good, and his attitude to law and order was said to be conservative (Alfred, 1976). To begin with, he and his disciples flaunted their disregard of 'respectability', displaying their hedonism in public and showing their commitment to the idea that man [sic] is just another animal, that the acts denoted 'sins' by the Christian are to be valued as sources of gratification and should be indulged in. However, drugs were excluded from this because they were illegal and because they reduced one's active control over the environment; for the same reason, while alcohol was used to enhance the imagination and reduce inhibitions, drunkenness was considered foolish and 'unmagical' (Alfred, 1976:186). Alfred alleges that this public display was subsequently toned down and the emphasis on dramatic display replaced by a stress on the hard work needed to amass magical knowledge.

According to Alfred, who studied the Church of Satan during its early years, 1968 to 1973, and was a member during the first of these five years, it did not appeal to young people: most members were over 30 (LaVey himself was in his middle thirties when he founded the Church) and many of those who were younger were in their late twenties. A recruitment campaign in Berkeley during 1968 met with little success (Alfred, 1976: 193). Alfred explained this as the result of the Church of Satan's hostility to drug-taking, but it should be remembered that this was the time of direct political action by Berkeley students, to whom the indirect rebellion offered by satanism might have seemed ineffectual. He also commented that while the Church at that time claimed 7,000 members (Gordon Melton refers to the claim as 70,000), there were only 400 or 500 active members receiving the newsletter, *The Cloven Hoof*. During the period in which he participated in them, the rituals were attended by about 20 to 30 members from a wider 'pool' numbering about 50 to 60. These were 'mostly middle-class white people in their forties, thirties and late twenties, including many professionals' (Alfred, 1976:194). Like LaVey himself and many neo-pagans (see Hutton in this volume) many of these were autodidacts who pursued their study of magic with great seriousness.

It is likely that the easy availability of LaVey's writings and the freedom to create independent groups rather than join the central organization of the Church of Satan made for a proliferation of small groups with different names, instead of the addition of branches to the Church of Satan itself. There appears to have been only one defection from the Church: it became Michael Aquino's Temple of Set, which, although much smaller, is the Church of Satan's main rival and is never mentioned by name. *The Black Flame* does refer to other affiliated organizations, mostly in the USA and Canada, although the establishment of two groups in New Zealand was noted in one issue. There is, for example, no branch in Britain, but two of the smaller independent satanist groups seem to resemble the Church of Satan quite closely and there may be individual members of the Church in Britain. As time went by, the Church of Satan was also concerned to distinguish itself from imitative groups or those that used the label of satanist as a pretext for other activities. Barton lists the characteristics of pseudo-Satanic groups in order to warn readers; the list reveals the Church of Satan's views by showing what they are against. Groups which offer the intending member sex, the killing of animals, or drugs, who claim direct revelations from Satan or talk of secrets accessible only to the initiate and of 'ethical' satanism, are to be avoided. The attitude of individuals and groups to LaVey's works, which appear to have become a sacred canon despite the insistence on members writing their own rituals and using their own experience, is a definitive test. Particular types of groups to be generally avoided are: feminist Wiccans, who are said to 'practice more male-bashing than magic' (Barton, 1990: 127); New Age groups 'draped in satanic trappings'; 'jargon-laden Christians masquerading as Satanists' (these are believed to be undercover missionaries); and what are described as "pen-pals and lonely hearts social groups", presumably those who advertise for members, which the Church of Satan does not. However, Barton also writes approvingly of affiliated groups that share the same goals, even if they emphasize one type of imagery over another. On the other hand, if they wish to use the name of the Church of Satan or speak as its representative, they must join the organization and pay the subscription. Decentralization did not result in a decrease of LaVey's authority either; until his death he was said to be keeping 'a tight rein' on the Church and planning its future development.

THE TEMPLE OF SET

The Temple of Set was founded in California in 1975 by a group of[8] dissidents from the Church of Satan, led by Michael Aquino, a former US army officer. According to some accounts (e.g. Harvey 1995a), they were displeased at the publicity the organization had received and criticized LaVey for, as they claimed, turning satanism into a form of show-business. They declared that they wished to restore the high moral purpose with which the Church had been founded, but the organization that ensued became rather different from that of the parent organization, being more like some of the self-improvement movements than the Church of Satan, although the Temple of Set's origin is apparent in some features of the ritual practice of its members. They also share with the Church of Satan the concept of the Black Flame, the symbol of knowledge and of scepticism towards the received wisdom of established religions. They emphasize knowledge and learning about magic more than the bodily liberation which the Church of Satan preaches. Unlike the Church of Satan they do not seek publicity, although the leaders may be available for interview and the head of the British section is seen on television on most occasions when programmes about satanism are made. However, Aquino's writings – *The Book of Coming Forth by Night* (1975) and *Black Magic in Theory and Practice* (1992) – are not widely available except to members. Harvey's published research on satanism in Britain gives a full account of the Temple of Set and is the main source for the following account, except where other references are given.

The name chosen by Michael Aquino makes clear the greater emphasis in this group on the lore and magic attibuted to ancient Egypt. In this it resembles the order of the Golden Dawn more than the Church of Satan, although its system of grades is unlike that of the Golden Dawn or other magical groups. Set is generally equated with Satan, although some members may distinguish between them. While the 'official view' is probably that he is a person, a 'real being', he is not worshipped but approached as a friend. His gift of the Black Flame (knowledge) to mankind offers the opportunity to members to become fully themselves. In this they share an ideal of self-development with the Church of Satan but place much greater emphasis on it. They are expected to 'become', that is, become truer to themselves, and they quote the dictum: 'As Set was, we are; as Set is, we will be'. The term *xeper*, which is used for this process, is glossed by Harvey as 'individual transcendence', presumably of a former self.

The Temple of Set emphasizes what it is that distinguishes human beings from the natural order: the intellect. They are thus different from the Church of Satan which emphasizes what humanity has in common with animals. They stress the urge to 'know', to be independent in thought and not to accept others' judgements or opinions. It is this questioning intelligence that is Set's gift to humanity; Setians do not regard it as the result of evolution. Harvey quotes a Setian as saying: 'Knowledge is achieved by learning, working, experimenting, experiencing and thinking. Faith is the true evil. Blind unquestioning faith . . .'. The gift of intellect imposes an obligation to use it, and to subordinate oneself to faith or to play up one's physical nature are wrong.

Setians distinguish between an 'objective universe', the natural world, and the 'subjective universe', which is the individual's personal perspective. In this and other major principles of magical theory they resemble other magicians, including the Church of Satan. They follow Crowley in believing that magick is causing change to occur in the objective universe in accordance with one's Will. A change in the subjective universe is believed to cause a similar and proportionate change in the objective universe. Objects, costumes, music and rituals that have an impact on the individual are aids to this process. Setians recognize the distinction also made by LaVey between Greater (ritual) and Lesser (the everyday manipulation of persons and things) magick. Aquino's book *Black Magic in Theory and Practice* contains an example of Greater Black Magic ritual, and other ceremonies may be created for particular occasions (Harvey, 1997: 289). These take a similar form to the rituals used by all ceremonial magicians, which is not surprising because the Temple of Set is best understood as an association for magicians. It is concerned solely with magical skills and has no regular occasions that are celebrated by fixed rituals. Unlike all other neo-pagans, Setians do not use a calendar of festivals, not even treating Walpurgisnacht as a festival, although certain pagan festivals may be seen as appropriate for social gatherings. However, most of the activities of the Temple of Set's members are solitary, involving the study and practice of magic.

The rituals of the Temple of Set resemble those of other magicians in structure and form, although both groups of satanists so far discussed are distinguishable from neo-pagan magicians by the fact that they do not use a circle as a 'working space'. Satanists' rituals raise power to benefit themselves and they therefore see no need to contain the energy raised or protect themselves from anything invoked. Both the Temple of Set and the Church of Satan ring a bell nine times to clear and purify the atmosphere at the beginning and to intensify the effect of the ritual, and both close it by admitting pollution at the end. Whether this is derived from the Black Mass, as Harvey suggests, is not entirely clear, given that LaVey, who initially devised these rituals, made clear his view that the Black Mass was never a serious satanic ritual but more a parody for the amusement of clients of the purveyors of shocking sexual pastimes.

The Temple of Set considers that the ritual or magic of all other groups is white, while theirs is black. In this they differ from the Church of Satan, who follow LaVey (and Crowley's) dictum that there is no difference between white and black magic. For Setians, these labels do not refer to moral qualities but to the Gnostic distinction (also used by LaVey) between other-directed and self-directed action. Black refers to the fact that their magic is self-consciously self-benefitting. Given the other-directed nature of other religions, this seems to be splitting hairs, for, at least in Christian terms, selfish actions are wrong and might well be designated 'black'. All satanists appear to share the distinction between Right Hand and Left Hand Magick and the Temple of Set is no exception.

Organization

The Temple of Set has a strictly hierarchical structure consisting of six levels, known as degrees: I. Setian ; II. Adept ; III. Priest/Priestess ; IV. Magister/Magistra Templi ; V. Magus/Maga ; and VI. Ipsissimus/Ipsissima. The Temple of Set's insignia is a silver pentagram in a circle and each degree is marked by a different coloured background to it. In this they resemble the early Church of Satan who also had a graded series of insignia, although the colour distinctions were abandoned with the decentralization and the image in the Church of Satan regalia was that of the Baphomet. Unlike other groups of magicians, the Temple of Set does not expect all its members to progress towards the highest grade; most are expected to remain as Adepts, that is at the second degree, which recognizes an individual as a competent magician. While all Adepts are expected to improve their magical skills by accumulating experience and deeper learning, the higher degrees are not a recognition of achievements in magical skills but represent offices believed to be conferred by Set and recognized as conferring priestly duties and responsibilities within the Temple. The ruling body of the Temple consists of the initiates of the highest degrees, of whom the senior priest in Britain is one, and is called the Council of Nine. An annual conclave brings the Council and other higher initiates, as well as ordinary members, together.

Priests and priestesses are responsible for running the Temple and its local groups or Pylons. While Pylons facilitate meetings between members who live in the same region, any member can attend a meeting of any Pylon. Harvey lists four Pylons in Britain but one is a correspondence Pylon concerned with a region outside Britain. In addition, the Temple is divided into Orders, each representing an intellectual interest and supervised by a IV degree initiate as GrandMaster of the Order. In this respect the Temple is conceived of as like a university, with subject departments or faculties, led by a professor. Harvey summarizes the description given of 11 different orders ranging from the Five Senses to Nietzsche and notes that: 'Each order has its own insignia, reading list and publications' (Harvey, 1997:4). Adepts are expected to specialize in one order and develop an expertise in it. It is not stated whether, if they wish to, members may belong to more than one order.

Unlike the Church of Satan, the Temple of Set has a British branch, although it is not large. Its leader David Austen is frequently called upon to appear on television as a representative of satanists and has an equivocal relationship with the rest of the pagan community that has expressed itself on occasion in violent reaction to any perceived criticism of the founder, Aquino. While Harvey records that some of the British Setians who completed his questionnaire voted Labour, Liberal or Liberal Democrat, the general views expressed by Austen are much more right wing.

There is little evidence of branches of the Temple of Set in other European countries, although the Temple has corresponding members elsewhere who may be quite numerous as a special Pylon is concerned with them. The Black Circle in Bergen, Norway, is an off-shoot of the Temple of Set but is now independent.[9] In 1992 Gordon Melton estimated the number of members of the Temple of Set in the USA to be about 500 and Harvey suggested a figure of around 50 in Britain , noting however that their senior priest, David Austen, told him that the Temple was growing. One pagan informant has suggested that Harvey's figures are generally underestimates but another who attended a supposedly large gathering of the Temple of Set in London said there were only about a dozen members there, and a member of the Pagan Federation claimed that Harvey's figure was about right. It seems unlikely that there are more than 100 members of the Temple of Set in Britain at the very most and the total may be considerably fewer.

THE PROCESS-CHURCH OF THE FINAL JUDGEMENT

While this group has long been dissolved, it was responsible for generating a good deal of the publicity accruing to the satanists during its existence. It was also rather different from both the other groups, in that its members lived together as one or more communes, whereas other satanist groups have been more conventional in undertaking only part-time activities. Moreover, it is difficult to decide whether it was a truly satanist organization, given that Satan was only one member of its pantheon. Nevertheless, it caused much alarm in its heyday when it was accused of forced sex and murder. Rumours that it has been revived are still accompanied by expressions of apprehension.

In the early 1960s, two members of the Church of Scientology, Robert and Mary Anne de Grimston Moore, who had been working as therapists left to set up in business for themselves to develop the techniques used by the Scientologists even further. They called their approach 'Compulsions Analysis' and claimed that it enabled individuals to realize their full potential. Their technique was named a 'Process', after the Scientology technique. Soon their success enabled them to rent premises in Mayfair. Their group therapy sessions produced strong bonds between themselves and their clients to the point where they realized they had created a new religion, which was ultimately to be called The Process-Church of the Final Judgement. About 30 of them left London to found the ideal community and after some years spent wandering from place to place, including a period of proselytization in London and similar trips in the USA, they settled in eastern North America. They had by then had some contact with Anton LaVey and added Satan and Lucifer to their worship of Jehovah, with the result that they were soon labelled devil-worshippers. Once communities were established in the USA they supported themselves by begging in the street, where they were highly visible figures. They wore black garments with a huge figure of the Goat God on their chests, and in New Orleans they wore dramatic purple capes, although these were later exchanged for black ones. Nevertheless, their appearance was still sufficiently dramatic to become counter-productive so they changed the uniform to one of sober grey. At the time of this change they had been wrongly accused of having trained Charles Manson to commit the series of horrific murders that took place in 1969 (this accusation is still associated with the name). Money was very short and rifts developed within the leadership. In 1974 the group split. By the end of the decade the remnants of the Process were to be found in Texas and Utah as quite different religious/therapy groups.

The Process regarded their gods, who eventually numbered four when Jesus was added to the other three, as inner realities rather than deities. They were therefore not worshipped. The sociologist Bainbridge, whose study of them is the main source of information about them, has described their theology as constantly changing, being largely written by Robert who continued to elaborate his ideas up to the point of his departure. He has described how 'Processeans used the gods as a personality theory, holding that different individuals were closer to one or two of the deities than to the others' (Bainbridge, 1978: 302). Satan had two aspects: the Higher represented 'detachment, mysticism, otherworldliness, magic and asceticism', while his lower aspect was the province of 'lust, abandon, violence, excess and indulgence'. In relation to the other gods, Satan was an intensifier, both of the self-control demanded by Jehovah and also of the self-indulgence of Lucifer. In the theory of quadruple gods, each individual was associated with a combination of two gods and the combination explained not only the personality of the individuals con-cerned but also their relationships with one another. An elaborately dualistic structure of opposition and combination was constructed on this basis but it had more to do with explaining the internal dynamics of the group than those of the universe.

There is little here of the traditional Satan, although the terms for the gods/inner realities were drawn from a Judaeo-Christian background. Nor was there anything to compare with the magical activities of the other satanist groups that were established in California at much the same time that the Process communes were undergoing their various changes. There was no worship and no magic so there were no rituals directed to Satan nor magic invoking dark powers; and the communal life of the Proces-seans, including their sexual life, was strictly regulated rather than orgiastic. At times it was clear that the leaders were exploiting other members, who collected funds which were inequitably divided. However, there was little here to justify the label satanic. The Process was, as Bainbridge has termed it, a 'deviant psychotherapy group' rather than a religious one – let alone a satanic cult.

OTHER SATANIST GROUPS

The Black Flame is bought by many satanists outside the Church of Satan and knits small groups and individuals into a loose network of satanists. There are said to be differences of outlook and practice among these groups, but most of those referred to in the literature follow the general line established by LaVey. The differences emphasised by the Temple of Set that allegedly set them off from all other groups are organizational and theoretical; their practice of magic appears to be similar to those of other satanists.

Gordon Melton lists six satanist groups in the USA of which four were allegedly defunct; Harvey lists two in Britain: The Order of the Nine Angles and Dark Lily. Many more editors of satanist magazines were listed in *The Black Flame* and mention was made of small groups establishing themselves in various parts of the world, including Australia and New Zealand. In Norway, arson attacks on churches have been attributed to satanists; certainly one of three persons convicted for burning down an ancient stave-church in Bergen proclaimed himself a satanist at the time but the authors of subsequent attacks were less reliably identified. In Sweden there have been incidents of churches and graveyards being vandalized but by whom is not clear. It is noticeable that satanism appears to be limited to Christian parts of the world. If there are followers of LaVey or Aquino in India or Japan they do not communicate with other satanists via *The Black Flame*.

NUMBERS OF SATANISTS

It is impossible to know with any accuracy how many satanists there are altogether, whether within one country or internationally, and any figures given, including those given here, are guesses – more or less informed, but still guesses. There are many reasons for estimates to be biassed. Those who perceive satanism as a danger to society, particularly the more evangelistic Christians among them, exaggerate numbers to emphasize the threat. Extremists claim that every class and subdvision of society has been infiltrated and that satanists are to be found everywhere – in cities, small towns, in farms and villages. No evidence is offered for the numbers that are adduced to support such claims. Any satanist organization is probably also tempted to exaggerate the size of its membership to show its appeal. However, even the most neutral observer cannot make a completely accurate count of satanists because of the difficulties entailed in identifying who they are. Attempts have been made to assess their numbers but they inevitably founder on two main problems: how to locate satanists who are not members of any organization, and how to judge whether those who buy satanist magazines or wear satanic emblems are 'really' satanists or not, since even if they call themselves satanists, members of the main satanist groups may not consider them to be so. There seems, however, to be agreement between observers and the more established or 'visible' satanists that the adolescents who call themselves satanists, scrawl pentagrams and the number 666 on walls and play the type of rock music associated with satanism, are more often than not merely posing, adopting an image that proclaims a rebelliousness that is not lasting or serious. The source of their ideas is more likely to be horror videos and films or the novels of Dennis Wheatley and their film versions, than writings containing the philosophical ideas of satanist leaders or the principles of high magic. The label 'satanic' may also be attributed to deeds such as serial murder, particularly of children, that are generally considered to involve great evil without there being evidence of any satanist organization behind the acts. This is a moral judgement rather than a descriptive label but it confuses the issue.

One serious attempt in 1989 by the owner of a British occult bookshop to conduct an objective national census of all occultists (Occult Census, 1989) reported a very low percentage of respondents who could be called satanists. Only 4 percent of the total of slightly over 1,000, that is 40 individual respondents, recorded themselves as 'committed satanists'. Another 6 percent claimed a 'serious interest' while the largest category, amounting to 15 percent, were those who merely indicated their curiosity about satanism. Three-quarters of the respondents reported no interest at all. The actual figures extrapolated from this Census are less significant than the conclusion that satanists are a very small minority among occultists, who themselves represent a minority within the population at large. Another estimate is that of Harvey (1995a), based on his research among satanists. He reports estimates for Britain ranging from 5.5 million (Phillips on the television programme 'Viewpoint', see Thomas, 1993) to 3,000 (the 1994 UK Christian Handbook). His own estimate is of less than 100 individuals in six organized groups (of which one is the Temple of Set) plus a (probably) more numerous fringe of individuals who are interested in the groups' ideas. Those who are sufficiently interested to buy satanist magazines probably outnumber the members of groups and are themselves outnumbered by the curious and the sensation-seekers, mostly adolescents. The pattern confirms that established by the Occult Census, and the figures for those committed to, or seriously interested in, satanism in Britain are likely to be between 100 and 250 – certainly no more than 400, which is negligible in a population of about 60 million.

For the USA, the figures are equally doubtful and there has been no attempt at a national census, which would be a much more difficult undertaking in such a very large country. No figures, whether reliable or otherwise, can be put on the membership of satanist groups elsewhere either. There are said to be branches of the main satanist churches in various parts of Europe outside Britain and they also exist in New Zealand and possibly in Australia. Where the smaller groups and individuals are concerned it is impossible to be sure but there is no doubt that there is an international movement, albeit tiny. The circulation figures of the main satanist magazine *The Black Flame*, which, although published by the Church of Satan, is read very widely among satanists and has been credited with maintaining a sense of community among them, might offer a rather crude means of estimating the size of the satanist community. Unfortunately, it was not possible to obtain information about them.

SECTION 3

Heathenism / Odinism

Within the neo-pagan movement are groups that are particularly suscep-
tible to being seen as satanists and have some attitudes in common with
them. These are the Odinists or Heathens. Although they have been
visibly increasing in recent years, they represent a well-established interest
in recreating the pre-Christian religion of 'north-eastern Europe' or of the
'Norse and Anglo-Saxon peoples'. They may be referred to as Odinists,
after the Norse High God, Odin. The various different groups of this
persuasion have developed their own rituals, symbols and forms of worship
although they have some common features. Heathens may be mistaken
for satanists, partly because their appearance seems to resemble that
expected of satanists. They also raise similar concerns among observers.
These are political and social as much as religious, and concern anxiety
about the encouragement of interpersonal violence and, more particularly
of right-wing militant elitism. Heathenism may be seen as resembling the
occult interests of some high-ranking members of the Nazis in pre-war
Germany. Like satanism, it does seem to encourage racism, anti-Semitism
and an aggressive stance to any opposition among its members. To those
for whom these ideas represent the revival of Nazism and hence the
greatest evil, there is little difference between the two. It is important,
therefore, to make clear what the differences actually are.

Since Christianity did not become the majority religion in Scandinavia
(unlike the case in Britain) until the eleventh or twelfth centuries, more is
known about the religion it superseded than about other pagan religions
in Europe. Nevertheless, the ideas and rituals of modern Heathens are not
accurate revivals of the ancient religions of the Norsemen,[10] Anglo-Saxons
or Teutons, but select from them in ways that seem appropriate to the
modern Heathens, much as neo-pagans have done with other pagan
traditions, such as the Celtic or Druidry. The various different groups of
the Heathen persuasion have developed their own rituals, symbols and
forms of worship but they do have some common features. These will be
discussed briefly below, both because they clarify what is not satanist and
also point to similar areas of political and social, rather than religious,
concern.

According to Harvey (1995b) there are Heathen groups throughout
Scandinavia and Western Europe, in North America and Australasia. Since

1973 one form of Heathenism has been an officially recognized religion in Iceland; its marriages and other rituals thus have the same standing there as Christian ones. There is no single organization to which all Odinist/ Heathen groups belong but some groups have branches in other countries – for example, the British Odinic Rite has French and German sections – while others have links with other similar groups. Heathen groups are not mutually exclusive and individuals may belong to more than one group.

Odinists/Heathens have certain characteristic symbols: runes, the hammer of Thor and the swastika. In ancient Scandinavia the runes served as an alphabet but this function appears not to have been taken over by neo-Heathens, who are mainly concerned with their magical qualities. The runes are used in a variety of symbolic ways in magic, fortune-telling and rituals; they are carved on wood to form talismans or charms, or combined, as bindrunes, for use in magic. Some Pagans who do not describe themselves as Heathens also make use of them in magic. The hammer of Thor may be used in rituals to invoke the god whose symbol it is, or, in the form of a pendant worn round the neck, it may serve, like the cross, as a sign of religious allegiance. Government-funded research in Sweden on neo-Nazi groups indicated that similar insignia were being used by some of them (Hélène Lööw, pers. comm.). The swastika, a former symbol of the sun in Norse cosmology, should differ from the form of it used as insignia by the Nazis: in the Norse swastika the arms turn in the opposite direction. Often, however, there is no apparent difference and it is therefore this symbol that has aroused most alarm, both among minorities such as the Jews, who associate the symbol with the Holocaust, and among older Europeans who remember the German invasion of their countries during World War II.

Harvey describes Heathen groups as concerned with ecology and shamanism like other pagans. However, another source states that an Odinist magazine reports that 'few are interested in ecology'. Certainly the Odinist magazines read for this essay gave little indication of an interest in modern ecological issues, unlike pagan publications. Where shaminism is concerned, a tradition of herbal magic that was originally considered morally dubious has been turned into a shamanic means of entering into relationship with the gods. In this, Heathenism demonstrates clearly that, so far from being a revival of an ancient religion, it is a part of the neo-pagan movement, sharing its love of magical innovation and indifference to authenticity.

Two issues distinguish Odinists from other pagans: their attitude to gods and to race. Heathens are clearly polytheistic, while there is a tendency among other groups to associate different gods together as aspects of the Goddess. More has been written about the pre-Christian religions of northern Europe, which were practised longer than those of the more southern regions, the latter being first affected by the religion of the Roman Empire and then Christianized at a relatively early stage. The Roman Empire did not include the north and Christianity therefore came late to it. Heathen views on gods and goddesses are consequently clearer and more uniform than those in other traditions, where different views may be held within the same group (Harvey 1995b: 66). Heathens acknowledge a plurality of gods, divided into two categories – the Aesir and the Vanir. The former are referred to in the name Asatrú – those who honour the Aesir – and some heathens today call themselves Vanatrú – those who honour the Vanir. It is Asatrú that is recognized in Iceland. The gods and goddesses are treated as persons with whom human beings enter into reciprocal relationships, which is quite different from the normal semi-indifferent attitude of other pagans to deities that are hazy, remote or seen as forces of nature rather than persons. In this, the influence of the fuller literature on old Norse cosmology can be seen.

The second and most important difference between Heathens and other neopagans lies in the former's attitude to race. Their view is that each 'race' has a particular tradition to which it has some inherited psychic or genetic affinity, so that, for example, Odinism is particularly suited to Northern Europeans. It is not altogether clear what is meant by race but it seems to mean a physically defined group with a particular culture – an ethnic group in more modern terms. Heathens reject the use of words with Latin or Greek origins as belonging to another, southern, tradition, preferring, where possible, to use terms with what they consider to be a Norse derivation. An example of this is their preference for 'heathen' rather than 'pagan' as a description. Their objection to Christianity is on similar grounds: that it is not part of the Northern tradition. Heathens object strongly to multiculturalism and to pluralism of any sort. In Scandinavia where the governments have accepted large numbers of refugees from the 'South' (a new label for what was formerly the Third World), this attitude can be interpreted as a reaction to recent events. Something similar may be true of Britain too, although here immigration is less recent and was ended some years ago, so that it is hard to see this racism simply as a direct reaction to immigration.

Harvey states that not all Heathens take such a racist view of others. Some see other traditions as 'equally valid for other peoples' and others make clear that they are not claiming racial or cultural superiority (1995b: 65). However, he admits that relations with neo-pagans of other persuasions are not always amicable because of the Heathens right-wing views, their association of power with violence, and their commitment to an old-fashioned view of gender. A brief reading of the Odinist magazine, *The Raven Banner*, leaves one in no doubt as to its racist and right-wing views, which are brutally explicit. Even so, Odinism in Britain is much less clearly political than, for example, the extreme group Combat 18, one of whose members was given a prison sentence in September 1997 for distributing abusive literature and inciting the extreme harassment of a black boxer's mother. However, it seems likely that the sympathies of some Odinists and Heathens may lie with such extreme right-wing groups and there is a long history of overlapping membership between the two types of group.

It has been noted that the political outlook of members of the Church of Satan tended to be conservative and that LaVey was always against breaking the law, particularly where drugs were concerned. As we saw earlier, Alfred describes the membership as consisting of 'mostly middle-class white people in their forties, thirties and late twenties, including many professionals', which would be consistent with this. The membership of the Temple of Set, classified by Harvey, was slightly more varied, ranging from a chef to a telecommunications engineer. Although the group's political affiliations are said to include five people who voted for centre and left-wing parties, both the leader of the Temple of Set[11] and the founder of the Order of Nine Angles have both been members of a very right-wing organization, the British Movement. An article written in *The Black Flame* by Elizabeth Selwyn, who is clearly an American, refers to fascism as 'the English disease' and seems to consider all British satanists as likely to be fascists, although she absolves Black Lily, since it has got rid of its founder leader. Odinism has also been associated for at least 20 years with the rise of extreme right-wing politics and, as has just been noted, Heathen groups may express very right-wing, racist views. A Norwegian expert on neo-paganism stated that in Scandinavia young men had been leaving satanism for the new Norse groups, claiming that both LaVey and Acquino, like their predecessor Aleister Crowley, were too soft and too ready to leave events to magical manipulation. These included the self-styled satanist, formerly known as 'The Count' (possibly a reference to Count Dracula) who was responsible for burning a stave church in Norway and is currently in prison for murder. He announced that he rejected his former identity, was no longer a satanist and was renaming himself Fenrir, the Wolf, a figure of significance in old Norse mythology (Hartveit, pers. comm.). In Sweden, research on neo-Nazi groups has shown them to be adopting symbols drawn from Old Norse folklore, of which the Viking axe, hammer and the swastika (derived from the Norse symbol of the sun) are the most frequent and disquieting to liberal observers. In the rest of Europe too the rise of neo-Nazism has coincided with the increasing popularity of Old Norse religions. To date, not enough research has been done to establish whether there is a causal link here or even to permit any clear distinction to be drawn between Odinist groups with right-wing ideas and extreme right-wing political organizations using symbolism drawn from Norse mythology.

The oldest Odinist Group is said to have been founded in Australia in the 1930s but to have moved to Britain subsequently – when is not clear. There are thus two groups both named the Order of the Odinic Rite, but one is generally accepted as the older. It is the latter that publishes the right-wing magazine, *Raven Banner*. Other Heathen groups in Britain are: Odinshof, Hammarens Ordens Sallskap and the Rune Gild. The last is represented in America as well and all the groups have connections in Europe, not merely in the northwest but also in France and Germany. In the USA, the Asatrú Alliance, the Asatrú Folk Assembly, the Odinist Fellowship and the Ring of Troth are well established. They seem in one respect to be much more successful than other pagans in the attempt to recreate an ancient pagan religion, because they do not seek to combine post-Christian learned magic with the religious traditions of an earlier period, but concern themselves with belief and ritual practice from a single cultural system. They are quite distinct from satanists, who are dedicated magicians and although some Odinists may have links with right-wing groups as individuals and may even be members of neo-nazi organizations, many of the Odinist groups seem to be primarily religious in orientation.

Satanic Abuse Mythology

The phrase 'satanic abuse mythology' is intended to serve as a label for a particular set of beliefs that has spread very widely through the Western world. Neither the existence of satanist churches nor the Christian theology of evil were directly and solely responsible for these beliefs, although both were contributory factors, together with Christian folk mythology. According to those that held them there were covert organizations, said by some to be international in scope, that met in secret at night to perform rituals of devil-worship. These rituals consisted of the sorts of atrocious actions that characterized their perpetrators as inhuman. The action that accounted for the term 'satanic abuse mythology' was the sexual abuse of children, which was allegedly an integral part of the ritual, although this was not all that occurred in it according to the accounts. The groups who worshipped Satan in this way were alleged to be composed of people from all walks of life, including the very highest; it was the fact that members included the rich and powerful that afforded them protection, along with the skills of those who could conceal the evidence of their crimes.

In books and articles denouncing the satanist threat, the little-known fact that satanist groups existed was used to support the allegations. When sceptics pointed out that the accusations seemed to derive from Christian ideas, the reality of some form of satanism could be used in rebuttal. It was argued that it was not necessary to be a Christian and believe in Satan oneself to accept that such rituals were taking place, for it was those involved in satanist religions, whose secret rituals these were, who believed in him. Since most people to whom these remarks were addressed had no idea what the rituals of satanist groups like the Church of Satan were actually like, the argument sounded convincing. Others, who did know, became convinced that the whole truth was not being revealed by the groups they knew about. Belief in the truth of the allegations was so strong that contrary evidence had little effect.

While the mainstream and 'official' cults deny the charges of sacrificial ritual and blood-lust, there are many less formal covens of worshippers and pseudo-satanic sects, some resorting to a kind of ritual . . . that provides the blood, sex and disgust that the detractors [sic] of satanic worship insist is prevalent. (Parker, 1993:242).

A close reading of the book from which this quote is taken fails to discover any evidence for the existence of the 'pesudo-satanic sects' – other than the supposition that if the known satanist groups are not guilty of the horrible rituals, there must be others who are.

THE SOCIAL CONTEXT OF THE MYTH

The foundation of magical groups like the Church of Satan, the Temple of Set and the smaller satanist organizations did not take place in a social vacuum but as part of a marked resurgence of interest in spiritual concerns in the aftermath of World War II and the conflicts in Korea and Vietnam . This became apparent as several new social movements began to take shape in Western societies. First the 'beatniks', then the 'flower children' or 'hippies' attracted public attention, because their pursuit of peace through the development of a new way of life overturned so many social conventions. Their critics saw their communal way of life as associated with drug-taking, with the absence of marriage or, as some called it, sexual promiscuity, and with complete indifference to the world of formal education and employment. These were young adults with relatively affluent and educated parents, who rejected the society they had been brought up in, holding it responsible not merely for the failure to improve the lives of human beings in the world but for introducing new evils in the form of terrible military weapons and the destruction of the global environment for profit. Their approach to their philosophy was romantic and idealistic, they provided an example rather than proselytizing, and they were successful, up to a point. For several years the movement seemed to be spreading, most visibly at universities across the Western world.

In addition to the social movement of peaceful protest, this period also saw the establishment of New Religions among Western societies. The convenient term 'New Religious Movements', in current usage among sociologists (Barker, 1989), will be used to distinguish all these groups from the traditional, established religious organizations, for they have much in common, despite widely different theologies. Some members of Western societies converted to what were considered by their compatriots to be 'exotic' religions, such as various different sects of Buddhism. Others joined new and dissident Christian movements that were established by charismatic leaders, like the Reverend Moon, who founded the World Unification Church. Some New Religious Movements described themselves as Christian, although doctrinally they seem somewhat heretical and run the risk of being rejected by other Christian churches on that score. Other New Religious Movements were, and are, definitely and self-consciously not Christian. The developing occult movement produced a kaleidoscope of diverse groups, including neo-pagans, druids, wiccans (witches) and ceremonial magicians, as well as the Satanists described earlier and the Heathens who are now emerging – although only a few of these have increased sufficiently in size or been publicized to the point where the general public are aware of them. Still other groups, such as Scientology, Exegesis and Transcendental Meditation, belong to what Paul Heelas has called the 'self-religions' (Heelas, 1982), locating the ultimate truth within the individual and devoted to improving their members spiritual and emotional strength. In this they have a good deal in common with the satanist organizations already described.

The whole movement appeared to be seeking, in its diverse ways, a spirituality that, it was clearly felt, traditional Christianity no longer provided. The different groups also shared a rejection of rationalism and of science as the means of improving life for humanity, regarding them as having failed to achieve moral was well as technological progress and, worse, with having provided the means to cause environmental and human destruction on a vast scale. They were all to some degree under attack from sections of the Christian Church as well, particularly from the New Christians, who have referred to all New Religious Movements as satanist on occasion. However, the fact of holding some views in common and being faced with hostility from the same source has not resulted in a united stance; on the contrary, the various groups have competed with one another and engaged in mutual denigration.

The members of the established Christian community were not immune themselves to the general current of thought and it effected developments within the Churches. While the Roman Catholic and Anglican established churches were losing members, new movements within the fundamentalist wings paralleled the rise of interest in new religions. The house church movement, the charismatic movement, exorcism, and belief in the possibility of direct communications from God (e.g., the 'word of knowledge' that reveals when a fellow member of a congregation has been a victim of satanic abuse), are all part of a fundamentalist revival which started much earlier in the century with The Jehovah's Witnesses, the Seventh-Day Adventists and the Assemblies of God, but which has now gone on to effect changes inside even the more traditional denominations as well. As one example of this one can cite the fact that the exorcism of spirits or demons, once relegated by most denominations to the quaint mediaeval past of the Church, is now widespread; even the Church of England has priests in every diocese responsible for what is now called deliverance. Some of these evangelizing groups, like the Baptist Church that became the Jesus Army, became indistinguishable from new religions, just as some new religions considered themselves Christian. There might be a considerable difference between the perceptions of members and those of outsiders and in the case of some groups, it might be hard for an observer to decide whether they were religious revivals within the Christian Church or New Religions.

As Hutton has pointed out elsewhere in this volume, the recruits to the religious revival and to New Religious Movements, have much in common. They are drawn largely from the urban middle class, from the independent sections of it, and share a concern for the state of the world in general. Structurally the groups are similar, showing a diversity of practice and a tendency to split over disagreements between members or to dissolve and reform. There are similar features in their religious practices as well: possession by spirits is the basis of shamanism among neo-pagans, and among charismatic Christians speaking in tongues manifests the descent of the Holy Spirit into members of the congregation. A belief in the efficacy of magic, common to occultists and neo-pagans, resembles the faith in the healing ministry and the laying on of hands among New Christians. Ian Cotton's study of New Christians has pointed out the close parallels between their conversion experiences and visions and the effects of recent therapeutic practices such as primal scream therapy and the practices of the self-religions (Cotton, 1995). Another common thread in all these various sections of the religious revival is an apparently romantic reaction against a rationalist world view and an emphasis on direct and personal experience as against learning as the basis of knowledge. This epistemology, as has often been pointed out, resembles that of the psychotherapeutic professions and it is probably no accident that the post-war period saw these latter also spread and develop in significance.

The major differences between the New Christians and the New Pagans are directly relevant to the question of satanic mythology. Hutton describes those who joined the neo-pagan movement as autodidacts, interested in learning and in exploring new subjects; this is not true of the fundamentalists who are traditional in their outlook, derive all their knowledge from the Bible and are convinced that theirs is the only true religion. Neo-pagans are eclectic, tolerant of other religions and do not proselytize; the New Christians are determined to spread their faith and see themselves as engaged in a battle against all other religions which are tools of Satan. For while there might be little apparent difference between the Christian faith in the efficacy of prayer and the neo-pagan's confidence that magic causes change through the operation of the magical will, the powers they invoke in this way are perceived as radically different. New Christians are opposed to any divergence from the Christian faith as laid down in the Bible and may interpret this as evidence of the devil's influence and a source of danger to Christian, that is Western, civilization.

Preaching against Satan is a feature of revivalist church services and of meetings of the New Christians. Warnings include pointing out his ultimate aim of defeating God by bringing the whole world under his sway, and descriptions of his methods – seduction and temptation through minor sins and then blackmail and other forms of coercion. The Devil is seen as seeking an opening to lure or coerce individuals, particularly the young, into his service. Some activities that may seem harmless enough in themselves provide Satan with this opportunity; others are demonstrations of his success or of his power. These general ideas are given life by using contemporary events as illustrations of them. Two New Christians told Ian Cotton that they had been warned that taking drugs risked involvement with the satanic and when they had done so on one occasion they had seen the Devil in the room and were saved from him only by calling on Christ. Some Christians also believed that the approaching end of the second millennium since the birth of Christ heralded the events foretold in the Book of Revelations – the triumph of evil and the destruction of the earth before the Second Coming. The spread of other world religions such as Islam and Buddhism was used as a demonstration of the truth of this, and the rise of pagan cults was, *par excellence*, taken as proof that worshipping the devil in the guise of false gods was spreading.

A HISTORY OF ACCUSATIONS OF SATANISM

The central features of beliefs in satanism have a historical background of great antiquity, as historians (and this series of volumes) have shown. From time to time, these beliefs have resulted in accusations against living people, where fears have been given substance and hence acted to confirm the beliefs. The past is used by believers in satanism as a source of episodes that are seen as providing evidence for the great antiquity, not of the ideas but of the practices they describe. Thus, the allegations made against heretics like the Cathars are taken as indicating the existence of a satanic sect and a number of other episodes may also be used in the same way. In tracing a brief history of the development of the idea of satanism, the modern relevance of some of its features can be demonstrated.

Charges of holding secret meetings where rites of incredible depravity took place predate the spread of Christianity through Europe according to Norman Cohn, who traces the idea back as far as the first century before Christ and recounts various fictions concerning secret cannibal feasts held by conspirators that were promulgated at the time. By the second century AD Christians were being accused of infanticide, cannibalism and incest and a decade or so later, in 177, similar accusations resulted in the torture and death of the whole Christian community in Lyons. Their remains were burnt and thrown into the Rhone, a fate not accorded to the bodies of any other criminals, even traitors. These early episodes are difficult to handle in terms of the satanic mythology and they are not often mentioned, except to remark that satanism predates Christianity.

After the conversion of Europe to Christianity, it was the Christians who made these same allegations against those who were perceived as enemies of the Christian Church. Sects like the Montanists in Phrygia and the Manichaeans were suspected of infant sacrifice and of mixing children's blood with meal to make ritual bread of it. This last was a claim made by St Augustine that was to be repeated time and again as an accusation hurled at the Jews in the centuries to come.[12] Cohn describes how, 'As the centuries passed the powers of darkness loomed larger and larger in these tales, until they came to occupy the very centre of the stage' (Cohn, 1975:17). By the time that the Church was embattled against heretical Christian sects, the myth had become one of a ritual of devil worship with demons present and Satan presiding overall. The ritual had become the inverse of the Christian Mass. During the Middle Ages heretics were regularly accused of versions of these rites. In the twentieth century people again assert that those accused were guilty, although historical research has detailed the falsity of the accusations against them.

The Knights Templar were more formidable adversaries for the Church to choose as opponents than most heretics, yet the use of allegations of satanism helped Philip of France to bring them down and take possession of their enormous wealth to prevent his own financial ruin. From being a religious order with great power, as well as international bankers and traders enjoying great privileges, they were utterly destroyed. The crimes they were accused of were those levelled against the heretics, with the addition that they were said to worship an idol called Baphomet, which was smeared with the fat of roasted infants. The bodies of dead Templars were said to be burned and the ashes used for magical potions that were administered to new recruits. Questions about these allegations were put under torture and many of the Templars confessed, although many also recanted afterwards and 54 of these were burned when they refused to withdraw their recantations. This stopped any further recantations. The leaders were also burned, even though they had confessed, but on the scaffold on 18 March 1314 the grandmaster, Jacques de Molay, withdrew his own confession, proclaiming his guilt at having made it when nothing of what had been said was true. The historical evidence is sufficient to confirm his innocence (Cohn 1975 ch. 5).

The Knights Templar figure as satanists in many accounts where historical myth is used as proof of the antiquity of satanism. Their status as corrupt Catholic priests feeds the Protestant myth that Catholicism is a satanic religion; the allegations of homosexuality are accepted at face value. As has already been seen, the Church of Satan shares the anti-satanist view that the Templars worshipped Baphomet, despite the historical evidence showing that no such idol was found in the search of Templar property and the fact that various other interpetations have been given for the rumour. The idol is portrayed as the goat-god version of Satan, despite the contemporary allegations that it was a head. The powerful international organization of the Templars is the model for the myth of modern international satanism and may also have been the model for the myth of international Jewry, since the Templars controlled the world of banking and finance of their time.

Gilles de Rais, the companion and supporter of Jeanne d'Arc, is frequently instanced as a proven satanist. Having retired to his country estates at a young age, he was later accused of sorcery and of serious debaucheries with an incredible number of young boys whom he was alleged to have killed afterwards. Historians are divided on whether he was guilty or not; certainly he was tortured to force the confession he made, and although he was convicted of being a sorcerer there is evidence that he knew very little about the occult. Elliot Rose, who thinks he was probably a homosexual sadist, also remarks that the allegations must have been exaggerated in the telling (Rose, 1989 (1962):73). Even though there is no evidence at all that he was a satanist or that the boys were sacrificed in rituals of devil-worship, he is nevertheless commonly referred to by believers in the satanic myth as a satanist (e.g. Boyd, 1991:113).

The witch-hunts of the early modern period represent a crucial development in the satanic myth but are not referred to by modern anti-satanists, perhaps because it has long been accepted that the accusations made during them were largely untrue. What is less clear in the popular mind is that at the end of the Middle Ages there were two distinct uses made of magic: the learned and the popular. Among the educated, which often meant the clergy, there was interest in the phenomena of the natural world; learned magic was associated with the early beginnings of what would later be called the natural sciences. A distinction was drawn between natural and demonic magic, the former dealing with the 'hidden powers' in nature, the latter having to do with conjuring demons to perform what man alone could not do. While the distinction was clear in principle, in practice it might be hard to maintain and there was suspicion that those who practised natural magic might invoke demons as well. There is a direct parallel here with the modern occultists whose practice of magic resembles that of the magi rather than the popular magic that was later outlawed as devil-worship.

To some early modern clerics, more rigidly purist in their ideas, all magic involved the demonic and this view came to prevail. This affected the activities of the other class of magicians – the wise men and woman among the peasants whose knowledge of charms and use of magic to heal, to find thieves and to recover what they had stolen, was important in the rural areas. Keith Thomas has shown how in England the Church was offering its own specifics for these ills, so that its attempts to stop the practice of traditional white magic by claiming it was of the devil smacked of self-interest (Thomas, 1973). The Church also decreed that black magic or sorcery, the witchcraft that was believed to cause sickness and misfortune, was also associated with the Devil. All magic, it was said, obtained its power through a contract made with the Devil and witches were his servants.

It was a short step from this to the idea of assemblies of evil beings meeting to worship their master the devil. The final idea of the witches sabbath was composed of various strands that had been added to the myth of the conspiratorial feast. The eating of murdered children and the indulging in sexual orgies were retained but other details were brought in from other images and folk beliefs at different times. These included the *osculum infame* (the kiss on the anus or buttocks that servants of Satan must offer as a sign of their servitude and that has been seen as an obscene parody of kissing the Pope's ring), the flight to the sabbath, and the idea that witches had animal familiars. The lasting effect of the persecution unleashed was probably the establishment of the idea of devil-worship and the witches' sabbath as a folk-belief. The modern myth is a descendant of it; despite the failure to mention the ideas that animated the witchhunts, it is the idea of the witches sabbath that has contributed the framework of alleged satanism. As in the past, local elements may be incorporated into particular accounts, but the main features of the witches secret meeting to worship the devil remain.

This mythology was revived as a direct result of the New Christians' struggle against other religions. Fundamentalist Christians had always opposed Freemasonry and previous dissident Christian sects such as the Seventh Day Adventists, condemning them as the devil's work; from the 1960s onwards they also campaigned against the practices of the hippies and against New Religions as manifestations of Satan. The neo-pagans, particularly the witches (it was only later that the evangelicals learnt to call them Wiccans) were, from the first, deemed to be servants of Satan and their rites, about which little was known, to be modern forms of devil worship. The term 'cult' was used to refer to all New Religions, particularly those that were small and unconventional and the term quickly took on a derogatory inflection. Christian campaigning organizations in both the USA and Britain described themselves as being anti-cult. The term 'cult-cop' was used in North America to describe those policemen and women who became 'experts' in satanism and who propagated the myth in lectures and workshops.

New evils were added to the campaign as time went on. Some came from the beliefs of New Christians about the dangers of modern amuse-ments. Practices such as reading horoscopes, telling fortunes by using tarot cards or a crystal ball, and practicing spiritualism through engaging mediums or using ouija boards, were all likely to lead people to satanism. The focus of later campaigns were: heavy rock music, because certain bands used symbols such as 666 (the number of the Beast in the Apocalypse) and were said to transmit dangerous messages when their records were played backwards; the fantasy role-playing game Dungeons and Dragons; certain symbols like that of the Campaign for Nuclear Disarmament and that of the soap firm Proctor and Gamble in the USA, which led to a boycott of its products in the USA; and the World Wild Life Fund (WWLF) because of its ecological concerns which were characterized as pagan nature-worship (the Duke of Edinburgh has been characterized as a satanist because he is President of the WWLF). To the dedicated New Christian even the practice in primary schools of celebrat-ing Hallow'een with pumpkins and homemade figures of ghosts and witches put young children at risk. Stories about the dangers of Hal-low'een were already circulating in the USA during the 1970s. It was not until a decade later that campaigns to stop such practices in schools in Britain were reported in British newspapers.

The fundamentalists argued that just as marijuana was a comparatively innocuous drug but using it led directly to the use of hard drugs, so any of these dubious practices carried the risk of falling into Satan's power.[13] In his book published in 1973, the American evangelist and faith-healer Morris Cerullo lists all of them as part of the wave of satanism sweeping the country. (He records that the title of the book, *The Back Side of Satan*, represents Satan in flight from true Christians; the explanation leaves the reader wondering whether there is also a reference to the kiss that was alleged to represent fealty to Satan and speculating as to whether this was intentional).

As this example suggests, the religious revival first attracted attention in the USA and it was there too that the satanic abuse mythology arose. There has, however, been some disagreement over where precisely satanic abuse mythology started. The American folklorist William Ellis has argued that all the ingredients of the allegations were already present in British folk-lore and were exported to the USA (Ellis, 1993). It is true that one of the early allegedly satanic cults, The Process was founded in England, but as was shown earlier, this group was not typical of modern satanism and it did not fit the allegations of satanism either. Crowley too was British and influenced the occult movement in the USA but Ellis has pointed particularly to the fact that vampirism, that is blood-drinking, was more characteristic of cases in Britain, where folk-tales of vampires had a long history, as they do in Europe. It was this that led Ellis to consider a

British origin to the mythology. However, the view taken here is that it was a combination of features rather than any one of them that characterised what has become known as satanic abuse, and that this was first 'discovered' in the USA.

National variations in the allegations can indeed be detected, some of which, like the satanists dressed as clowns in the Dutch case in Oude Pekela, can be traced to particular allegations in the USA. On the other hand, some elements in the allegations that were distinctive to the USA were not transmitted as the mythology spread. One of these was the reports of mutilated animal carcasses being found that were considered as proof of the activities of satanists and which were largely absent from cases outside America.[14] Scares that children were to be kidnapped, like those that terrified a small town in New York state (Victor, 1991), were also prominent in satanic abuse mythology in the USA but rare elsewhere (Bromley, 1991). On balance, it can be said that if modern witchcraft was exported from Britain to America (Hutton, this volume) then satanic abuse mythology and the 'satanism scare' was imported in return.

THE COMPONENTS OF SATANIC ABUSE MYTHOLOGY

There are several strands in the mythology. The idea that children are abducted to be killed as sacrificial victims in evil rites is one such fundamental element. The cases of children who disappear and whose bodies are then discovered later are reported in the media and are used to show that it is still happening. Men like the Briton Fred West or the Belgian Dutroux, both of whom were responsible for the serial murders of children and teenagers are claimed to be satanists, their activities described as 'rituals', and efforts made to demonstrate their involvement in the occult. The fact that there is incontrovertible evidence to prove that these men tortured, abused and killed their victims has been claimed to 'prove' that satanism is a real threat, despite the fact that there is no evidence to suggest that either man was a member of a satanist group or was performing rituals when he committed his crimes. It appears that where crimes are unusually horrific, calling the perpetrator of them 'satanic' may be a moral designation as much as a literal description.

Cannibalism as part of satanic ritual is a regular, though not invariable, feature of the mythology. When beliefs in witchcraft were linked to ideas of devil-worship early in the sixteenth century, witches were also accused of cannibal feasts. Traces of this remain in the Witch in the folk-tale of Hansel and Gretel, who captures the two children to fatten them up in a cage for eating. Cannibalism does not feature in all historical accounts and the Templars, for instance, were not accused of it. But the idea that they sacrificed human beings to 'feed' their alleged idol, Baphomet, still defines human beings as food, thus breaking a fundamental taboo.

In all societies there are certain actions whose prohibition is taken for granted because such behaviour is seen as defining what is not human: the prohibitions concern food, sex and killing. Those that break them are inhuman in that they violate what are assumed to be basic qualities of human nature; they thus serve as symbols of supreme evil. The central acts of the rites of the Witches' Sabbath in the satanic myth are the public breaking of these prohibitions. The killing, rather than nurture, of the young, the use of human flesh as food and, finally, the orgies of perverted sex, all testify to the fact that witches and devil-worshippers are less than human. What form of sexuality is outlawed in the descriptions of evil beings may vary from time to time and place to place, as they must do since they are cultural prohibitions, not reflections of a universal human nature. Their alleged breach is best understood as a symbolic statement about evil, rather than as a factual description of reversals of human nature. Anal intercourse, bestiality, homosexuality, incest and finally, in the twentieth century, the sexual abuse of children, label the participants in the Witches Sabbath or any other 'satanic' ritual as beasts, not human beings.

Other fundamental elements also have a long history. The idea of secret meetings held by evil conspirators to plan the overthrow of the status quo, who then seal their pacts with one another by unspeakable rites, was first used against Christians, not by them (Cohn, 1970, 1975). At various periods during the centuries following the establishment of Christianity as the dominant religion in Europe, similar allegations were made against those whom the Church defined as its enemies – heretics, including the Cathars and Albigensians, theTemplars, the Franciscan Order, and the witches, who were denounced as devil-worshippers because their powers were said to derive from a secret pact with Satan. The Jews, who denied Christ's divinity and crucified Him, were associated with Satan and accusations made against them from time to time, most recently in the allegations of the Nazis that they killed Gentile children, especially boys, to use their blood in making of their ritual food. The Jewish term for their holy day, the sabbath, was and still is, used to denote the meeting of witches to worship the devil, like the earlier term for their meeting place: synagogue.[15] All these accusations might vary according to the nature of the people against whom they were directed but they associated satanism with accusations against identifiable people and groups.

While one can point to a historical continuity in the core elements of satanic mythology and their almost universal significance as definitions of the (in)human, this has not meant a lack of change. The twentieth-century version of the mythology reflects contemporary popular anxieties about children, concerning their sexual exploitation as well as the possibility of violence used against them or their deaths in infancy. Satanic rituals involving children may be said to have been photographed, video-recorded or filmed for sale, following media stories about the extent of child pornography. Children's sexual abuse as part of the rituals has become a common feature of alleged cases of satanism. It has featured in so many allegations that the term 'satanic abuse' is used to characterize them as a phenomenon and it is this that has propelled the mythology of satanism into the arena of state action. The prominence of children in accounts of satanic abuse or witchcraft has been explained as representing fears for the future in a society facing great uncertainties; it may also reflect fears that the horrors that befall children in other parts of the world, which are daily reported in the media, may one day occur to children in other societies that are as yet fortunate enough to be peaceful and well-fed.

Other more recent elements in satanic abuse mythology also refer to social controversies such as abortion. The controversy over abortion became a political issue in the USA where the New Christians were passionately committed to ending it, even to the point where violence was used against doctors and clinics who performed abortions. However, many Americans who were not New Christians were also opposed to easy abortion, so the reference to abortion, particularly to forced abortion, attracted wider support than the purely 'Christian' allegations.

National variations in the details of satanic abuse mythology can be identified and seem to reflect particular anxieties in the country concerned. In the USA, the majority of cases where children were said to have been ritually abused by satanists involved nursery schools − 'pre-schools' in American terminology. It has been pointed out that anxieties among women over leaving their children to the care of others easily become fears for their safety in those hands. In Britain, however, ritual abuse was alleged to involve the children's own parents, and the accusers were social workers and therapists rather than parents.

SOURCES OF ALLEGATIONS

New converts to fundamentalist Christianity would testify to their partici-pation in these satanic evils before they had 'found Christ' and to how they were led into worshipping the Devil; and some of their accounts were published. Cerullo gives a summary of one of these accounts, by Mike Warnke and two journalists, whose book, *The Satan-Seller* (Warnke, 1972) was widely read and quoted in the USA.[16] One of the most popular British accounts of a former devil worshipper, to judge by the number of reprintings it underwent, was published in the same year as Cerullo's book. Entitled *From Witchcraft to Christ*, it described witches engaged in rituals of devil-worship (Irvine, 1973). These converts were witnesses to the subtlety of Satan's temptations and to the power of Christian faith and prayer to save satanists; the depth of their (former) depravity was a measure of the strength of this power . In these early testimonies, drug-taking and dealing were very prominent and there were references to long hair and promiscuity which were seen as characteristic of 'hippies' and which were major public concerns in the 1970s. Prostitution was also a regular feature, usually representing the inevitable result of involvement with drugs.

The rituals described in these testimonies included animal sacrifice (usually of chickens or cats), nude women and sexual orgies. Blood from the sacrifice might be used in the ritual, for example it might be dripped on to a naked woman's body but human beings were not sacrificed in these early accounts. Warnke's account described fingers being cut off[17] and eaten but cannibalism was not a major theme. Other religions might be implicated, as when Cerullo describes the design on the membership ring of 'coven' members as featuring a crescent and star, the symbols of Islam.

Although in other respects these accounts represent modern versions of the early modern satanic myth, in that they are composed of the same elements, the differences show the effect of the intervening centuries: the witches do not fly to their Sabbath, either on animals (the Early Modern way) or on broomsticks (the later folklore version) and the Devil himself does not usually appear. Although sexual promiscuity is a feature of all versions, the modern survivor of satanism does not usually describe having intercourse with the Devil himself, as suspected witches were regularly described as doing during the witch-hunts of sixteenth- and seventeenth-century Europe.

The defining feature of satanic abuse mythology is that children are said to be being sexually abused and that these acts are an integral part of ritual addressed to the worship of Satan. This feature did not appear in the allegations referred to so far; neither Warnke, nor Cerullo nor, in Britain, Irvine, mentioned the presence of children at the gatherings that were described, let alone the sexual abuse and sacrifice of them. But while, in later allegations, variations on this theme are common and some allegations are extremely vague, sexual abuse is a core feature. This relates directly to the fact that it is a major public anxiety.

During the 1970s the problem of children being sexually abused by fathers and stepfathers was made public in the USA. Books such as Louise Armstrong's *Kiss Daddy Goodnight* (Armstrong, 1978) and accounts by child psychotherapists established that an unknown number of children were being subjected to various forms of sexual experience, including in some cases full intercourse. It was also learned that sexual abuse, as it was called, might start at a shockingly early age. The revelation followed the earlier discovery that babies and small children might be physically damaged by their parents (what became labelled as the 'battered baby' syndrome) and raised considerable alarm. What differentiated the two forms of abuse was that in cases of sexual abuse there were often no physical signs comparable to those that X-ray machines might reveal in a child's body and the vital, usually the only, source of information was therefore the child itself. For both these reasons, inducing the child to say what had happened became a focal issue and 'experts' in this field achieved considerable fame within their fields. Unlike the earlier discovery too, the memories of adults could be used to support the claim that sexual abuse was not a fantasy, as Freud had deemed it, but a reality. The children who said this was currently happening to them should be believed, since the memories of adults proved they were not lying.

Feminist concerns with violence against women contributed to the growth of satanic abuse mythology by insisting that women's accounts of the violence, comprising sexual and physical assault, that was used against them by men, be believed as they had not been previously. When women disclosed their memories of having been similarly abused in childhood these disclosures too were worthy of credence. The sexual abuse was sadistic and violent and, in some cases, it was recounted, had been so traumatic that all memory of it had been repressed; it was only when the victim entered therapy for other reasons that the original cause was revealed.

Thus, when evidence came to light that children were raped and beaten up, the feminists were in the forefront of those who campaigned for children to be believed. The discovery subsequently that women might also sexually abuse children and that networks of men might be involved in trafficking children, both as subjects for pornographic videos and for sex, added to the general anxiety about children. The murders of children were given great publicity in the press and rumours that children were being kidnapped for unspeakable purposes accompanied these horror stories. Some unusual cases, like that of the three-year-old who survived a terrible ordeal that was intended to kill her and who was able, remarkably, to identify her attacker, subsequently lent weight to claims that no accounts by children, however extreme, should be disbelieved. The argument that children 's disclosures should be believed turned into the slogan 'Believe the Children' and the dogma 'Children do not lie'.

One distinctive feature of satanic abuse mythology, that set it apart from other ideas of satanism or the actual beliefs and practices of satanist groups, is that it stimulated a rash of real cases in which allegations were made that seemed to offer the opportunity to uncover satanic activities and identify the satanists. Before this, claims about satanism being rampant had been couched in general terms; if actual cases were mentioned, usually only one or two, if any, of the satanists were identified. Moreover, all the cases in which adults were the victims referred to events that had occurred so many years before that action to discover and punish the perpetrators was not possible. With the advent of allegations that small children were being satanically abused the situation changed dramatically. In addition, in all the countries affected there were laws concerning the protection of children that were triggered by the allegations. The child victims brought the ideas out of the realm of belief into the world of action.

During the last 20 years, there has been a very large number of cases in a large number of countries where it has been alleged that rituals of devil worship have actually taken place. The allegations have not been simultaneous but have followed from one another as satanic abuse mythology spread from one country to another. They have been composed partly of the allegations of adults who described, usually to their therapists, their childhood experiences during which (they alleged) they were sexually abused during satanic rituals, and partly of allegations attributed to young children. These latter have been said to be 'the children's stories' and campaigning groups have taken 'Believe the Children' as their slogan or even, in one American case, their name.

Another peculiarity is that, despite police investigations being carried out and, in some cases, charges being brought against those perpetrators who were identified, independent material evidence to corroborate the accusations has never been found. Even in those cases where the charges have resulted in convictions, this outcome has been based on the testimony of the victims, in all but two cases in the USA. The exceptions have been cases in which the accused 'confessed', but, as in the other cases, there was no independent evidence that corroborated the admission that the accused had taken part in these rituals. These 'confessions' are of considerable interest and will be discussed further below.

THE SPREAD OF THE SATANIC ABUSE MYTHOLOGY

The first cases came to light in North America at the beginning of the eighties. Allegations by adults, such as *Michelle Remembers* (Pazder and Smith, 1980) and *Satan's Underground* (Stratford, 1988) were published in the USA, and subsequently, in 1984, the first case erupted. This was the case of the McMartin day-care centre in California, a case which was to take seven years to come to trial and proved to be the most expensive case in American legal history. For all the time and money it took, the case collapsed and the defendants were acquitted or released on hung verdicts.

Thereafter, cases spread across the USA like a rash. By the time that

David Finkelhor and his associates undertook their investigation into sexual abuse in day-care in 1985–6, they were able to find 36 cases of allegations[18] of what they called 'ritualistic abuse' that had occurred between 1983 and 1985 (Finkelhor *et al.*, 1988). Other cases emerged elsewhere, like those at Bakersfield in California in 1985, where the children were older and therefore not in day-care, and 34 of them were summarized for a special edition of the Memphis paper in 1988. These cases and the allegations of adults concerning their own satanic abuse as children were widely publicized, including appearances on the most popular television chat shows in the USA – the Oprah Winfrey show and the Bob Carson show. Such was the effect on the public of these cases, both those involving children and the publicly discussed cases involving adults, that some states changed the nature of testimony required in such cases, allowing convictions without what might in other jurisdictions be termed independent corroboration. On the basis of this unconfirmed evidence many people were imprisoned. Nathan and Snedeker dedicated their book to the 59 people who, in their opinion, were innocent of the charges against them, but who were still in prison in the USA in 1995 or who had already died there (Nathan and Snedeker, 1995).

In 1985, the year after the McMartin case, the allegations crossed international boundaries into Canada, with a case in Hamilton, Ontario. There had been connections with Canada in the McMartin case because the Canadian, Lawrence Pazder, co-author with his wife/patient Michelle, of the influential *Michelle Remembers* (Pazder and Smith, 1980) had come down to talk to parents. By then he had become a general adviser on satanic abuse. The ferment continued on both sides of the border and 1992 saw another very large case in Saskatchewan, which was not resolved until 1995 when it was quashed on the grounds that the children had been improperly questioned. By 1990 there were cases, either of adult survivors or of children, where satanic ritual was being alleged, across the country.

The movement also spread across the Atlantic. In 1986 there was a case in Holland, which included reference to underground tunnels, as the McMartin case had done. In 1987, following visits both ways across the Atlantic by evangelicals and experts on satanic abuse, cases began to occur in Britain. At the same time, Holland's most widely publicized case, in Oude Pekela, erupted. This was at first discussed as a case of organized abuse by a gang involved in producing mass pornography; it was not until much later that the notion of satanic abuse was mentioned by two persons involved in it. They achieved a good deal of publicity, particularly internationally, but their views were not taken seriously by the authorities. In the next six years, Britain suffered large numbers of cases, although only a handful had wide publicity. By 1993 when the Dutch Government instigated an enquiry, there had been some 20 cases in the Netherlands.

None of them had been substantiated. A police investigation found eight cases to consider in Sweden, none of which, it is said, produced any corroborative evidence. In Norway, one well-publicized case resulted in an acquittal for the principal accused. Cases in Germany have been less well publicized internationally but none of them appear to have resulted in convictions or in substantial evidence that such forms of abuse are actually happening.

Australia and New Zealand were not immune to the panic about ritual abuse; at the same time as cases were coming to light in continental Europe, Australia and New Zealand suffered a number of cases in which allegations of satanic abuse were prominent. In 1986 an international conference in Sydney brought many of America's 'experts' to Australia and it was the scene for a 'survivor's account of having recovered memories of sexual abuse by her father, an account which she published and which was widely publicized (Guillatt, 1996). However, it was not until two years later, after two television programmes on the subject of satanic abuse that a case resembling the McMartin case in very many details burst into Australian public awareness. Thereafter, there were numerous instances of allegations. A task force was set up in 1990 in the state of Victoria to investigate the claims but was disbanded after 16 months when no charges could be laid in any cases.

There are some national differences in these widely distributed cases. Most of them involving children in the USA, New Zealand and Australia concerned very young children in nursery schools and day-care centres. This was also the case in Oude Pekela in Holland, in Norway, where charges against a young man working in a nursery school resulted in his acquittal in court, and in a very similar case in New Zealand, where some workers in a school were dismissed from the case but the main accused was convicted and jailed. In Britain, by contrast, the accused were usually the parents of the children and it was not until 1994 that nursery schools were involved and then in only two cases. Clowns and nursery rhymes featured commonly in the USA cases, in Australia and in Holland, but not in Britain or Scandinavia. Careful attention to local newspapers has shown that the connections between various cases can be attributed to a compound of media publicity and the presence of individuals who are either disposed, by virtue of other ideas that they hold (some versions of feminism or of Christianity, for example) to believe the allegations, or who are making a place for themselves as 'experts'. The international spread of allegations is not an indication that the same organization is operating in all the places where allegations are made; rather, transmission of the mythology from place to place reflects the interconnectedness of societies whose cultures have a good deal in common. In particular, they share definitions of evil and a determination to eradicate it.

All the cases referred to have occurred in areas of the world where the culture is imbued with Christianity and particularly with Protestant Christianity. The rash spread from America to other English speaking countries, either where there were native speakers of English or where there was a high degree of competence in English as a second language. Catholic countries and those where English is not a second language or is not widely used have been relatively immune. France, for example, has remained relatively free, even of adult 'survivor' stories, although that may partly be the result of the work of Sherill Mulhern, an anthropologist who has undertaken research on the psychotherapeutic genesis of adult stories in her native USA (Mulhern, 1991) and who is much respected in her adopted country, France. Satanic abuse mythology, however, is very clearly a social problem of the West and must be explained in terms of western culture.

SOURCES OF ALLEGATIONS

There are two sources of allegations of satanic abuse: adults and children. Not only is the nature of the primary evidence that is associated with them entirely different, but the roles of the adults who report the allegations tend to differ also. Whereas adults, largely women but a few men, give accounts of what has happened to them to sympathetic adults who are often therapists, but may also be counsellors at rape crisis centres or Christian churches, children's 'evidence' consists not merely of what they say, which is often fragmentary or apparently unintelligible and needing considerable interpretation, but also their behaviour which is believed to be indicative of what they have undergone. The role of the reporter/interpreter is much greater where the cases of children are concerned, but as will shortly be apparent this is not the whole story. Adolescents, whose stories are coherent narratives, fall between the two categories on most criteria.

Adult survivors
Adults who have suffered serious trauma in their past are commonly termed 'survivors' by analogy with those who survived the Holocaust, although in the case of survivors of incest the experience may not have actually endangered their lives. Survivors of satanic abuse are commonly women and it is also characteristic that they have had periods of mental illness in their lives that have not yielded permanently to treatment. There are a number of diagnoses that appear in their records; on an impression-istic view, since no research on sufficiently large numbers has yet been

undertaken, it seems that they may be diagnosed schizophrenic or as having borderline personality disorder. Some survivors have become Christians and resemble the 'trophies of grace' whose accounts of escape from former wickedness have been mentioned already. The accounts of satanic abuse are typically cumulative, in that the most horrifying details are not given immediately but emerge gradually. These accounts have preceded the identification of cases involving children and have often predisposed those who believe them to accept similar stories associated with children; in all countries, some of these survivors' accounts have been published, even if only in newspapers or on television. It is therefore not surprising that there are similarities in the stories that they tell; common features concern extreme sexual abuse, the killing of adults, children and babies, forced abortion and the eating of human flesh and drinking of human blood. In some cases, animal sacrifice may substitute for, or be performed in addition to, human sacrifice. These acts are said to be part of rituals performed by groups, often very large gatherings, of men and women who may be gowned and hooded or dressed in other unusual costumes.

Despite the fact that it has been claimed that a forceful reason for believing these accounts is their similarity, there are marked differences, both in what the rituals are said to consist of and in the attendant circumstances. Some survivors incriminate themselves, saying that they were forced to take part in the rituals and perform sacrifices. Others claim that they resisted any attempts to make them sexually abuse or kill children. The symbols involved may be described as hexagrams [sic] or five-pointed stars, Baphomets, inverted crosses, runes, the number 666 or other satanic symbols. Even if the costumes appear the same they are often of different colours. The ritual acts belong to the categories of actions already described as characteristic of supreme evil but within broad similarities there are many variations. Given that an established characteristic of ritual actions is their fixity – rituals *must* be carried out in a certain way – this variability and the fact that it is ignored weakens the credibility of the accounts.

Changes can also be seen that seem to relate both to the passage of time and to the location of cases. Thus, the first allegations commonly included acounts of women and girls being used as 'brood mares' (breeders in North American terminology), who were impregnated regularly so as to provide babies for sacrifice or, alternatively to be forcibly aborted for the foetus to be sacrificed. The first mention of these features, and probably the model for later versions, was the published account by Lauren Stratford, *Satan's Underground*. Later survivors' accounts mostly lack this detail. Similarly, new details are incorporated, such as the use of runaway children or derelicts and tramps for human sacrifices, and the use of tarpaulins or plastic sheets to ensure that no traces that might form forensic evidence remain.

The later details appear to refer to arguments about the credibility of accounts and are introduced in the wake of objections. *Satan's Underground* was shown to be a fake by a careful journalistic investigation, so the detail characteristic of it was dropped. Similarly, the absence of any forensic evidence, even when murder had been committed, resulted in the incorporation of details which would account for this. One detail that accounted for the absence of bodies was the use of portable crematoria, a detail transferred from the USA to Britain.

There is no purpose to be served by detailing all the variations and changes in accounts. Enough has been shown to indicate that although there are similarities, there are also enough differences to make it unlikely that the accounts refer to a single organization, whether national or international. The lack of supporting evidence has aroused considerable scepticism, particularly since it appears to be true in all the countries where cases have been investigated. The accounts of survivors are thus the sole evidence for the existence of the satanist cults. It is here that the role of the hearers of such accounts is significant because they take them at face value and claim they must be believed. They are both the guarantors and publicists of the stories.

There are various points at which the roles of the listener and supporter of a survivor may be vital to that survivor's account. To begin with, it is only if the listener is prepared to accept what is said as true that such accounts will be heard at all. It is well established that only those who are prepared to accept the truth of whatever is said are likely to elicit them. There is an identifiable input here from a certain type of feminism. Following campaigns to believe the victims of rape and of domestic battering, in these circles it has become a matter of dogma that the stories of women who are victims must be accepted. Valerie Sinason and Robert Hale in their chapter in a book on satanic abuse edited by the former (Sinason, 1994) go as far as to claim that a secondary trauma may be caused by the failure to believe a survivor (Sinason and Hale, 1994). This is a new approach to patients, the more conventional being that while the account may be 'emotionally true' for the patient, the therapist cannot know whether it is actually true (Adshead, 1994).

In other cases, the 'victim', although feeling that something is wrong in her life, appears to have no memory of such events; in these cases it is a therapist or counsellor who induces the memory. Research has been published (Mulhern, 1991) that makes clear that these 'memories' retrieved in therapy are constructions, the product of the relationship between therapist and patient. Techniques such as hypnosis and 'regression therapy' have been identified as particularly likely to generate such constructions.

They are fictions although they may not be recognized as such by either party . Their resemblance to other similar stories is explained by the wide dissemination of information on 'satanic abuse' in all the forms of the media. This issue of 'repressed' or 'false' memories is of great importance in the psychological disciplines, since it concerns the basis of psychoanalysis, the notion of 'repression'. The debate that has been provoked still continues but is too complex to deal with in the space available here.

Another issue, evoked even earlier in the course of the construction of satanic abuse mythology, and which has also been a cause of controversy, is the diagnosis, not uncommonly applied to 'survivors', of Multiple Personality Disorder (MPD). This diagnosis, which is formally recognized in the USA but not elsewhere, refers to a condition whereby the patient displays several distinct 'personalities' which are often contradictory in character. The number of personalities displayed has increased rapidly over time; patients with 100 personalities are not unknown. MPD is said to have been caused by trauma in early childhood and before the 1980s cases were extremely rare. They have become increasingly common and are now attributed to sexual abuse in childhood, particularly satanic abuse. There are some psychiatrists and therapists who even claim that MPD is diagnostic for satanic abuse, that is, that all patients diagnosed as having MPD must have been satanically abused. Research in the USA has shown that the diagnosis of ritual or satanic abuse has most often been made by a small minority of clinicians and that these believe the claims despite lack of reliable evidence for them (Bottoms *et al.*, 1996). Those amongst them who are fundamentalist Christian in outlook may claim that one of the chief problems of the therapist is to distinguish between personalities that are actually intrusive demons, requiring exorcism rather than therapy, and true personalities (Friesen, 1991).

Children's cases

The cases of children differ from those of adults in that it is usually only adolescent children who give coherent narratives of satanic abuse. As I have argued elsewhere (La Fontaine, 1998) these stories are best treated like those of adult survivors, which they resemble in most details. The main difference occurs in the context of the allegations; teenagers may be in care when they start talking about having been satanically abused. They may therefore tell their stories to a wider range of persons than adults – to foster-parents, workers in children's homes or social workers, as well as to therapists and counsellors. There are few cases involving adolescents discussed outside Britain; an exception to this may be the Swedish police's investigation of eight cases to which I have unfortunately been unable to obtain access.

Young children's accounts of what is interpreted as 'satanic abuse' are strongly influenced by adults. While it has been invariably said that children are revealing that they have been satanically abused, a scrutiny of the case files makes it clear that much of what is claimed as children's own stories is a construction by adults. Children may make 'odd' unintelligible remarks and later, when encouraged to do so, may elaborate material into episodes, but it is much more common for the childrens' 'evidence' to be elicited by questioning, either by anxious parents or in interviews by experts. The number of these interviews, the leading character of questions and the pressure put on children have all given cause for concern. The variation in what children have said in these conditions is very wide indeed and it is only by ignoring most of it that the claim that there is similarity in the accounts can be justified. There are similarities that can sometimes be traced to common folk-lore, to television programmes and adult conversations but there are also highly idiosyncratic features. Of the 84 British cases involving allegations of satanic abuse, 51 had features shared by no other case and of these several had more than one feature of this kind. In the American case known as the McMartin pre-school case, the allegations of one child alone were described as a 'word salad', and there were 'hundreds' of children who after having been interviewed produced similar statements. There was little consistency, even within one case, let alone between cases.

In the cases involving children, particularly young children, behaviour of various sorts was used to supplement interviews, especially when these were, as often happened, inconclusive. A Californian social worker, who later became an international 'expert' on satanic abuse, produced a list of behavioural symptoms from cases, which like several others became a list of 'indicators' against which a child's behaviour could be measured to see if they indicated satnic abuse. Since many of these indicators were non-specific signs of disturbance, such as bed-wetting, nightmares or temper tantrums, and others, such as 'erotic behaviour', depended entirely on the observer's interpretation, it was relatively easy for anxious social workers or foster-parents who obtained these lists to match them to the behaviour of the child(ren) about whom they were worried. Once 'diagnosed' in this way, the child would be interviewed in order to produce corroboration. In this way, the satanic abuse mythology was transferred from case to case in country after country.

Confessions

Two cases in which there were allegations of satanic abuse are distinguished among all the others by the fact that they produced confessions in the accused. In one, the alleged victims were already adult, while in the other, allegations were made about young children. The cases were constructed in much the way that has been described above. In the first case, the accused were the owner of the pre-school, Frank, and his wife, Ileana, the latter aged only 17 at the time. Both were immigrants, although from different Latin American countries, and they ran a child-minding service in their home in an affluent suburb of a Florida town. Ileana's confession, which resulted in her husband being convicted of having abused the children in satanic ceremonies, was later withdrawn. She claimed that she had been pressured to produce it and told the Chaplain of the prison in which she spent considerable periods locked up in isolation that she was afraid of her lawyer. Certainly, he changed her defence plea, arguing that she was herself only a child who had suffered similar abuse from Frank. Evidence emerged that he had hit her, at least on one occasion. A psychologist testified that Ileana would have been under Frank's domination and likely to do anything he required of her. Psychologists also worked with her to 'bring back her memory' of the abuse (Nathan and Snedeker, 1995:173). A pair of psychologists whose business was named Behaviour Changers had at least 35 sessions with Ileana, even waking her at night to interview her. She became disoriented and was told she suffered from blackouts; she was told to recount her nightmares and soon she began to dream what the pyschologists suggested. She finally made a statement confessing to several counts of having sexually abused children. She served her sentence of three and a half years in prison and was deported to Honduras. In 1994 she signed a long sworn deposition describing her ordeal and withdrawing the statement it had produced.

The second confession was made by the father of adult daughters who accused him of having ritually abused them (Ofshe, 1992; Ofshe and Watters, 1994). All the family were members of a fundamentalist church. One of the girls attended a feminist retreat sponsored by their church and recovered 'memories' of the abuse; she was later supported by her sister who confirmed it. Their father, Paul Ingram, was a part-time policeman and was aware of the view that both victims and perpetrators might repress their memories of what had happened. When accused he therefore said he had no memory of the abuse but that if his daughters had accused him he must be guilty because they would not lie. His colleagues who interrogated him repeatedly suggested that he had a devil in him or that he did not remember because he was afflicted with multiple personalities, one of whom had been responsible. Ingram began to induce himself to experience trance-like periods in which he attempted to visualise the abuse, which he finally succeeded in doing. A cult expert, Richard Ofshe, was called in to identify what Ingram had began to refer to; he recognized that the memory was confabulated. Ofshe tested this by asking Ingram to recall an entirely imaginary incident, which he succeeded in doing. However, by the time Ofshe presented his report, Ingram had been convicted and sentenced. In prison, when interrogation ceased and he stopped trying to recall incidents, he began to realize that his 'confession' was false; he recanted his testimony but was refused leave to appeal and remains in prison.

These are the only confessions of satanic abuse that appear to have been made; they are certainly the only ones that have been investigated and the results recorded. They indicate how it is possible for pressure and self-delusion to produce the appearance of confessions that may then be cited to 'prove' that the existence of satanic abuse is a reality. Historians have often wondered what induced women during the early modern 'witch-craze' to produce what seemed to be entirely voluntry confessions. This material provides some suggestions as to how that may have happened. While repeated interviews produce their own form of pressure, it is not necessary to use physical torture to induce vulnerable people to confess. Ileana Foster was alone in a country not her own and subject to techniques that had the avowed intention of making her change her mind. It may perhaps be a measure of her innocence that it took so long for this to happen.

Frank Ingram, on the other hand, was a Christian and a police reservist who knew something about the sexual abuse of children and who believed in the power of the devil to make human beings sin most terribly. Acting on the suggestions of his interrogators, his self-hypnosis successfully enabled him to imagine scenes in which this happened. It was his unwillingness to believe that his daughters were lying that started the process of his destruction.

Notes

1 This section draws mainly on the work of Cavendish, Cohn, Kieck-hefer, Russell and Taylor; the particular books consulted are listed in the bibliography but are not cited in detail, to avoid cluttering the text with references.

2 In fact, the Black Mass was a comparatively recent idea and seems always to have been a parody of Catholic ritual rather than acting as satanic ritual or even as black magic. However, the idea of the Black Mass has become part of folklore without there being much idea of what it entails. Witches may even be said to perform a Black Mass, which is out of keeping with the original views of witches.

3 The name is written *Argenteum Astrum* by Sutcliffe (1996:126) and there are other variants. The one used here is Lamb's (1977:22).

4 Gareth Medway, to whom I am most grateful for having read my draft and thereby saved me from several slips and errors, has also pointed out that some people have argued that Seth is the same as Satan, but that in his view the etymology on which this is based is flawed. I have also drawn on the manuscript he is preparing for publication, which he was generous enough to let me see.

5 Tantrism is an Indian philosophical and magical system that allows the magickian to dispense with the Western labelling of magic as good and evil. Left-Hand Path magick refers to the transgression of certain food taboos and incorporates sexual intercourse into the ritual. It is designated as Left Hand, not because it is evil, but because it is occult and concerned with the liberation of the individual from social conditioning (Sutcliffe, 1995:110–11).

6 Gnostics were Christian heretical sects that developed in the early years of Christianity. Their ideas were influenced by Zoroastrianism and even, according to some authorities, by Buddhism. Their signifi-cance here is that they were religious dualists, according immense power to the anti-God, Satan. They believed that Satan could be both worshipped and magically manipulated. Some Gnostics believed Satan to be the Lord of the material world, while the spiritual was God's realm. The Gnostic heresy was eventually crushed by Christianity but it was revived to some extent by the, equally heretical, Cathars in the twelfth century. Modern understandings of *gnosis* as distinct from

Gnosticism emphasize a form of knowing where the 'knower becomes immersed to the point of identity in that which is known.' (Sutcliffe, 1996:119).

7 According to the caption on the photograph of LaVey in *The Black Flame* that announced the birth of his son, whom he is holding, she is the baby's mother.

8 Alfred refers to some priests [sic] who attempted to introduce innovations in the Church of Satan but were 'disciplined so severely that they left', who may be the founders of the Temple of Set.

9 Karl Milton Hartveit, personal communication. His two books, *Modern Occultism* (1988) and *Magic and Satanism* (1993) have unfortunately not yet been translated into English from Norwegian.

10 They do not, for example, sacrifice horses.

11 Austen is also said to have been a Mormon; he has certainly written an article that shows an intimate knowledge of what he describes as the initiation rites of the Church of Latter Day Saints.

12 Indeed, at a seminar in 1993, a social worker told a workshop I was running how on Jewish holy days she and her Jewish colleagues had regularly to endure jokes about their slaughtering infants to make matso (unleavened) bread.

13 The first half of this equation has been shown to be over-simplified, but it was generally believed in the 1970s. The parallel that was drawn with satanism played on parents' fears for their children.

14 On investigation, those animals that had not died of disease were shown to have been killed on the roads or by predators; the carcasses might also have been mutilated subsequently by scavengers.

15 Some ingenuity has been shown in devising etymologies that avoid this conclusion, so as to dissociate allegations of satanism from the blood-libel, but they are not convincing.

16 Cerullo does not list this work in his bibliography although it was published a year before his own and his acquaintance with Warnke is well-attested.

17 Curiously, the mutilations were not noticed by outsiders, even when they had been repeated several times.

18 This study concerned cases that had not been substantiated in any way, but that had merely been reported to the investigators as having involved ritual abuse. Some of them were subsequently shown to be false.

PART 3

The Witch, her Victim, the Unwitcher and the Researcher: The Continued Existence of Traditional Witchcraft

Willem de Blécourt

In 1921 at the port of Naples, so the story goes, customs officers stopped an old woman who refused to show the contents of a suspicious parcel. When they took it from her and examined it, they found 'a lamb's head wrapped round with a woman's hair, which was attached to the former by a kind of steel comb and forty-three nails driven into the head'. Information about this discovery spread from the Custom's station into the surrounding area. There, the old woman was immediately defined as a witch and set upon by a crowd. She was rescued by the customs officers and the police, but to pacify the crowd the lamb's head had to be handed over, although the woman pleaded against it. It was brought to a nearby church where 'a priest was obliged, much against his will, to satisfy the superstitions of the crowd and to celebrate a kind of ceremony to nullify the evil effect of the old woman's witchery'. After the priest had extracted the nails, the head was burnt outside the church.

This event is reported in the British Sunday newspaper *The Observer* of 15 May 1921 and subsequently in the journal *Folklore* (32: 210–11). In this way, the report was cut loose from the original event (if it ever occurred) and turned into an oddity, classified as 'Collectanea', as something to be collected like an exotic butterfly. It was presented as an example – not, however, of how customs officers interfered with the material and spiritual property of the anonymous old woman and how they failed to keep the information about it within the confines of the station. On the contrary it was an example of how 'the people', also described by the paper as 'the crowd' and 'the mob', still clung to 'old beliefs and superstitions'. Conveniently, it was an Italian 'mob', far enough removed from the centre of British civilization not to be unsettling. There was no report or speculation about what exactly the woman wanted to accomplish with her spell and why it even should have been evil. (This is probably because the head would have evoked images of innocence and of Christ, the lamb of God. This would have taken any attempt towards an explanation right into the heart of Western morality).

The newspaper message thus referred to the sensational, the exotic and the peripheral, to the past and to the lower classes. Are these then the appropriate parameters for characterizing twentieth-century European witchcraft? Is witchcraft mainly a feature of the so-called 'dark middle ages' and of 'primitive people'? Is it doomed to be marginalized in a rational and rationalized society? Part of the answers to these questions depends on the way witchcraft stories are presented. The message related above can be easily added to by others. In 1920, four men were charged at the court of Bordeaux, France, for assaulting an abbot whom they accused of having enchanted a woman miracle worker (*NYT* 5 January 1920). In 1922 an Italian woman went on trial for having cast a spell on an sick child (*NYT* 26 October 1922). A year later, a French peasant tried to burn alive a woman who he was convinced had bewitched his pigs (*NYT* 23 October 1923). 'German witchcraft story explodes when veterinarian discovers natural cause for cow's failure to give milk', read a report in 1926 (*NYT* 21 May). In 1929, there were cases from France, Portugal, Yugoslavia and Russia (*NYT* 9 April, 14 and 28 July, 6 August). These are just a few examples taken from the 1920s index of the *New York Times*. Although this newspaper did not mention any cases from Britain, others did, like the *Times* of 15 September 1926. A man from Devonshire reportedly left his wife, a cunning woman, because she accused him of having bewitched her and their child (Davies, 1947: 197). No European country was without traces of witchcraft.

If all these tantalizing reports were presented in full, together with those found in Denmark (Henningsen, 1989: 127–30, 138–9) in the Dutch province of Drenthe (de Blécourt, 1990: 273–4) and in France (Lancelin, 1911: 194–209), it would be quite easy to convey the impression that Europe was as ridden with witchcraft in the early twentieth century as it was during the time of the persecutions – especially so if the newspaper accounts are considered to reveal only the tip of the proverbial iceberg. This also applies to the middle of the twentieth century, for which period newspapers mention cases in Italy, Austria, England, France, Germany (Auhofer, 1960: 112–3) and Wallonia (Beckman, 1987: 78). Other sources seem to support this impression. 'The rural country belief in witchcraft, with its ill will, forespelling and sympathetic magic has left plenty of traces all over the country,' wrote folklorist Katharine Briggs about the British isles, 'and the actual belief itself is still lurking among unsophisticated people' (1970: 609–10). In 1956 about 8 percent of the inhabitants of the Federal Republic of Germany were inclined to consider the possibility of the existence of witches. At the time, 8 percent amounted to about 4 million people (Schöck, 1978: 9). In 1986 the figure was raised to 34 percent, that is to say over 20 million people (Schöck, 1991: 42).

We have to be cautious, however. Briggs' observation is merely based on selective folklore accounts and they report a phenomenon rather than the scope of it. There are also several difficulties in assessing the value of a witchcraft survey. (The value of newspaper reports will be discussed below). To start with, only a representative proportion of the West German population will have been interviewed, possibly one or two thousand in all. It is not certain whether representativeness in, for instance, the case of washing powder or political preference is similar to representativeness in belief in witchcraft. A German folklore survey from 1933 shows a remarkably uneven geographical distribution of witchcraft beliefs (Zender, 1977: 156), which was probably not taken into account when the later surveys were interpreted and the percentage found was extrapolated to all the inhabitants of Germany. With witchcraft beliefs there is hardly any possibility of readjusting statistics, as there is no feedback (as in the case of votes). Also, since witchcraft is known to be an extremely difficult subject to talk about, people may not have responded truthfully (Paul, 1993: 106–7). But even if the figures are more or less correct, what would they have measured? The question 'do you believe in people who are able to bewitch others?' could, without further explication, imply both the full repertoire of a witchcraft discourse and a vague notion of inter-human influences. It could even be taken in a metaphorical, romantic sense. On the whole, the question mainly refers to a latent belief that is not translated into actual witchcraft accusations. In the form of a mere belief, witchcraft can be rather harmless, since events are needed to activate a belief. As a Flemish author has remarked: 'if there are no more witches, it is hard to believe in them' (van Eyen, 1989b: 71). One actual witchcraft case may thus carry more cultural weight than thousands of passive believers. Finally, data on Germany do not of course reveal anything about witchcraft in the rest of Europe.

To evaluate the occurrence and absence of twentieth-century European witchcraft, research is needed which is based on different sources covering the same area and period. Synchronically this research needs to be systematic and exhaustive. Diachronically it needs to be serial. The current state of the art degrades these requirements to mere wishful thinking. All we are allowed from the existing literature are occasional glimpses that are superficial most of the time and only occasionally provide genuine insights. Moreover, while in some countries, like France, Germany and Hungary, a certain kind of research tradition has been established, in others, like Britain, it is virtually absent. This makes it impossible even to start comparing different regional or national trends in the twentieth-century practice of witchcraft. The shortage of serial research also precludes informed links with earlier events.

If there is a general lack of twentieth-century witchcraft research, there is also the problem of the accessibility, or rather relative inaccessibility, of the research that has been done. The *International Folklore Bibliography*, compiled since 1917 and therefore carrying most of the relevant titles on twentieth-century witchcraft (but certainly not all), lists works that are published in so many different languages that it takes a linguist rather than an anthropologist to read them all. Also, without a proper central witchcraft library, books and articles have to be consulted all over Europe. Since no one has even tried to compile any national overview of twentieth-century witchcraft, the present chapter will understandably contain many gaps. In this situation a sensational newspaper article may, for the time being, be all there is to start with.

STUDIES OF WITCHCRAFT

Historical research on European witchcraft has become a specialism. It has its historiography and bibliographical surveys, as well as its conferences and debates. The amount of attention is mostly due to the historians' fascination with the criminal trials of people suspected of witchcraft and the devil worship this always implied. The period after the last burnings or hangings has been grossly neglected, as if suspicions and accusations suddenly died out with the decision to stop prosecuting witches. The twentieth century, historically an arbitrary period anyway, has hardly been regarded as specifically relevant for the study of witchcraft. Most scholars subscribe to the disenchantment thesis that leaves no place for irrational research subjects such as witchcraft. The few existing studies convey the isolated character of their subject; if there is a common theory at all, it is anthropological and originated from the western researcher's confrontation with foreign and usually subjugated people. Evans-Pritchard's witchcraft monograph on the African Zande is one of the few books referred to internationally (Schöck, 1978: 28; Favret-Saada, 1980: 14, 195; Hauschild, 1982: 158; de Pina-Cabral, 1986: 186). Intellectual exchanges on witchcraft within Europe are conspicuous by their absence. As a consequence, a state of the art survey of twentieth-century European witchcraft research has to be written from scratch.

Witchcraft has always been one of the paragons of otherness; its study was undertaken by outside observers who initially did not have any part in it. In twentieth-century Europe there have been at least four professional groups which have been concerned with witchcraft and have provided sources and offered the occasional analyses and interpretations. There are the folklorists, who by the early twentieth century 'produced little more than "miscellanies", rag-bags of supposedly amusing facts, which are nearly always the same, and very rarely have any originality or wit to recommend them' (Caro Baroja, 1965: 225). The custom of using witchcraft texts as fillers has been widespread and can also be found among criminologists, who have published them as quaint examples of 'criminal superstition' (Baumhauer, 1984: 114). Together with journalists the criminologists can be ranked among the champions of rationality who have campaigned against witchcraft. In the course of the century the collections of both folklorists and criminologists have been set up more systematically and have risen above the level of mere curiosities. The fourth group consists of anthropologists who after the demise of colonialism in the second half of the twentieth century turned to Europe and especially to the Mediterranean countries to practise their participant and observational fieldwork. Probably because of its Southern-European visibility, most anthropologists have focused on the evil eye, 'a modern form of optical witchcraft' (Gilmore, 1987: 168).

In the following sections I will present the main results of these different disciplinary approaches to witchcraft. (The contributions of a fifth group, namely psychiatrists, are hardly significant, cf. Favret-Saada, 1980: 250–66; Gaboriau, 1985; Dundes, 1992: 212). In order to evoke debate as well as to invite new research I have opted for a thematic treatment concentrating on the intricacies of reconstructing the contemporary manifestations of an abstract witchcraft discourse. This abstraction enables us to consider distinct expressions in a wider European framework, without losing sight of their local and regional embeddedness. The presentation moves from descriptions of the different kinds of witchcraft, via a discussion of the positions the researchers have occupied within the discourse, to the various sources and how they can be analysed and placed into wider contexts. Since this necessitates the use of very concrete examples, a certain bias in favour of Dutch source material (which was most easily accessible) may have crept in. Undoubtedly, analyses of newspaper articles or legend texts from other parts of Europe would have produced slightly different outcomes; what matters here is to illustrate the kind of material available, the sorts of questions that can be levelled at it, and the possible answers that are to be discovered. I have refrained from skimming legend collections and systematically indexing every specific witchcraft trait or motif from all over Europe. Although an insight into the geographical distribution of such phenomena as the bewitching of butter churning, the various cooking tests to tease out witches or the notion of witches' tails would certainly cast light on the contexts, derivations and mutual influences of local witchcraft discourses, such a vast enterprise fell outside the scope of this essay.

Within an area as large and as densely populated as Europe it is impossible to establish particular patterns that have a general range. This is quite apparent in the matter of the gender of witches. Most authors agree that witchcraft primarily concerned women (Vuorela, 1967: 13; Cutileiro, 1971: 276; Pitt-Rivers, 1971: 198; Schöck, 1978: 127), but to overlook male participants in the discourse, its masculine aspects, and male witches would be detrimental to an account of people's experience. I have nevertheless used the feminine pronoun throughout when referring to witches in general. This may occasionally cause some confusion when authors quoted have addressed both female and male witches as male. Above all, the question may arise of what a witch, strictly speaking, is. The focus on the witchcraft discourse means that witches are primarily defined by their being called witches, by others or by themselves. But the English word 'witch' may not correspond exactly to the concepts in other languages which have been translated as 'witch'. The most important distinction that tends to get lost in translations is the one between practised witchcraft and ascribed witchcraft, that is between the witchcraft people perform and witchcraft people are *said* to perform. When we consider this quotation: 'A Spanish journalist, at the beginning of the present century (. . .), claimed that witches were still making a living by selling philtres and spells to bewitch, cure and kill, and by practising the art of conjuration and divination' (Caro Baroja, 1965: 240), it clearly refers to practised witchcraft. Like the French 'sorcière', which can either be translated as 'witch' or as 'cunning woman', terms in other South-European languages apparently also carry this double meaning. This does not imply though that every European conjurer, diviner, cunning woman, fortuneteller, charmer or blesser can be considered a witch and thus be a subject of this essay. For these specialists did not live under the name of 'witch' everywhere and it is confusing to make them into witches, as is done, for instance, in the German translation of Ernesto de Martino's *Sud e magia*, where the Italian 'rimidiante' (healer) is erroneously translated as 'Hexe' (witch) (1982: 20; the French translation has 'guériseusse'; 1963: 18–9). The Greek *magissa* 'is usually translated as "witch," [while] in fact it is cognate with "magician"' (Dionisopoulos-Mass, 1976: 54). As a Portuguese researcher remarked: 'Even though people fear and talk derisively of such specialists, they certainly do not confuse them with witches in the proper sense of the word' (de Pina-Cabral, 1986: 190). 'No one will admit being a witch,' it is said of Denmark, 'while there is no secret about being a cunning woman' (Rockwell, 1978: 86). Danish witches are mainly ascribed witches. Likewise in the sentence: 'Others were pronounced to be witches because they transgressed the moral code of the community' (Dömötör, 1982: 144); this also concerns ascribed witchcraft and its practitioners do not have to practise any witchcraft at all. To complicate matters, witchcraft can also be ascribed to a professional witch. As the line has to be drawn somewhere, I have chosen to discuss practised witchcraft mainly when it implies bewitching and unwitching (and not fortune-telling or healing in the more general sense). Cunning folk figure primarily as experts in counter witchcraft.

If not everyone is a witch who is named as such, one can also be considered a witch without being called so.

On ordinary occasions, if witches are to be mentioned at all, it is only by allusion and through ambiguous sentences. For instance, the speaker declares he is '*badly neighboured*'; he enigmatically alludes to '*the other bastard*' or to that '*filth*' without ever daring to add a proper name (Favret-Saada, 1980: 65; cf. 98–9).

As a French cunning man said about a farmer: '*apparently he's been playing tricks again but only on animals*' (Favret-Saada, 1980: 69). In Germany being bewitched is described as 'someone has caused him grief', or the expressions 'evil force' and 'evil people' are employed (Bartholdy, 1969: 36; Schöck, 1978: 92). A last example of the tabooing of witches and the use of euphemisms or circumscriptions from Hungary shows 'surrogate titles' for 'illness demons, witch, nightmare and devil' such as 'the comely woman, the evil, the wicked one, the not-pure one, the bewitching spirit, etc.' (Zentai, 1976: 253). This brings to the fore another ambiguity in the (abstract) witchcraft discourse which affects the delineation of witches from different 'supernatural' or 'magical' beings, like nightmares, were-wolves, revenants, fairies and such. Briefly, in some times and places they overlap, in others they are distinct. As witches are complex enough by themselves, the overlaps are not taken as a pretext to discuss European 'folk beliefs', 'popular mythology', 'superstitions' or whatever term is used to cover the collection of non-religious, non-medical or non-scientific concepts, especially since their assembling has been arranged by outsiders (folklorists or ethnologists) and may not reveal indigenous ordering.

For this synthesis I have used publications in English, German, Dutch and French that, if only sometimes, went beyond mere descriptions. Publications about witchcraft among European emigrants elsewhere (in the Americas, for instance; cf. Williams, 1938; Migliore, 1997) have not been considered, nor have I included witchcraft material to do with the numerous immigrants who in the twentieth century have come to live in Europe from elsewhere (see for bewitched Italian immigrants in Switzer-land: Risso and Böker, 1964). I have come across hardly anything covering this aspect of what is strictly speaking also 'European witchcraft' (cf. Camus, 1988: 142–3). Like many of the other features of European witchcraft discourses that are dealt with in this essay, this may become the subject of future research.

TYPES OF WITCHCRAFT

Twentieth-century European witchcraft comes in many guises. Recently women in Amsterdam invited their sisters to join them in the 'Night of the Witches' (an evening in late May 1997). 'Women, reclaim the streets!!! Dress like a witch!' they announced. The witch-figure, riding her broomstick, has become one of the trade-marks of a specific kind of radical feminism (cf. Bovenschen, 1977; Katschnig-Fasch, 1987: 385–6), referring to a timeless tradition. 'Nothing has been lost,' a German witch exclaimed. 'Once again we know everything we knew before' (cf. Treiber, 1991). As Diane Purkiss concluded in a play with the formal and substantial levels of analysis: 'The figures of the witch and the Goddess and the truths they contain are eternal, but also constantly subject to historical loss and forgetfulness, constantly requiring to be rediscovered' (1996: 49). This self-proclaimed and city-based witch will not occupy us much here. Presented as timeless, she reveals herself as a basically nineteenth-century invention, more linked to male interpretations of historic witches, 'as a male fantasy about what feminitiy should be' (Purkiss, 1996: 39; see also Unverhau, 1990), than to age-old village traditions.

For similar reasons, the fairy-tale witch and her descendants in plays, operas (Hörandner, 1987: 353), films, fantasy novels and computer games will be omitted as well. Though an intrinsic part of twentieth-century Western education and thus prominent in European consciousness, the fairy-tale witch is primarily a figure of the imagination (cf. Scherf, 1987), like the Russian *Baba-Iaga* (Mouchketique, 1992). In this way she differs from the witch that people believed to be real. This distinction may seem nonsensical, especially to those who do not grant reality to any kind of witch. Yet in cultural analysis, and particularly in witchcraft studies, one has to take seriously the opinions of those who are the objects of study. As witches are cultural constructs, not existing in any biological sense (although some would have them equipped with extra senses), it is only through words and images that we can access them. Within this context it is important to distinguish between witches in forms of art, on the one hand, and people who are constructed as witches, on the other. In what sense or to what extent art-forms influence witchcraft discourse and subsequent behaviour is not clear as yet (cf. Dingeldein, 1985). But since products of art, fairy-tales among them, are generally (at least in Western Europe) situated within the middle and upper layers of society, whereas the nineteenth- and twentieth-century witches came into being through lower-class accusations, interaction between the two will have been limited. 'Only the witch in which one does not believe any longer becomes a fairy-tale witch,' remarked Manfred Grätz, 'if one can frighten anyone with her at all, it is children' (1988: 128). Folklorists keep stressing that in those cases where we do find fairy-tales and witchcraft legends discussed on the same occasions, narrator and audience clearly differentiate between the fantastic character of the tale and the possible truth of the legend (for instance: Dömötör, 1982: 145; Kurotschkin, 1992: 199; Gottschalk, 1995: 162).

To isolate the fairy-tale witch and the feminist witch from twentieth-century European witchcraft tradition is, admittedly, very arbitrary. All instances of contemporary witchcraft are in one way or another related to earlier ones, whether in form, content or interpretation. But the continuity of a tradition also depends on the participants and on the genre they assign to the tradition. In this way we can discern different witchcraft traditions, each with different witch-figures. On an everyday level witchcraft is neither a feminist symbol, nor a pagan religion, or a fantasy. It is primarily seen as a crime, as a deviation from social norms within a community. In all likelihood this everyday witchcraft dates from pre-Christian times. By the nineteenth century (if not before), however, it had become totally integrated into Christianity. Witchcraft is also gendered; accusations are used to direct women to their 'proper' place in society. But it contains no secret knowledge, nor any proto-feminist organization. In everyday life witchcraft is as real as God, Christ, Mary and (to Catholics) the saints – probably even more so, since people are more likely to meet a witch in person than any of these supernatural beings.

The main kind of witchcraft discussed in this essay is best defined as misfortune ascribed to other human beings. Although its twentieth-century manifestations would have been recognizable by fifteenth-century Europeans (the other traditions would have been alien to them), this does not imply that witchcraft has not changed since then. It acquired demon-ological aspects, for instance, which were later dropped by most intellec-tuals and exchanged for equally degrading labels such as superstition, backwardness and irrationality. Its connection with natural disasters such as thunderstorms and crop failures dwindled or disappeared as it became aimed at individual households and even individuals, instead of whole communities (see the contribution of Marijke Gijswijt-Hofstra to Witch-craft and Magic in Europe: The Eighteenth and Nineteenth Centuries). Most of all, the witchcraft discourse lost adherents. Group after group, whether enlightened schoolteachers, liberal farmers, university-trained doctors or zealous agricultural consultants (to name but a few), left the witchcraft discourse and started to describe their personal misfortune in non-personal terms. Alternatively, they blamed it on their own failure rather than on their neighbour's evil influence.

Traditional witchcraft is centred around harm. Elsewhere, I have called this main type of witchcraft *bewitching* (de Blécourt, 1990). It includes damage done to people, especially to little children, and to livestock. It can be instrumental in the failure of the churning of butter and it can devastate crops. Even an occasional engine can falter because of witchcraft. To quote the French anthropologist Jeanne Favret-Saada: 'animals and people become sterile, fall ill or die, cows abort or lose their milk, plantations [plantings] rot or dry, buildings burn or collapse, machines break down, and sales drop drastically' (1989: 42; 1986: 30). These different misfortunes can be considered as separate subtypes of bewitchment; they do not need all to occur in the same place and period. Bewitching also defines its counterparts: *unwitching* and *witching*. According to the inescapable logic of the witchcraft discourse, harm caused by humans through witchcraft can be undone by them. Every bewitchment needs an unwitchment. In most parts of Europe this is best accomplished by the witch herself and victims of witchcraft need, therefore, to find means to identify her (or him).

While bewitching is mainly ascribed (although there are instances of people actively exercising witchcraft), unwitching has to be acted out, generally in the form of a blessing or a ritual. This act also conforms retrospectively to the validity of the witchcraft interpretation; witchcraft discourse abounds in this sort of circular thinking. Witching, that is the accumulation of wealth by witchcraft, is a less frequently occurring type of witchcraft, although it is based on the same premise of equilibrium as bewitching. If misfortune can be due to witchcraft, so can fortune. A successful person, so it has been remarked about the Galician Serbs, 'is necessarily in communication with the Devil, or his assistants' (Koenig, 1937: 61). As the Norwegian folklorists Bente Alver and Torunn Selberg observe: 'we also find the idea that those who were the best off were those who were suspected of witchcraft' (1988: 28). In an egalitarian society, the individual's luck and profit can easily be considered as the result of unsocial dealings.

There is also a fourth type of witchcraft, *scolding*, which is hardly mentioned in the literature. Among the few examples is the Austrian series of curses against women: 'You're a witch – you look like a witch – damned witch' (Schipflinger, 1944: 13). It concerns witchcraft accusations that do not seem to refer directly to any of the three other types of witchcraft. Instead, through these accusations people, mostly women, are compared to witches; they are grouped among evil people without having perpetrated any specific debauchery. They correspond to the image of the stereotypical witch as 'an independent adult woman who does not conform to the male idea of proper female behaviour' (Larner, 1984: 84). Already noticeable in early modern times (cf. de Blécourt, 1990: 132, 154–7), this type of witchcraft is also revealed through (unpublished) twentieth-century folklore surveys. At least in the Netherlands some informants replied to the question whether there were still witches in their village by saying that superstition had died out but that some women were still called 'witch'. For example, one was said to be 'ill-mannered and strong, [and] is known in the neighbourhood as intolerant and quarrelsome' (cf. de Blécourt, 1989: 249). Folklorists ignored such remarks as their interest was focused on everything 'magical' (cf. Jalby, 1971: 259–85; Schmidt, 1972: 132). To their local contacts mentioning this 'non-superstitious' witchcraft was a way to appear helpful without having to degrade the name of their village. The scolding could also have stood out more clearly because of the disappearance of bewitchments. We can consider this type as a derivative of the other types; it is also possible to see it as one of the assumptions underlying accusations of bewitchment. Women who are already denounced as witch-like are the most likely targets in cases of bewitchment. 'She was a bad cook, the food was inedible, her household was dirty, in short she was not a proper housewife' was said about a woman accused of witchcraft in Oberschwaben (Schöck, 1978: 201).

With these four types the content of witchcraft is briefly summarized. In the sections that follow more extended examples will be given. Here, I would like to address briefly the issue of the combination of the first three types. In my Dutch research from which the types are derived, they generally appear separated, substantively as well as spatially and socially, as in relation to the presumed actor. Unwitching specialists were very rarely accused of bewitching while a witchcraft accusation did not imply counter-witchcraft as a public occupation (an ascribed witch was not as a rule known as a practising witch). A man accused of witching seemed not to have been thought to have accomplished it by bewitching. Within the region under observation, Drenthe, it was usually a woman from the neighbourhood who bewitched someone. Witching men were mostly located in a neighbouring village or hamlet and unwitching experts were always outsiders, who certainly in the nineteenth and early twentieth centuries lived outside the province (de Blécourt, 1990). Elsewhere, however, connections have been documented, as in the case of Austria where diligent and successful farmers were said to have magically taken the milk from their filthy and debased neighbours (cited in Schäfer, 1955: 36). Favret-Saada used the metaphor of communicating vessels in this respect: as one farm 'fills up with riches, health and life, the other empties out to the point of ruin or death' (1989: 43). Others, following the anthropologist George Foster (1965), suggested the theory of 'limited good' here (which ignores the influence of outside markets; cf. Foster 1972: 199). As another example of fluid boundaries between the types we can consider the battle between unwitcher and witch where the successful unwitcher in a sense has bewitched the witch (Kruse, 1951: 59; Vuorela, 1967: 75–6; Dionisopoulos-Mass, 1976: 54; Favret-Saada, 1980: 71).

Whatever combination occurs, in general bewitching, professional unwitching and witching should not be assumed beforehand to be exercised by the same person.

Apart from cultural definitions of witchcraft, attention has to be paid to the social dimension. 'What is important,' wrote Favret-Saada, 'is less to decode what is said than to understand who is speaking and to whom' (1980: 14). Witchcraft discourse is constituted in a triangle of the most involved participants: the victim, the witch and the expert. The construction of a bewitchment is subject to a process that in many ways resembles the construction of illness. It starts with the diagnosis, it goes through all the stages of discussion and consultation, and it (preferably) ends with a cure. What sets it apart from illness is that it presupposes another human as the perpetrator. As illness has its healing experts to guide the patient through the phases of this process, so witchcraft has its unwitching experts: the witch–doctors, the witch–expellers, the cunning folk. In Catholic areas priests have often fulfilled this function (cf. de Blécourt, 1994). In the few regions where unwitchers have been subject to systematical research, a majority of them turns out to be men (Schöck, 1978: 141; Daras, 1983: 157; cf. de Blécourt, 1991: 165). Therefore, in opposition to the female witches, I refer to them as male. Their counter-witchcraft is basically a practised one and it consists of medicine, advise, and rituals. To the bewitched the unwitcher appears benevolent, while he is an arch-enemy of the witch. The triangle is riddled with tension.

THE RESEARCHER'S POSITION

One of the most outstanding differences between historical and present-day witchcraft research is the incorporation of the present-day researcher in the witchcraft discourse. When in the field, talking to the main protagonists, it is impossible not to become part of the witchcraft triangle, impossible not to take sides. This is most eloquently expressed by Favret-Saada (1980), who has become famous for her research in western France (originally published in 1977). Having established that in witchcraft words are crucial, she criticises the mere collection and storing of these words for academic purposes; words 'are power, and not knowledge or information'. Although the publishing and translation of her book is by itself a betrayal of this principle (even if its style and structure are not, cf. Jonas, 1993), what she is concerned about is how the researcher communicates with her subjects of research, with her interlocutors. 'In witchcraft, words wage war. Anyone talking about it is a belligerent, the ethnographer like everyone else'. What counts is not only the position of the researcher but her mental and emotional attitude. 'There is no room for uninvolved observers,' she categorically states. 'A mere desire for information is the sign of a naïve or hypocritical person who must be at once frightened off' (Favret-Saada, 1980: 9–11). The crux is one of understanding; to stay uninvolved is to fail to 'grasp what is at stake in a witchcraft crisis' (Favret-Saada, 1980: 227).

The choice presented to Favret-Saada was clear. Either she would have to be 'caught', that is gripped, by the witchcraft discourse, or 'not caught'. For a responsible researcher the latter was out of the question, the more so since the people she wanted to investigate would not talk to her if she remained an outsider. As she later revealed: 'they started talking to me only (. . .) when reactions escaping my voluntary control showed them that I was affected by the real – often devastating – impact of certain words and ritual acts' (Favret-Saada, 1990: 191). When 'caught', she could either be bewitched or be in the process of becoming an unwitcher (1980: 17). Wanting to understand the witchcraft discourse, the position of the 'alleged witch' was closed off to her. This was hardly regrettable, 'since witches always claim that they do not believe in spells, object to the discourse of witchcraft, and appeal to the language of positivism'. Witches and bewitched do not communicate (Favret-Saada, 1980: 20).

Vis-à-vis the unwitching expert, the position of the researcher resembles that of the bewitched. Both the bewitched and the unwitcher partake in the witchcraft discourse; both belong to the same party, aligned against the witch. Here there is some flexibility. Favret-Saada was either regarded as a victim of witchcraft, or as a pupil of her unwitcher (cf. Camus, 1988: 20). When the expert is interviewed by an interested outsider he will only yield trivial answers. There is 'a barrier, then, of silence and duplicity: the diviner can only admit "*dealing with that*" in front of someone who puts forward a personal request for divination' (Favret-Saada, 1980: 21).

As an anthropologist, Favret-Saada raged at folklorists who favour their own theories above the explanations of the believers. Folklorists, in the words of the title of one of the appendices to her book, had 'ignorance as a profession' (1980: 227ff). In general, they are indeed a welcome target for anthropological scorn. Their only asset is to have collected information that would otherwise have been lost (as we will see below), even if they have made the wrong selections and have obstructed rather than enabled insights into contemporary witchcraft. There are, of course, exceptions which, with the development of folklore into ethnography and cultural studies, may well turn into the rule. After all, Favret-Saada's folklorists are French and from a previous period (see, e.g., Jalby, 1974).

The Tübingen (Germany) folklorist Inge Schöck, whose book appeared only shortly after Favret-Saada's, preferred to take sides with the witch. Addressing the isolation witches experienced within a community of witch believers, Schöck points out that this can become unbearable. 'How difficult and depressing such situations can get is signalled by the legal complaints against witch believers, by the attempt to escape the unbearable cohabitation, or, more drastic, by suicide as a last resort' (1978: 17). This was impossible to ignore. Her own basic attitude towards witchcraft could only be rationalistic. 'We should take seriously the veto of people accused as witches against the role witch believers generally try to impose upon them' (Schöck, 1978: 18). This had grave consequences for her fieldwork. Frau N, one of the accused witches whom Schöck discovered, declined an interview as she did not feel strong enough to relive the events. Schöck also refrained from interviewing local believers in this case, for the allegations against the woman were still rampant. 'The gossip about the case and the discrimination against the family would very probably have grown in force again' (1978: 179). Indeed, earlier investigations by a student in the Allgäu had resulted in a new eruption of witchcraft rumours (Schöck, 1978: 41; cf. Favret-Saada, 1980: 59).

The involvement of the researcher can also cause confusion. This is shown in the case of Johann Kruse, a north-German campaigner against witchcraft and particularly against cunning folk. With the rise of his public profile, suspected 'witches' sent him letters to ask for his help against their superstitious aggressors. He also occasionally received letters asking his advice as a witch-doctor (Schöck, 1978: 129, 195; Hauschild, 1980: 149–50, 1981: 556). Far from being an entertaining anecdote, this instance shows the dominance of the witchcraft discourse. In view of Kruse's motives the error may have been a total misunderstanding (Baumhauer, 1984: 75), but for the bewitched it was only logical, since the newspapers portrayed Kruse as a powerful expert on witches (cf. Gijswijt-Hofstra, 1997: 119). The French anthropologist Dominique Camus found himself in a similar situation when he was asked to operate as a magical expert by a woman whom he had told about his anthropological work. In her opinion, studying witchcraft could only result in becoming its practitioner (1988: 187). The witchcraft discourse did not allow a neutral attitude.

How then should we consider a combination of the two opposite positions of witch and bewitched? Does support for the witch automatically lead to a failure to understand witch-believers, bewitched and unwitcher? Or more important, is there any possible justification for ignoring the plight of the ostracized witch? French researchers seem to consider the last question irrelevant since they do not address it. When Favret-Saada discusses the position of the witch, she ends by stating the unlikeliness of the existence of actively operating witches. 'No one (. . .) calls himself a witch; it is not a position from which one can speak,' she explains. 'The witch is the person referred to by those who utter the discourse on witchcraft (bewitched and unwitchers), and he only figures in it as the subject of a statement' (1980: 24). In a system in which the witch is only identified by the bewitched, it is implied, her place in the community does not change while she is still alive. Consequently, one does not have to take it into account.

The neglect of the witch as a social being is one of the weak spots in Favret-Saada's otherwise unsurpassed approach (cf. Beck-Braach, 1993: 85–6). Possibly peasants in western France resorted to a different, less sociable witchcraft system than elsewhere in Europe, one in which it was not absolutely necessary to identify the witch in order to make her withdraw her spell. 'In recounting an unbewitching, typical stories omit the methods used in identifying a witch, but they always describe the ritual aimed at overcoming him, the great scene of the magical clash' (Favret-Saada, 1989: 44; we will look at this problem in more detail later on). It may also be that the witch's invisibility followed from the fact that she did not belong to the same discourse as the unwitcher (Camus, 1988: 15). The witch was nevertheless created by that very discourse. Without her, the witchcraft discourse would have lost its foundation. And in France as elsewhere, the witch was not only a 'projection' (Gaboriau, 1987: 106), but also the result of a label projected onto 'some familiar person (a neighbour, for example)' (Favret-Saada, 1980: 8).

The witchcraft discourse of the witch believers seems to be incompatible with the rationalistic way 'witches' define themselves. To expect otherwise, however, would imply that a witch should comply with her role. Her use of the rationalistic discourse can be seen as a defence (Favret-Sasda, 1980: 187), as a denial of the accusations levelled at her. She may even be a believer herself. As a German researcher wrote: 'In most cases the witch is as superstitious as the other villagers – only with the restriction, made by herself, that she is sure about not being a witch herself. She does not doubt the existence of witches' (Schäfer, 1959: 60). In a similar way, the anthropologists' interlocutors may switch between the two discourses, as we have seen from the example of the diviner. Why should this eventually be an impossible feat for the anthropologist? Initially she is an outsider, pigeonholed as a representative of the 'press, television, the Church, the medical profession, all the national organs of ideological control'. The people she wants to study dislike being ridiculed for their unsurpassed 'backwardness and stupidity' (Favret-Saada, 1990: 191). Perhaps they fear being criminalized and prosecuted. Therefore, the anthropologist needs to be initiated, to learn the peasant discourse in order to communicate on the same level as her interlocutors, without external power constraints. This takes time and it may never be totally accomplished. But does it preclude discourse switching? Does it prohibit any conciliation with the other side?

At least for the purpose of this essay the dilemma can be surmounted.

The evaluation of twentieth-century witchcraft research is similar to that of historical witchcraft research as it is one step removed from fieldwork experience. Reading texts only creates a distant involvement. As for the criteria of assessment, however, there is still a choice. Either all research that is not informed by the witchcraft discourse can be declared worthless. Or we can attempt to recognize possible traces of the discourse in the reports of people who did not submerge themselves so completely in it, even if this implies the disadvantage of missing its hidden, ambiguous aspects.

JOURNALISTS AND FOLKLORISTS

In a critique of Anglo-Saxon anthropologists who failed to acknowledge the occurrence of rural witchcraft in twentieth-century Europe, Favret-Saada pointed to the work of folklorists, to press reports about 'murders of presumed witches and trials of unbewitchers', as well as to unspecified ethnographic publications. On the level of 'a so widely attested social fact' (Favret-Saada, 1989: 40), where it is simply a matter of recognizing the existence of witchcraft, the writings of 'uncaught' authors do seem to have some value after all. The four sources mentioned are indeed the main writings of those who encountered witchcraft (diaries of the main protagonists have yet to turn up), but newspaper accounts, legends, trial reports and fieldwork narratives are all more or less biased or at least selective. In this section we will take a closer look at the production of newspaper accounts and legends.

Newspapers and newsagencies are dependent on correspondents and on other newspapers for news about witchcraft. It always erupts locally and if a local newspaper finds it too sensitive an issue, the regional paper has less inhibitions. Distance, both in a social and in a geographical sense can facilitate the reporting of witchcraft. For it is news, especially because it is deemed old and in contrast to the modernity and rationality newspapers stand for. 'You wouldn't think this to be happening here on the arrival of the twentieth century!' a Frisian reporter exclaimed (*Nieuw Advertentieblad* 15 December 1900). 'In the middle of our fatherland belief in witches prospers as it did in the darkest Middle-Ages,' a Dutch weekly wrote in the early 1920s (*Het Leven* 16: 1368). 'Are we returning to the middle-ages?' the Rotterdam correspondent of the *Telegraaf,* one of the main papers of the Netherlands, asked his readers a few years later (7 July 1926). 'In Sarzbüttel the Middle-Ages make their appearance,' ran the headlines in German newspapers. 'Witchcraze in 1954 in spite of TV, radar and atoms' (Baumhauer, 1984: 218). A similar notion is to be found in French newspapers: 'Five hours from Paris, I have discovered the Middle-Ages,' thus *l'Express* of 17 October 1955 (Bouteiller, 1958: 217). 'Electric pylons stand over the grass-land, tractors are driven along the tarred sunken lanes . . . but medieval superstitions still prevail,' wrote a French journalist in 1965 (Favret-Saada, 1980: 34). The general attitude has been one of condemnation. Through publication, reporters hoped, villagers would realize their mistakes and properly join the twentieth century.

A witchcraft case can only enter the public sphere when the knowledge about it transgresses the boundaries of the household. Since witches are hardly designated within one's nuclear family, the witch usually has to come from outside and since force is often needed to compel her to lift the spell from her victim, most instances of witchcraft become known sooner or later. 'In a Dorset village,' wrote a certain Dr B. from Poole in 1935, 'an old woman lives whose back and chest are covered with scars. She was accused of bewitching someone, and the victim made her take off the spell by "Blood"' (*Folklore* 46: 171). Scratching the witch, a regular feature of British witchcraft, is in comparison to Dutch cases one of the more violent means to generate unwitching. It can even be worse. According to the *Rhein-Neckar-Zeitung*, a regional German paper, several farms were burned down because the residents were suspected of witch-craft (14 October 1956). For a similar reason a Franconian mechanic burnt down a widow's home (*Times* 9 June 1962; see also about this case: Wagner, 1970: 354–5; Schöck, 1978: 190–2). Polish newspapers reported an attempted burning in 1957 and one in which the 'witch' perished 'in the flames of her own house' in 1984 (Schiffmann, 1988: 150–1). Newspaper stories have ranged from the normal, but exotic enough for the reporter to take notice of, to the extraordinary. In the course of the twentieth century, newspapers seem to have concentrated on the more sensational aspects of witchcraft. After all, the usual unwitching did not need to result in the witch's death. When a witchcraft event went public, it did not have to be publicized.

The journalist's interest in witchcraft appears to be superficial; his story has to be ready in a few hours and he hardly has the time to investigate. At best he can write small follow-ups, such as the following example from Frisia: 'The father of the bewitched child has changed his opinion. He has thrown out the witch-doctor's medicine and has called for a medical practitioner to visit the patient' (*Provinciale Drentsche & Asser Courant* 14 February 1912). Checking newspaper stories for their reliability through interviews is not always easy; the reports may have influenced the informant's memory, or even have formed the basis for it. Where Dutch collectors of legends have come upon the same events as those reported by newspapers, they have usually not discovered more information. The newspaper reports are usually much more detailed than the specific legend texts, the more so since they provide exact dates. 'We have countless reports in the folklore records on the ill-treatment of witches (. . .), but we are never told *when* a witch was beaten till the blood flowed,' argued Danish historian Gustav Henningsen when stressing the importance of including newspapers in witchcraft research (1989: 149). Nevertheless, legends reveal a different kind of reality by the quantity in which they were collected; they depict witchcraft as a part of daily life far more profoundly than newspapers are ever able to do.

Folklorists started to form legend collections in the nineteenth century and proceeded collecting far into the twentieth century. In some areas of Europe this was done more intensively and systematically than in others, but altogether tens, if not hundreds of thousands of texts on witchcraft alone have been noted down and stored. Some of these texts are published but only a few have been analysed. The idea was to use them for learned monographs, on witchcraft for instance, but that hardly happened (see for exceptions Vuorela, 1967; Pinies, 1983). The original presuppositions behind the collecting had hardly anything to do with genuine interest in contemporary cultures. Superstitions, including witchcraft, were taken as the oral equivalent of archaeological remains. They were the mental relics of times long past, mainly to be found in the remote parts of the countryside. Backwardness in the romantic sense was revered rather than rebuked. Witch families, according to Jacob Grimm and his epigones, were the descendants of pre-Christian priestesses (cf. Schöck, 1978: 19–22; Hauschild, 1981: 546). Later folklorists renounced their attempts to reconstruct ancient animistic systems (although the custom survived longer in eastern Europe than in the west; cf. Dömötör, 1982; Pócs, 1989b). They adopted a literary approach, renamed superstitions as 'folk beliefs' and came to regard collecting as a means to map the distribution of these beliefs, supported by vague notions about disappearing narrative cultures. Yet they held on to their trusted definition of the legend. As a text about beliefs, its content was non-religious and non-scientific. 'Folk-belief,' to quote only one definition from many similar ones, 'is the belief in the effect and observability of powers that are inexplicable by natural laws and not founded in religious doctrine' (Kaufmann, 1960: 83).

What it embodied for the believers (in other situations still known as superstitious peasants) did not count. As a result the collections are curiously selective and devoid of contexts. Showing witchcraft and other 'beliefs' as an intrinsic element of people's outlook, they conceal the rest of it. Where witchcraft was narrated in the past tense and recorded by the folklorist correspondingly, other memories were edited out. In the ensuing legend text the questions of the collector were omitted and the discussions between the informants were ignored. It was a perfect example of miscommunication, also in terms of time. While the folklorist enticed the informant by asking about stories about the past in general and gradually brought the subject to somewhat mysterious happenings, the informant could oblige the folklorist by using the past as a device to obscure the present, since 'a *discourse* on the past is perhaps not quite the same as a past *event*' (Favret-Saada, 1980: 65).

But the folklorist persisted, the more so when the advantages of oral interviews over data collecting through written surveys had become apparent. The picture Favret-Saada painted of him is accurate but limited. He certainly received evasive answers to his queries about witches such as: '*they no longer exist*'; '*that was in the old days*'; (. . .) '*they exist but not here*' (Favret-Saada, 1980: 16; Favret-Saada and Contreras, 1981: 31–2). He was also a local (though somewhat better educated) who spoke the dialect and when people did not know any stories he persevered until he found the ones who did. Legend collectors spent years roaming the countryside surrounding their homes and therefore gained some trust. What they lacked in depth, they gained in breadth. Through numerous texts we learn about witchcraft events from a more or less removed past and we do hear the voices of genuine believers. Occasionally, we even hear them disagreeing and joking, as in the following fragment recorded in Hungary (Dégh and Vázsonyi, 1972: 105). The text is taken up at a point where people have just discussed the idea that a witch cannot die until someone is willing to receive her power. Her orchard is also magically protected:

Mrs R.   I have heard it too, but I am not sure about it.

Mrs E.   God would not let this happen. I wonder . . .

Mrs S.   Who is it?

Mr K.   (*to Mr A*) You know them, why don't you speak up?

Mr A.   Of course. She lives close by the Catholic Church.

Mr E.   On the corner, next to the cemetery?

Mr K.   That's right. And you know about her son? She has a son, a handsome young man.

Mr A.   He doesn't get a wife, no matter how handsome he is.

Mr K.   He cannot marry, neither can her daughter. No one wants her daughter.

Mrs F.   No, because of her mother. The witch.

Mrs S.   I don't believe this.

Mr T.   I do, I do. . . . This is a good excuse for the boys. Is it not more sensible to stay a bachelor? (*He laughs.*) Smart fellow, didn't let himself to get pushed around.

In this session the taperecorder was hidden and only Mrs E. knew about it. Most of the legend texts, however, are presented as a monologue. And the few taperecordings are not always as revealing as this Hungarian example. (Dutch published transcripts, for instance, merely show the collector asking an informant to repeat the legends that were told on an earlier occasion. They do not add a new dimension to the storytelling event). When discussions are left out of the texts, they cannot be assessed either. They may show the process of a witchcraft discourse in decline, they may also enforce the discourse. 'Unbelief serves as a catalyst to show the facts to be true,' a French folklorist observed (Pinies, 1983: 23). Likewise, joking about witchcraft can be interpreted as an instance of disbelief or as a compensation for 'the fear of the power of witches' (Lehnert-Leven, 1995: 134).

Both the journalist and the folklorist have denied witchcraft its place in contemporary, rationalized and disenchanted society. If witchcraft still persists, then it is an anachronism, belonging to the past. In the journalist's perception, this is the dark, superstitious past of the Middle-Ages. The folklorist projects witchcraft back into an idealized prehistorical period. In both cases, their objectives do not include an understanding of the contemporary witchcraft discourse. Their informants are not their interlocutors. These last points are aptly illustrated by a meeting between a Flemish folklorist and an octogenarian. The folklorist, who systematically worked his way through every village of his region, asked the man if he could name certain women as witches. He was rather direct in his questions. 'I am not going to name them,' the man replied. 'But it is for the university, sir!' the researcher countered. He got two names and that was all (Penneman, 1972: 122). As his colleague from a neighbouring area concluded: 'It was especially difficult [for the informants] to tell [me] witch legends, as these often referred to people still alive and the telling might be dangerous' (van den Berg, 1960: 29).

SLIEDRECHT, 1926

In 1926 Dutch newspapers reported on a bewitchment in Sliedrecht, a town north-west of Dordrecht, along the river Merwede. 'At the dyke in Sliedrecht,' according to the *Telegraaf*, 'lives the family V. For the last six months the nineteen-year old Gezina V. has suffered from a curious illness. She suffers from a kind of fatty degeneration, which shows the more because of her small stature.' As she was also often bedridden and weak in the head and as the family doctor had apparently exhausted his skills, the family followed the advice of a backdoor neighbour, the elderly woman Mrs M. They consulted the witch-doctor of Gorinchem, a saddler who practised as unwitcher to earn some extra money.

> The moment he saw the girl, his diagnosis was fixed: the girl was enchanted by a witch. Now the difficulty was to discover the witch. For only she would be able to break the enchantment. Mrs. V.

immediately accepted the verdict of the witch-doctor as the only true solution. Were not the trees on her land withered? – What? the witch-doctor asked, are the trees on your land withered? Then you have to look for the witch in your near vicinity! But how to find out who actually was the evil spirit? The witch-doctor also knew the solution to this question. 'Go home,' he oracled, 'and the woman, who is the first to inquire after the well-being of the girl, is harbouring the evil spirit, with which the poor child is bewitched. She is the main character!' He mumbled a formula and started to prepare a potion, which he gave to Mrs. V. 'You should – so he continued – let the witch drink from this potion and she will be willing to bless your daughter, so that the enchantment will stop and she will become healthy and merry again!'

Back home, they met their nextdoor neighbour Mrs K., who inquired after the girl's health. This identified her as the witch. The family, consisting of the mother, the daughter and her maternal grandfather, gathered together with Mrs M. and some days later they lured Mrs. K. to their house. At this point the journalist presented the story from the suspected witch's point of view.

'They had always acted weird,' said Mrs. K. about her neighbours. 'And they always spoke about witchcraft. But I had never seen them as weird as that morning. I enter good-naturedly and I find the whole family sitting around the table. Is it someone's birthday? I ask. Then the old man began to speak. Yes Mrs. K., he said, you have now come here and we will tell you now for good. We know all about it. So what do you know then, I ask. We know that you enter our home with your spirit. You have the girl in your power. And the trees on the land are withered. That girl, who becomes so heavy, she was made that way by you. And now we demand that you end it. Don't deny it. We tested it with the bible and the key and the key turned to your house. I did not understand any of it.'

Then the sick girl announced that they should drink wine. Mrs K. did not see whether they poured her wine out of a different bottle, because they kept her distracted. But the wine tasted sourish and she felt her lip withdrawing. Later it was discovered that her lips looked bluish. As soon as she had finished her wine, they wanted her to bless the girl. It made her very upset and she wanted to go home to prepare lunch for her son. But they did not let her go. 'Now you are here, you stay here,' they all shouted in confusion. And the daughter kept asking: 'You should bless me, for you are able to bewitch'. Mrs V. urged her: 'Just say "God bless you", then my daughter will recover'. They offered her money and they threatened to use force, after which Mrs K.'s wish to leave was stronger than ever. Only when her son kicked down the door, did they let her go (7 July 1926). In the next few days stories about the case circulated locally and lots of people went to see the house for themselves. Mrs. K. moved away from the neighbourhood and Mrs. V. and her daughter planned to leave Sliedrecht altogether. It turned out that a local handy woman had stirred up the whole incident. Her grandchild had been bewitched earlier and on the advice of the Gorinchem unwitcher a black chicken had been boiled alive to lure the witch (*Telegraaf* 11 July 1926).

These two newspaper texts offer just one example of the way witchcraft cases were rendered public. They hardly conceal the reporter's indignation about people's gullibility and the witch-doctor's exploitation of it. Notwithstanding the irony in the reporter's wording, there is no reason to cast doubt on his description. The Sliedrecht case, although one of the last to be reported in the Netherlands, was fairly typical (cf. de Blécourt, 1996: 346–50). It featured all the participants in the witchcraft discourse, from Mrs M., the 'annunciator' to the bewitched Miss L., from the unwitcher from Gorinchem to the witch Mrs K. At the time, women played the main part in the witchcraft matters at private and neighbourhood level; in this particular case both husbands are totally absent. On the whole men played a marginal role as figures of authority. The case had the repetitive form of bewitching (or the reinterpretation of previous events in terms of witchcraft). It referred to the two most pronounced (at least in the protestant Netherlands) forms of identification: the chicken test and the book and key test. It comprised luring, forcing and the attempt at blessing. Only years later was the clue revealed. According to a local superintendent, interviewed in 1962, the bewitched girl had been pregnant (Kooijman, 1988: nr. 333). Such a misdiagnosis was not uncommon either (cf. de Blécourt, 1990: 177). The case also presents one of those instances in which different sources overlap, enabling us to obtain some idea about the memory of the folklorist's informant. In the legend text the two most sensational events had been merged and the chicken test had been transplanted on to the girl's case.

The Sliedrecht case can also be approached from the perspective of the witch-doctor. His name was Lambertus Lelie and he was the last of a line of male witch-doctors (de Waardt, 1991: 290–1), which alone shows that he was fully integrated in the regional witchcraft system and no outsider to it (cf. Favret-Saada, 1980: 31). A bricklayer who visited Lelie in 1921 told a reporter that he was left alone in a room and heard an infernal racket. The witch-doctor charged ten guilders for a consultation and then sold him a potion, which helped him to defecate a toad (*Het Leven* 16: 1369). Another man was told that he harboured a stoat in his body. Occasionally, men could still fall victim to bewitchments. Other reports are less prosaic. In 1908, for instance the unwitcher told a woman that she had been bewitched by a man (*PD&AC* 17 March 1908). The full picture of the unwitcher, however fragmentary, has to be compiled from different sources. 'People went to Gorkum when they thought themselves to be bewitched. There the witch-doctor lived,' a factory-worker related in 1963. 'He gave them a jar with medicines and ordered: "Take care to keep the jar out of sight of the witch, otherwise it will burst". Then people anxiously entered Brakel [a village] holding the jar under their coats' (Kooijman, 1988: nr. 2102). Dates were rarely given. In the same year a clerk mentioned an indefinite 'in the old days' (nr. 2448) and a peasant, who only remembered that people went to the Gorinchem unwitcher for a bewitched girl, said: 'What kind of man he was, I don't know. For it is such a long time since I heard the story' (nr. 2051). Lelie died in 1944, but already in 1934 a local doctor and student of folk medicine mentioned that lately the unwitcher did not seem to practise his trade anymore.

Lelie must have been rather popular. People consulted him from within a radius of 15 kilometres from his residence, judging from the places where in the early 1960s he was still remembered. When we look at the 1934 statements, the radius can even be extended to approximately 20 kilometres (cf. Geldof, 1979: 157). This may be an indication of the man's shrinking influence. It can also be explained by the mechanism of reporting witchcraft, in which proximity in time translated into geographical distance and vice versa. Apart from the doctor's remark, the only 1934 report from the area close to Gorinchem places the unwitcher about half a century in the past.

FOLKLORE INDEXES

The enormous mass of material accumulated by folklorists has caused problems of cataloguing and indexing. For fairy-tales or other clearly structured narrative genres like anecdotes or migratory legends, it has paid to compile type indexes. Within tale types, it is possible to indicate 'motifs', small narrative elements that can be found in different types. The tale of Hansel and Gretel, type number ATh 327, for example, consists of motifs like 'Children abandoned' (S301), 'Ogre's gingerbread house lures child' (G412.1) and 'Ogre burned in his own oven' (G512.3.2.1). Witches do not figure as the main protagonists everywhere (Aarne and Thompson, 1973: 116–17). Similar motifs can occur in different genres and 'a motif may be in itself a short and simple story,' which 'may not be related to any of the types. The account of a witch's taking milk from a neighbor's cow by squeezing an axe handle or a towel (D2083.3.1) seems to be an example of this kind of motif' (Baughman, 1966: xi). This was one reason why hardly any type catalogues of 'belief-legends' have been published. Among the few that have is a Dutch catalogue (Sinninghe, 1943), which acquired some international standing. But its necessary elaboration and refinement became stranded in fraud, ignorance and squabbles between Dutch and Flemish folklorists (de Blécourt, 1981).

In the 1960s, attempts at an international legend codification by researchers who wanted to facilitate international comparisons and to trace the diffusion of tales, did not succeed either. This was hardly surprising, as the number and variety of legends was so vast that the venture was doomed to failure before it had even started. Many of the legends were merely remarks and pieces of memory (hence they were called *memorates*) that sometimes acquired some narrative structure in the telling, but mostly had their origins in events rather than in tales. Yet the legend texts had to be ordered somehow, not only to make them accessible, but also to provide the discipline of folklore with the academic aura it so badly needed after World War II. In the case of publication, it was sometimes decided to order legends by locality or narrator instead of by theme. Then the legend contents still had to be made accessible by indexes. Initial analyses were, therefore, made and some form of structure did arise.

Classificatory systems and indexes are not only methodological tools; they also show principles for structuring knowledge. It remains to be seen, however, whose knowledge this concerns, the local informant's or the researcher's assumptions about it. International indexes, for instance, can hardly do justice to local or even national peculiarities. The *Motif-index* of folk narratives, according to its conceiver Stith Thompson, 'makes no assumption that items listed next to each other have any generic relationship, but only that they belong to the same logical categories' (1946: 423). Logic, then, is the unifying and universally governing norm for ordering diverse data. As the folklorists never agreed on one system, they apparently each applied their own different kind of logic.

The structure of the systems used is beyond question. As a (open) tree-structure, it enjoys a long standing tradition within European academia. What is in dispute (explicitly or implicitly) is the categorization of legends within that structure. Witchcraft itself is generally considered as a main category, although the *Motif-index*, derived as it is from fairy-tales, has different sections for magic (especially D2050: destructive magic power) and witches (G200), which are ranked in the section on ogres. The principal witchcraft pattern, consisting of the opposition between the witch's deed and its undoing, is found in every system. General themes, like witches changing into animals, or particular forms of bewitchment are recurrent on a lower level. Yet the mutual relations of the themes and classifications within the systems vary. Variation also ensues when the different systems are compared to each other.

In her landmark contribution on witchcraft in the *Handwörterbuch des deutschen Aberglaubens* (Dictionary of German superstitions) Lily Weiser-Aall (1931) distinguished between the witch's practice and capacities, how people became witches, where they lived, how they spoke and how they died. Further categories were reserved for the identification of witches and for defence against them. The lemma ends with a small section on witches in proverbs and sayings. The sequence within the structure of this overview progresses from bewitchments to unwitchments. Some of the sub-categories also show this movement. The weather witch, who can produce thunder, rain, hail, whirlwind and frost, can be overcome by sounding bells and shooting. Counter-witchcraft in the case of milk witches includes cooking the milk (with or without nails), beating it or putting objects into it. When other mischief of witches is discussed, however, unwitching methods are left out, only to return as a general category later on. Cooking again appears, involving now the urine of a bewitched child, together with burning, shooting and hitting bewitched animals and objects. The internal logic is somewhat flawed since the same themes emerge at different places in the system.

A similar inconsistency is to be seen in the *Motif-index* and especially in the extended index on the British Isles and North America (Baughman, 1966), also within the section on witches. Unwitchment, to take one example, is ranked under such diverse subcategories as 'Characteristics of Witch', 'Recognition of Witches' and 'Witch overcome and escaped'. Thus the motive 'Witch is made to say "May God bless you" instead of "My God bless you" to remove spell' (G224.1(a)) is primarily a characteristic of the witch, whereas 'Burning heart of animal, usually one of the victims of the witch, will bring witch to scene to stop burning' (G257.1(a)) belongs to the sub-category of recognition, and 'Burning heart of cow or bullock to break spell of witch' (G271.4.1(aa)) to overcoming witches. This may of course point to slightly different accents in the legend texts the index was based on, but on a logical level it is disputable whether one should choose between recognizing and overcoming the witch (which are usually phases of the same process anyhow) or concentrate on the action itself, in this case burning.

A dictionary article like Weiser-Aall's builds up a composite picture of the witch, 'a multi-coloured, almost confusing portrait' (Schöck, 1978: 99). Witches (or their souls) can change into cats, pigs and hares. They also appear as bears, bees, billy-goats, lizards, magpies, ducks, owls, flies, foxes, goats, etc, etc. The only animals forbidden to them are those which the Christian creed designates as symbols of purity, like lambs, pigeons and swallows (Weiser-Aall, 1931: 1869). Although one of the *Motif-index*'s aims may be to differentiate rather than to synthesize, it creates a similar impression: witches can change into any animal, from domestic to wild, from mammals to birds, insects and reptiles. The underlying assumption is that even if there are many forms of witches, they still belong to the same 'belief'. Set against the individual tales, however, the combination of these shapes hardly makes any sense. Only in fairy-tales and ballads can wizards change into different animals; in legends witches normally use only one other shape, if they change at all.

Legend texts do not lend themselves to universal classification schemes. Although the fairy-tale index has been dubbed the 'Linnæus of the fairy-tale students' (Lüthi, 1979: 16), types and motifs are not equivalent to genuses and species. Bringing together themes found in different witchcraft legends abstracts them from their original place in localized and time-bound witchcraft discourses. It relates legends and motifs to each other, instead of to their production and reception. Meanwhile, important elements are disregarded because of their non-'magical' character. In the *Handwörterbuch* the bewitching of humans is barely mentioned. Likewise, in the *Motif-index* the relevance of social categories is not recognized and there is thus no differentiation between the bewitching of adults and children, or men and women, or even adolescent girls. From legend texts one of the most striking characteristics of the witch that appears is her being a neighbour of the bewitched, but this is not acknowledged in the indexes. Moreover, by separating legends about the same events or about the same witches and by regrouping them according to 'magical' content, bewitching and unwitching disappear as constitutive parts of a process. Such a process can start with the indigenous interpretation of different kinds of misfortune in terms of witchcraft, particularly because of their 'extraordinary repetition' (Favret-Saada, 1980: 6; Schöck, 1978: 105–6). To study this process, we have to return to the sources and find out what they tell us about the actual events. Entries in dictionaries and indexes can be helpful here mainly in so as far as they refer us to large quantities of original material.

LEGEND REPERTOIRES

Out of the folklorists' work on witchcraft two approaches emerge which may help to render witchcraft legends useful for the understanding of witchcraft discourses. We can either concentrate on a particular trait in the legends, or focus our attention on a regional or local level. The pursuit of either possibility has largely remained descriptive so far. Only in relation to the 'evil eye' complex, a form of bewitchment by looking, have interpretations been suggested (see below).

Yet at a regional or local level it is also hard to ascertain whether or not a witchcraft discourse can be reconstructed by just combining witchcraft legends told by different people. If communication is considered to be a condition of the discourse, in the absence of dialogues and discussions we can only surmise that statements by individuals (made to folklorists) form part of an encompassing system. It seems evident for villagers to have had access to different repertoires; 'quite contradictory cosmogonies may exist side by side', as the Hungarian folklorist Tekla Dömötör remarked (1982: 18). But can this not also apply to the level of witchcraft discourses? Is, for instance, the idea that witchcraft is hereditary and predestined compatible with the notion that witchcraft can be learned (Schöck, 1978: 101; Gottschalk, 1995: 162–163)? Or does it concern different discourses that are rooted in different social structures (cf. Jenkins, 1977)? Can notions of gender be more dominant than those of witchcraft in the sense that stories about male witches are not easily interchangeable with stories about female witches and may even belong to a separate discourse? In short, can a witchcraft discourse be unitary and indivisible, even locally?

Regional publications in which witchcraft legends are discussed as part of a preconceived, superimposed system are obviously hardly helpful in answering these questions, although they may contain interesting details. They merely repeat the failures of the supernational indexes and surveys as criticized in the previous section. In her discussion of witchcraft legends from Westmünsterland (Germany) the Germanist Gabriele Gotschalk (1995), for instance, recapitulates legends about how one becomes a witch, about witches' gatherings, metamorphoses into animals (mainly cats and hares), bewitchments and unbewitchments. Her colleague Christl Lehnert-Leven has completed a similar project on witchcraft legends from Westphalia. She, however, remarks that the legends about witches' gatherings 'curiously' appear as 'totally extricated from causing harm' (1995: 137), that is from bewitchments. A similar observation has been made by the Hungarian folklorist Zoltán Kovács in his study on means and methods of identifying witches. Russian legends about the recognition of witches in churches and more specifically in 'the chair of St. Lucia' (or Luca) miss a certain kind of concreteness, 'do not join organically in the other witch-craft legends' and look like prescriptions rather than experiences (1977: 249).

One of the ways in which we can gain more insight into local witchcraft discourses is to examine the legends of individual informants. A rather random selection from the legends which were collected in the summer of 1963 in the Kempen, a region east of Antwerp, indeed reveals that different people had different repertoires (which is only to be expected). It also reveals individual attitudes towards witchcraft which are more varied than the dichotomy between 'superstitious' witch believers and 'rational' sceptics, or the division into critical, indifferent and believing attitudes towards legends (Kaufmann, 1960: 89–90) lead us to expect.

Thus a 79-year-old woman from the hamlet of Pulderbos, from whom 12 witchcraft texts were noted down, told the folklorist how a priest pronouncing the 'dominus vobiscum' (God be with thee) was able to recognize witches in the church because of the beehives that appeared on their heads (Daras, 1964: nr. 1476). This woman knew the legend about the witch who flew to the winecellar in Cologne (nr. 830) and she 'had often heard' about witches stealing butter (nr. 1054). She also knew about a case in which a witch had been unable to die until a priest 'read her to death' (nr. 1793) and that it was possible to torment people with the aid of a book of spells (nr. 1947). Once, a witch had taken a pair of scissors into the church and had destroyed the coats of other women 'out of jealousy' (nr. 1161). On the whole her legends have an anecdotal quality. They refer more to tales, to notions about witchcraft that circulated in the area (and far beyond), than to actual experiences, although she localized some of the legends. When she came close to narrating events they had turned anecdotal in the telling, for instance when she told about her husband who had visited a woman 'who had the name of being a witch'. The poor man had got lost on his way home and had only arrived the following morning (nr. 1107). The only concrete bewitchment she recounted was about her parents who had suffered from headache and had been sent to a cloister by the doctor. There a monk had said: 'There is something to witchcraft, but not as much as the people say' (nr. 2071). Even that was a formula (Daras, 1983: 149). In the woman's stories the witches themselves remain elusive. If we presume that she kept silent towards the folklorist about her more direct involvement (which is unlikely), her taking refuge in already existing opinions and tales was still a certain way of speaking, a certain narrative mode that could be adopted.

The stories of the woman from Pulderbos stand in sharp contrast to those told by a 61-year-old woman who lived in St Antonius-Brecht. This second woman also knew that the priest could spot witches in the church. 'The past was full of those things!' (nrs 1451, 1452). The bulk of her legends, however, concerned her experiences with one particular witch, whom she named in full. 'How did it all start? Well, how long have we been punished with that Mie van Nuffelen?' Delving into her memory she found that it had started just after her wedding (presumably around 1920). She had lost her ring and Mie had found it at a spot where they had already looked 10 times. 'If she could do this with a blessed ring, how strong must she have been?' (nr. 1207). Mie was unable to have children and she had told the woman that she too would never conceive. Thereupon the woman consulted the monks in a nearby village and gave birth within a year (nr. 881).

Other neighbours were less fortunate. The witch had borrowed some salt from a grinder which had caused him to lose his grindstones (nr.

1148). Children who had touched her became ill (nr. 882). When the informant's aunt had stepped into Mie's footprint, she had looked back (nr. 1530). One of the main victims was the witch's own daughter-in-law. Her family met with one misfortune after another. A new cow died and a child lost a lot of weight. The other children saw a black dog and screamed the whole time. The local priest advised her to see the Capuchins in Antwerp. Since the daughter-in-law was unfamiliar with the city, the informant accompanied her. 'She kept crying, so I had to do the talking'. They got 'something strong', a 'long lesson' which they had to read for nine days in a row. The witch 'never did have any power no more!' (nr. 982, cf. nr. 987). And when witches could not inflict harm on others, they had to injure themselves. After the women had visited Antwerp, Mie had writhed in agony and had lost half a bucket of blood each day (nr. 1099). This informant was rather experienced in dealing with unwitchers. Clergymen sweated it out, she claimed, and they also needed buckets of water to restore their power (nr. 2027). She and her neighbour also consulted a lay unwitcher (nr. 1622). For her, the reality of witchcraft was reinforced through these visits. They also provided her with a means to handle it and she could even become a mediator between bewitched and unwitcher.

Witchcraft was discussed in several ways, depending on the narrator's degree of involvement. The issue of the univocal witchcraft discourse is closely linked to the credibility of the legends. Between the rationalistic denial of witchcraft on the one hand and the certainty of the truth of one's experience of it on the other intermediate positions were taken. In the context of repertoires as they were related to a folklorist (which is often the only context that can be reconstructed) single stories acquire something of the meaning of the whole repertoire. To recognise witches in church, to take up Kovács topic, would be more anecdotal within the repertoire of the first woman whereas it would lend more support to the omnipresence of witches in the second. Similar motifs and tale types could thus become charged with slightly different meanings. This is even more apparent when a story referred to an event. When told by a sceptic, it could still contain the same narrative elements as when told by a believer. (In both cases the setting is determined by the interviewing folklorist).

The relation between repertoire and narrative is not totally unilateral, however; since the range of meanings of an individual narrative is limited, the narrative also affects the repertoire. The tale about the journey to the winecellar, for instance, was also told elsewhere in the province of Antwerp (Roeck, 1966: 149), as indeed with different destinations all over Europe. It is 'an entertaining story' (Bošković-Stulli, 1992: 148), structured around fixed motifs, such as the formula 'over thick and over thin', which in the story is rendered into 'through thick and thin' by the man following the witch (G 242.7.g; the Dutch language version is more expressive as it has the protagonists travel over and through hedges). Even if this tale had been told in the first person, most of the audience would have recognized it as a tale and not as an experience. Folklorists have classified it as a migratory legend (ML 5006*), which can also feature fairies instead of witches (Briggs, 1971).

Within witchcraft legends we have thus to differentiate according to narrative mode and narrative genre. As with other representations of the witch, here the question is also whether there are mutual influences between the different modes and genres. Furthermore, the function of the different modes and genres within a particular witchcraft discourse needs to be established. In any case, the Frisian witch Alle Tet used the winecellar story in the first person to instill women with even more awe of her than they already had. 'I've been to the winecellar in Spain, last night. My oh my, how many drinks I had. I took the broomstick, sat on it and hop it went through the air' (Wytzes, 1995: 99). In order to understand witchcraft tales it is also significant to know who told which tale to whom.

GENDERED LEGENDS

Are twentieth-century witchcraft discourses gendered? Or to apply the question to folklore material: do men and women have different reper-toires of witchcraft legends? As the necessary research is largely missing or unsatisfactory, the answer must again remain tentative. Thus, Ton Dekker concluded in his essay about Dutch witchcraft legends: 'Both men and women tell stories about witches and sorcerers and in the process make very negative remarks about people of their own sex. There is no question of a gender-specific preference for stories about witches and sorcerers' (1991: 188). Dekker was mainly interested in the differences between male witches (sorcerers in his terminology) and female ones and he did not look for specific repertoires. But there are indeed very specific stories about male witches, for instance those included in the *Motif-index* under number G295*: 'Witch (usual male) does impossible deeds (usually with the aid of the devil)'. These feats are summarized on the basis of a German collection: 'to win all card games, to make little devils appear as well as phantom animals, dogs, soldiers, pigeons and black mice, to make the pottery in the cupboard rattle, to change burned cards into new ones, to keep away mice and rats from the corn and foxes from the chicken yard, to make snappy dogs harmless and to silence them, to make tables dance, to change oneself into a broom bush, to lure squirrels and cats, to immobilize disagreeable people and thiefs' (Kaufmann, 1960: 100; the list

contains many magician's tricks; cf. Favret-Saada, 1986: 42). If it is possible
to indicate more or less separate male and female repertoires, stories about
male witches can be expected to occur in male repertoires. This is not the
place for a re-study of the 6,000 legends Dekker based his analysis on. All
that can be done is to use some of his material to cast doubt on the above
conclusion.

In the early sixties the collector Engelbert Heupers pillaged the countryside of the province of Utrecht and adjacent areas for legends (Heupers,
1979; 1981; 1984). He was one of the two most prolific Dutch collectors
of witchcraft legends. Among others he notated 29 versions of the legend
about the farmhand who spread muck within a day (a variant of ATh
820). This tale was exclusively narrated by men. In the same region the
legends about men who sent a playing card (jack of spades or ace of clubs)
to fetch a drink also belonged to the male domain. Out of the 15 legends
collected, only one was told by a woman and she placed it in a male
setting: at the factory where her father used to work (Heupers, nr. 1542).
Male witches who immobilized people or horses occurred in 20 texts, 17
of which were taken down from men. The remaining three were told
about the (female) informant's father (nrs 521, 643) or about 'rough men'
(nr. 2952). According to Dekker, the acts of male witches were characterized by these three themes (1991: 189–90). At least in the centre of the
Netherlands these tales about typical male witchcraft were male tales. This
finding probably has a wider relevance. Only about a fifth of the
corresponding legends in the collection of Daras (1964) came from women
informants and here we also find indications that they heard them from
their brother (nr. 1863) or their father (nr. 1872).

There are more legends with a gender-specific content. Most of the
changes witches undergo are into cats or hares (Wittmann, 1933: 30–7),
which already provides a much less complicated picture than the previous
enumerations of animals. In most parts of Europe the standard legends
recount how witches in animal form were wounded and still showed the
wounds when back in human shape. These structurally similar legends
may belong to the same discourse; they can also be separated in terms of
concepts about domesticity (cats) and wildness (hares), or according to the
gender of the narrator. For hares were shot and hunting was a male
preserve. The Irish legend about the woman who is hunted while in the
shape of a hare 'can be read as an attempted rape of the old woman by
the man, or at the very least as an expression of the battle of the sexes' (ní
Dhuibhne, 1993: 79). In the Irish case the gender of the informants was
not taken into consideration; in Scandinavian hare legends, however,
'legends of how a milkhare is shot by a man (. . .) are exclusively male'.
Also the 'trollhare tradition is a wholly male tradition', 'a sportman's yarn'.
In Scandinavia, there are three sorts of (geographically distinct) legendary

hares. The trollhare is apparently unconnected to any human being and the milkhare is made by a witch to steal milk. Besides, witches can transform themselves into hares too and steal milk. People who informed the folklorists about the last group 'belong to both sexes', probably because whole communities were dependent on the milk (Nildin-Wall and Wall, 1993). Whether tales about the mere shooting of witchhares have circulated mainly among men is unclear as yet.

When particular witchcraft legends are confined to a male sphere, male witchcraft discourses have at least different accentuations when compared to female ones. To gain a clearer idea of how this comes about in daily practice, we can return to the legends from the Kempen. They constitute one of the largest Belgium collections and therefore lend themselves to some statistical analysis. Hervé Daras spoke to 327 people about witchcraft. As usual with male researchers, he contacted many more men than women, respectively 215 and 112. His male informants, however, told less tales per person than his female informants; out of 1,419 witchcraft legends 887 were told by men and 532 by women, which amounts to an average of 4.7 legends per woman and 4.1 per man. Women's propensity for witchcraft stories becomes even more transparent when we notice that 42 percent of the women told five or more stories against only 31 percent of the men. In itself this quantitative distinction does not necessarily demonstrate differences in content; women could simply have narrated more of the same. But a closer look at the largest repertoires shows, indeed, striking differences between the repertoires of men and women, although the picture is complicated by the different stances they took on witchcraft. At this stage of the research, it is therefore impossible to arrive at 'typical' male or female repertoires or discourses within a certain region. On the basis of different individual repertoires we can at the most reach conclusions about different narrative modes.

Among men there was a preference for witching, not in the sense that it was directly aimed at material profit, but because it certainly expressed cultural power. My previous discussion of male legend types has already hinted at this. There were also plainly male traditions. Thus, a 57-year-old butcher at Halle quoted his father and uncle. Although he mentioned bewitchments and even a particular witch, he emphasized the witch's extraordinary deeds. One witch was seen reading on several occasions (nrs. 1083, 1534), a stone thrown at a cat bounced back (nr. 1279), a farmhand was immobilized by the farmer he worked for (nr. 1893). The informant's father had once met a girl at a fair and accompagnied her home. 'They say that you are a witch, but I don't believe it,' the man told the girl. 'Stand on my toes,' she commanded him. Heavy thunder sounded and they flew straight into the air. The father saw 52 steeples. 'When are we going home?' he asked. Boom! Suddenly they were sitting on a heath with a cup of wine in their hands. He asked again. Boom! The girl vanished and he held only a shoe (nr. 1151).

A bicycle repair man did not mention any bewitchments at all. His universe was inhabited by cats. One night he saw 500 of them leaving a witch's house. In a minute they were gone (nr. 1197). His father had once kicked at a cat, whereupon 50 of the beasts had surrounded him (nr. 1292). One of his friends had conducted a conversation with a cat (nr. 1261). To shoot a hare, one needed consecrated gunpowder (nr. 1388). The bicycle man was also convinced of witches' ability to fly. When his father had visited a pub some way from his home, the landlady (who was known as a witch) had asked him about a couple of trees near his place. 'I often rested in them,' she explained (nr. 1213). Other men had their own favourite tall tales. A slaughterer from Grobbendonk was fascinated by the power of men. He himself had seen a man controlling fire; this man had had some training for the priesthood and in former times priests were taught evil before they learned good (nr. 2096). A shepherd had rendered two thiefs immobile (nr. 1876) and one of the slaughterer's acquaintances had sent rats to young men who had made fun of him (nr. 1967). These magicians were also able to do harm. His cousin had once visited a powerful male fortune-teller in Mechelen to find out who had stolen his money. Afterwards he got into trouble with his cows, a child fell ill and he had to visit the white monks (Bernardines) of Bornem (nr. 2009). 'I've never had anything to do with it myself,' said a farmer from Zoersel (nr. 1660). So he related the yarns of other men. One had found his house full of cats which began to sing when he tried to whip them out (nr. 1323). Another met a witch in the form of a white hare (nr. 1439). Cats used to gather at night at a mill. A curious labourer hit one of them and the following day found the miller's wife ill (nr. 1445; a well-known migratory legend). A man from Pulderbos, according to the farmer, had lost his way when returning from a visit to his girlfriend. He had found a house, full of young women who had all thrown their arms around his neck. He was offered a cup of wine and pronounced a toast: 'To God's health!' Then he found himself alone on a heath (nr. 1913).

When men had experienced bewitchments in their own households this made their repertoires much less anecdotal and distant. The new cow of a labourer did not drink for nine days and he had to consult the Dominicans at Lier to sort it out (nr. 1036). His son had been given a sweet by a woman. In the middle of the night he had shouted: 'Mum, dad, mum, dad, there she is again!' He had died when he was 11. 'Yes, I have walked hard roads,' the labourer commented (nr. 961). Witches he called 'good-for-nothings' (nrs. 1573, 1823). Walking to a nearby place, he had come upon a big tent in the woods. He was drawn inside where it was full of beautiful women and music. They asked him what he wanted, but before they had a chance to touch him he shouted: 'God bless all you witches!' and everything had disappeared (nr. 1908). Is it typical for someone who had first-hand experience with bewitchments to narrate this story in the first person?

The narrator's distance from bewitchments and witchments influenced male as well as female repertoires. Yet there is still a difference between the male anecdotal repertoires and the female one we looked at earlier, if only because of the typical male tales and men's preoccupation with power. There are even more indications of the occurrence of gendered repertoires. Clari-Anne Wytzes analysed the witchcraft legends of the two most intensively researched villages in the Netherlands, Soest in the province of Utrecht and the Frisian community of Harkema-Opeinde. She paid special attention to changes in the power structures within the legends (cf. the distinction made by Favret-Saada, 1989: 44) and found a different pattern in each village. In Soest most of the stories about bewitchments in which the witch was not overcome were told by men. In Harkema most of these stories were told by women. In the first village it was the women who fought against bewitchments, in the second one men played a bigger role (Wytzes, 1995: 52–3). This can be related in turn to the different religious profiles of the two places: Soest was predominantly Catholic and Harkema was mainly Protestant. Catholicism provided for more self-help against witchcraft, and in Soest, a Catholic enclave with far less cloisters within reach than for instance in the Kempen, women had to fight their own battles against witches. People in Harkema had access to a wide range of (lay) unwitching experts and as outside journeys were a male prerogative, men figured most in stories about the witch's defeat and also told more of them, even when the initial diagnosis was made by women.

WITCHCRAFT IN COURT

According to paganists the British witchcraft act was only repealed in 1951 and witches were prosecuted until then. They have thus contested the historians' claim that the turning point was in 1736 (cf. Bostridge, 1997: 180, 201). This disagreement shows the bias of both groups. In the 1736 Act the criminal focus switched from the apostasy of (mainly) ascribed witchcraft to the fraudulent aspects of practised witchcraft. Prosecution after 1736 concerned fortune-tellers, astrologers and later spirit mediums, people in whom historians of witchcraft have shown hardly any interest but who were among the forerunners of today's witch-covens. These professional magicians can hardly be considered as traditional witches, but in twentieth-century Britain bewitchments have still in fact appeared in several kinds of court cases. So far only a few isolated instances have emerged. The historian of 'popular' witchcraft Owen Davies has found two assault cases, one in 1918 and another in 1926 (1995: ch. 2). In about 1930 a farmer from Somerset took another to court over an allegation of witchcraft (Palmer, 1976: 61). As recently as 1976 the Salisbury County Court awarded 50 pence in damages because someone had sent a neighbour a chicken's heart spell (a heart transfixed with needles) through the post. It was 'the silliest case he had heard in over fifteen years,' the judge said (*Times* 19 July 1976).

German researchers of judicial sources have proceeded more systematically than anywhere else. They have identified the following petty crimes that could result from thinking and acting in terms of witchcraft: 'conjuring, cruelty to animals, violation of the law on livestock epidemics, violation of privacy, defamation, vile gossip, slander, assault, intimidation, all kinds of bodily injury, unlicensed practice of medicine'. Yet more serious crimes are listed: 'fraud, manslaughter, arson, homicide, murder and suicide, as well as false oaths and perjury' (Schäfer, 1955: 30–1). The criminologist Herbert Schäfer collected 95 such cases, dated between 1925 and 1956 (1959: x–xi). Obviously, in comparison to legends these are the more extreme and more salient cases, or at least those that have been published in full. Thus we read about a young couple who killed both their young children by keeping them awake and beating them, because they feared that they would fall victim to a witch if they fell asleep (Schäfer, 1955: 30; 1959: 69–71). If that is not gruesome enough, there is also the case of the labourer who cleaved his grandfather's skull with an axe because he thought the man had bewitched him. Afterwards the labourer hanged himself, leaving a note that he had wanted revenge for what was done to him. 'Don't be angry at me, I couldn't do otherwise' (Schäfer, 1955: 32; 1959: 65–6). The difference with the contents of legends may be due to a certain occupational blindness by the folklorists for 'such things as murder, suicide, and – somewhat milder – deception and defamation' that surrounded witchcraft legends (Baumhauer, 1984: 200). Court cases also stand out because the gravity of the conflict within the witchcraft triangle either forced one of the participants to step outside the witchcraft discourse and to resort to violence or to official problem solving, or provoked the authorities to interfere. Besides, judicial material has been selected for publication because of its relevance to several debates. It has served as illustration in the campaign against superstition and been used to convince judges to take witchcraft seriously. To this end a new kind of criminal, the *Okkulttäter* (literarily: the occult evildoer) was designated.

The North-German teacher Johann Kruse was of the opinion that a responsible nation had to protect its inhabitants against ridiculous accusations of witchcraft. But he found that daily practice was different: 'Most women who have become strongly suspected [of witchcraft] take care not to turn to the court for help. They rather bear the hardship' (1951: 127). At best the slanderer would get off with a small fine and the rumour about the women would spread even wider. Some judges decided on an acquittal since they were of the opinion that there were no more witches and the word 'witch' could therefore not be understood as an insult (Kruse, 1951: 128; Bartholdy, 1969: 5). In court witchcraft discourse clashed with the enlightened approach of the lawyers and judges. This came to the fore especially when unwitchers were implicated. Kruse cited a complaint by a labourer from Holstein against a healer who in the early 1930s had spread the story that the labourer's wife by her 'innate powers' had caused the affliction of a woman's leg. She had also made a girl sick by giving her chocolate and she had incited the headaches of another. These and other imputations had damaged the reputation of the labourer and his wife and he asked for reparations. The court, however, found mitigating circumstances for the accused healer; he had not fully realized 'the depravity of his acts'. The plaintif's honour could not have been affected, since it was 'precluded, that sensible people would take the accused's deeds and words seriously' (Kruse, 1951: 133). In other cases witnesses were very uncommunicative (Kruse, 1951: 130). Or, when unwitchers were prosecuted for fraud, their clients told the court that they had not been injured by them (Kruse, 1951: 138–9; Schäfer, 1955: 47). Rüdiger Bartholdy, himself an assistant judge, noticed that courts were seldom able to deal out punishments. Either the evidence was missing, or witnesses did not come forward. In the rare instances when witch-doctors were convicted it hardly hindered them (Bartholdy, 1969: 60). After 1945, according to Schäfer, German witch-doctors were only convicted because of their unlicensed practice of medicine (1959: 258). This merely increased their fame. The effects of judicial intervention were often contrary to what was intended by plaintifs and prosecutors.

In order to support the cases of the women designated as witches and to justify the seriousness of witchcraft insults Kruse as well as German judges had to acknowledge the social reality of witchcraft. The ensuing dilemma was partly solved by declaring witchcraft an anachronism. 'Many a judge merely sees an atavism in the witch-belief, a relapse into archaic times' (Bartholdy, 1969: 13). The most radical stance a researcher could take, however, was to construct as much distance as possible between himself and the 'believers'. To this end Schäfer created an opposition between the 'logical–rational world experience' and the 'magical-mystical outlook on life' (1955: 10). The last he objectified in a bleak picture of the superstitious person: 'He does not think independently anymore, he has stopped thinking, he disregards experience, acts against his instinct, his vital consciousness, for he belongs to the dark powers of this misbelief' (Schäfer., 1955: 24). The witch-believer was not exactly stupid, but was supplied with an 'undeveloped, not fully matured intelligence' and became easily subjected to all sorts of emotional passions (Schäfer, 1959: 41). Schäfer did not go as far as to suggest directly that women formed the largest proportion of the superstitious; his material did not allow it. Looking at the clients of witch-doctors, he found a majority of men. But statistics were misleading, he argued. It had to be taken into account that although among the 'rural classes women had not yet gained the independence to act externally', they could still have been the 'driving force in the background' (1959: 60).

Campaigners against the continuing, and in the 1950s even increasing, expression of witch belief considered the professional unwitchers to be one of its main driving forces. Therefore, the unwitcher's clients were not portrayed as perpetrators or as accomplices, but as his victims. The witch-doctor himself, together with 'magical healers' (blessers, magnetists and psychic healers) was categorized as an *Okkulttäter*, a special type of swindler. He was someone who broke judicial laws as well as social norms, by using occult methods or exploiting the occult and superstitious attitudes of the people who consulted him. It did not matter whether he was sincere or not (Schäfer, 1959: 5). Although it is possible to differentiate between a true and a false *Okkulttäter*, that is between one who is convinced of his own capabilities and one who knowingly commits fraud, between the 'fraudulent liar of superstitious style' and the 'pathological swindler' (Schafter, 1959: 251), in Schäfer's opinion both deserved a severe punishment (1959: 257). In an objective sense, according to Schäfer, both were deceiving their clients, for they stated facts that were not true (1959: 91). The witch-doctor was described even more negatively than the mere believer. Not only was he incapable of working regularly and orderly (1959: 95), he was also suffering from 'blindness towards the law' and a 'fanatical unwillingness to understand'. He was slightly schizophrenic and certainly psychopathic (1959:105), a typecasting later described as an 'utterly doubtful and risky enterprise' (Schöck, 1978: 142). For Schäfer, understanding witchcraft boiled down to translating its manifestations into rationalistic interpretations with total disregard for those participating in the witchcraft discourse.

The search for a method behind the superstitious madness, however condescending towards its subjects, nevertheless presupposed the notion of an indigenous system. If this was not to be found in such external interpretations as the psychology of the believers or the cataloguing of their tales, it had to reside somewhere in the contexts. In his study of witch-doctors and magical healers in Schleswig-Holstein, Bartholdy attempted to trace parallels between the old customary law and the basic rules of magical practice as this was still current in his time. By emphasizing the continuity of the phenomenon, the 'timeless basic attitude' of the believers with their 'archaic techniques of world control' (1969: 8, 10), he denied them a place in contemporary society, like so many others had done before him. Nevertheless, while exploring 'tradition's power to order' (1969: 26), he may have hit upon one of the underlying norms that ruled the relations within the witchcraft triangle. In a society where witchcraft was rampant, people feared gifts. Only during transitional events (like weddings) could they be freely given; otherwise they had to be reciprocated, at least by showing hospitality (1969: 22). An accusation of witchcraft referred to a disturbance of the social equilibrium. To reestablish it while still acknowledging the threat of the witch, she was kept in isolation; one did not accept anything from her and neither was it advisable to lend her anything.

SARZBÜTTEL, 1954

Courtroom material can present a much more profound picture of a local witchcraft discourse than the usual legend text. Certainly, the judicial system forces people into extraordinary situations and threatens them with punishment if they do not tell the 'truth'. Accused and witnesses also try to exonerate themselves and to justify their actions. In the process they reveal details that are not always noticed by outsiders. In this section we will have a look at fragments of texts produced during the 1954 trial of the witch-doctor Waldemar Eberling in the north-German village of Sarzbüttel (northwest of Hamburg), where the court of Itzehoe had moved for the occasion. Although I have not consulted the original dossier, because it is quite extensively quoted by the folklorist Joachim Baumhauer in his study on Johann Kruse, it can still furnish an idea of the prospects offered by judicial sources.

The Sarzbüttel case was 'one of the most spectacular witch trials of the post-war period' (Baumhauer, 1984: 76). It was experienced by the villagers as 'an interference in their traditional way of life' (Hauschild, 1980: 147). To protect accused and witnesses and because this was a condition for consulting and publishing the documents, Baumhauer used pseudonyms (1984: 364), which are adopted here as well. Only the main player, called Ebelmann by Baumhauer, was so well-known that it is relatively easy to reconstruct his identity through other writers' references (Schäfer, 1959: plates 15 and 16; Hauschild, 1980: 145; Pintschovius, 1991: 81). Eberling, a cabinet maker born in 1908, had become a healer by vocation. As he declared to the court:

Since I was fourteen, I have had sensory images. I saw God in front of me and the cross of Christ and it was as if a voice said to me: help other people! I would like to point out that during my youth I did not go away, these thoughts kept me occupied and I always had pity for the helpless and the ill. This was probably also because I have always been interested in nature, always loved it. Even as a child I could not bear it when an animal was slaughtered at home or in the neighbourhood. Maybe I have a soft nature (Baumhauer, 1984: 230).

The tradition of acquiring magical powers prescribed an alternation of sex between successors. Sometime later, in about 1927, Eberling was offered the opportunity to comply with this demand. When he was working in Dortmund, he told the court, an elderly woman had given him a book with prescriptions for treating illness. 'The woman told me I had the gift to help other people. But I hardly ever followed the prescriptions and instead acted only with God's help'. The woman, 'a real old witch', was suspect in Eberling's view anyway. Privately he declared that she was in league with the devil; another time, in front of his public, he referred to the 'scientific' discussions he had had with her (Baumhauer, 1984: 236). According to Schöck, these were typically defensive statements, only uttered in court; normally the origin of magical power was kept a mystery (1978: 138).

The witch-doctor and the court had different objectives. The prosecution, being urged by the individual complaints of people who had been accused of witchcraft by Eberling's actions, wanted to establish the extent to which he was punishable, either within the provisions of the law against the illegal practice of medicine or because of fraud or defamation. The court was not interested in the sociological context of the imputations, nor in their local meaning. As part of its investigations, it did, however, order a psychiatric report in which Eberling was declared to be a 'fanatical, psychopathical personality', but nevertheless responsible for his actions (Baumhauer, 1984: 220). (In his sketch of the *Okkulttäter* Schäfer eagerly quoted the psychiatrists' conclusions; 1959: 103–4). Only 10 to 15 years later psychiatrists would come to regard witchcraft as a way of communicating and a model of explanation rather than a delirium or a delusion (Risso and Böker, 1964: 63–4; Favret-Saada, 1980: 265). On his part Eberling seems to have used the proceedings to display his power as a healer and his standing within the region. If he came across as a strong personality who believed in himself (Baumhauer, 1984: 227), he accomplished this by observing the local patterns of expectation and by adopting a sincere, vulnerable bearing:

If it is claimed that I have become rich through my activity and made a lot of money, that is not true. I am even in debt. And at home we certainly don't live in luxury. During the day I have always been working in my workshop. The people I treated and helped, I always visited after working hours, so that my business did not suffer from it. I know that everyone has his enemies, and I think I have them too. It seems to me that many people are out to get me, want to see me punished. Furthermore I would like to stress, that this treatment which I use on people, also affects me. During these treatments I put myself into a state that demands inner strength. Hence I also often suffer from emotional depressions. I am very attached to my family and to my parents and if I was goaled for my activities or fined, my world would collapse. Thus I do not accept that I acted unlawfully, since I only wanted to do good and helped person after person (Baumhauer, 1984: 255).

On appeal Eberling was sentenced to four months imprisonment followed by probation and a fine of 400 marks (Baumhauer, 1984: 221). His influence in the village is documented in the statements of his patients and those who were brandished as the cause of their trouble (in this context the unwitcher never spoke about '*Hexen*', witches). The unwitcher's fame was mainly spread by word of mouth. One of his female patients testified that she had heard from him through a cousin whose father he had healed. As she and her children had been very ill for some time and had not found any relief through official medicine, she decided to follow her cousin's suggestion. When Eberling arrived he had blessed the children and advised her to look in their matresses. There, lumps of feathers were found (some in the form of a heart) as well as a cord with some knots in it. Their illnesses, Eberling declared, had been 'transmitted' by other people:

E. asked whether we had enemies in the village. We had to agree, my father in law had been mayor till the end of the war and held other offices as well. After the political overthrow people treated him very badly and those, who caused this, we had to consider our enemies. The name of Goos was also mentioned, because Goos was later mayor and had to decide about the deliveries. E. did not say anything to that, only nodded his head. One day E. was again with us, sitting on the sofa and suddenly he became very pale. When I asked him if he was not well, he explained that he had protected us from whatever was supposed to have harmed us. The one from which this originated had just passed our house. I looked out of the window and saw Claus Goos passing on his bike. That convinced me that I was right to think immediately of Goos when I was asked if I had ennemies in the village (Baumhauer, 1984: 267).

Witches were not named openly but their identity was hinted at by the unwitcher's probings. Another one of Eberling's patients, also a woman, had heard about him because he had been active in the neighbourhood before. She was pointed by him towards one of her neighbours.

> As far as I remember E. started to speak about an evil power. He said, we should no longer deal with a woman, who often came to see us. That was the evil power. We immediately hit upon Frau Clausen. She visited us most frequently. We also told E. right away, that this could only be our neighbour, Frau Clausen. Until then she had always helped us, at engagements, weddings, and other events. She used to be around a lot. We were always good friends with her. When she next came to us to bring apples to my daughter who was ill at the time, we did not talk to her and did not pay her any attention. We didn't eat any of the apples she gave to my daughter. We burnt them in the stove (Baumhauer, 1984: 280).

In another case Eberling himself identified the witch. As a witness revealed:

> E. had put his head in his hands, pondered deeply and thought seriously. Then E. said: 'She's just arrived at the house'. A little while later: 'Now she is outside'. Thereupon E. and Arnoldi went outside and E. said: 'There she goes'. But Arnoldi could not see anybody outside. After some time E. had remained in Arnoldi's inn and looked out of the window. As Frau Marx, the wife of the tailor Marx, who lived straight opposite Arnoldi, happened to come out of her house, E. said, while pointing outside with his finger: 'That is her' (Baumhauer, 1984: 273–4).

It is unclear whether there was a pattern in Eberling's accusations. Baumhauer, whose investigations were very thorough in other respects, did not look into the histories and family relations of the accused, nor did he pay much attention to the respective social positions of bewitched and witches. He only remarked that in the three cases where women had been implied no earlier conflicts had existed and that the unwitcher had used traditional methods (Baumhauer, 1984: 282). Although court material can be very detailed, it has to be augmented by other sources, the more so when it concerns contexts and backgrounds.

THE POWER OF THE UNWITCHER

The unwitcher occupies a key position in the witchcraft discourse. He is the expert, he operates as 'functionary of magic' (Schöck, 1978: 132). By actively propagating the discourse, he also keeps it alive. As Favret-Saada remarked in her field-work diary: 'If it is true that most of what people know about witchcraft stems from the unwitchers (. . .) they should be my most direct source of information' (Favret-Saada and Contreras, 1981: 157). This was before she was 'caught'; in her book she wrote: 'most witch stories are part of what the unwitcher teaches his patients' (1980: 144). Unwitchers are the public figures within the witchcraft triangle, yet they have to stay hidden from the authorities and sometimes even the anthropologists have been unable to find them. It was reported that in Czechia 'exorcists' were visited secretly, 'and no one was willing to discuss what procedures they employed or how much they received for their services' (Salzmann and Scheufler, 1974: 115). Their main means of advertising was by word of mouth (Schöck, 1978: 133; but cf. Camus, 1988: 61). When Favret-Saada made her acquaintance with her unwitcher madame Flora, this woman had already practised as a card-layer for 15 years, although she was still officially registered as a dress-maker for tax purposes (Favret-Saada and Contreras, 1981: 248). Unwitching is the more obscure as it is a procedure rather than a profession. Quite a few unwitchers have had an official trade, like the cabinet-maker Eberling or the saddler Lelie. They have mainly been, at least in western France and Germany, artisans, from 'modest social origin' (Schäfer, 1959: 93; Camus, 1988: 31–2; cf. Davies, 1997b: 92). When they found it hard to combine their material with their magical craft, because of patients' demands or because of the constraints that practising magic imposed upon them such as assiduous working hours (Camus, 1988: 89; Favret-Saada, 1989: 52), they could choose to become full-time magical experts. That does not, however, turn them necessarily into specialist unwitchers. Eberling can best be characterized as a healer, more specifically as a blesser who had a whole repertoire of charms (or prayers) at his disposal (Schäfer, 1959: 116; Bartholdy, 1969: 94; Baumhauer, 1984: 349). A fortuneteller like madame Flora discussed the main events in her client's life, and these only occasionally included witchcraft (see also Lisón Tolosana, 1994: 146–58). 'A typical witch-doctor, who confines himself to unwitching stables and cattle (. . .), who claims to be able to help bewitched people (. . .) certainly does not exist in this pure form in most of the cases' (Schöck, 1978: 139).

Whatever the unwitcher's level of specialization, his public stance is often demarcated by distance and strangeness. 'People prefer to choose their therapist beyond some boundary (. . .), in any case outside the network of acquaintanceship' (Favret-Saada, 1980: 20; cf. Pitt-Rivers, 1971: 193; Lisón Tolosana, 1994: 117). Dutch witch-doctors, Lelie among them, usually differed from most of their clients by adhering to a different religion (de Blécourt, 1989: 254; 1990: 245–6). They could easily be strangers as well (Kovács, 1977: 268–71). While Finns and Laps stood out amongst Swedish cunning folk, the latter distinguished themselves in other ways, by living far from others, by acting mystically, or by dressing in peculiar ways. Even their funerals attracted attention (Tillhagen, 1969: 142). This strangeness was a prerequisite for unwitching, which, after all, also amounted to the relief of social tension (even if it created it as well). 'As the white witch [unwitcher] deals mainly with the unfortunate effects of antisocial forces, the person who makes use of her services is in effect accusing his neighbours of giving vent to these forces' (de Pina-Cabral, 1986: 191).

Among unwitchers clergy took a special place, particularly catholic clergy (Schöck, 1978: 143), as they were even visited by protestants (Schöck, 1978: 99). Of the Catholic clergy those belonging to monastic orders were more popular unwitchers than local priests. According to Daras' Belgium informants the local priests may have been able to turn the wind away from a fire or to recognize witches in church, but their power dwindled to insignificance when compared to that of the regulars. The monks themselves (whom Daras systematically interviewed in the early 1980s) attributed this unanimously to the fact that their clients could remain anonymous. They also provided them with tangible counter magic such as blessed salt, holy water or medals to ward off evil influences (Daras, 1983: 131–2). An occasional reversal in the positions of regular and irregular clergy, seemingly due to a growing reluctance of the monks to accept the witchcraft discourse, confirms the notion of distance. At least one parish priest in the area where Favret-Saada researched had become a famous unwitcher, though only for people outside his village. 'Of course, he had not been acknowledged as such by the ecclesiastical hierarchy, only by his patients,' the anthropologist remarked (1980: 57). By the 1960s the time had gone 'when the profound distress of the bewitched was responded to by religion' (Favret-Saada. 1980: 143); Daras' informants also referred primarily to the earlier decades of the twentieth century (cf. Lisón Tolosana, 1994: 112). As most of the monks, and certainly their superiors, had come to regard witchcraft as superstitious, they had to be tricked into unwitching. 'My position is delicate,' one of them told Favret-Saada. 'If I say I don't believe in it, the villagers won't put their trust in me anymore. But all the same I cannot strengthen their superstition' (Favret-Saada and Contreras, 1981: 13). Others simply refused to practice exorcisms (Favret-Saada and Contreras, 1981: 170–1). People knew very well that the clergy did not solicit blessings. 'Often one had to commit them to help the stricken,' reported Daras (1983: 149). The attitudes of clergy and clients could thus differ severely. What was offered as an exorcism or a benediction could easily be taken as an unwitching, according to the historian Willem Frijhoff (1991: 168), himself a former priest. At a theoretical level, however, this subtle divergence evaporates. The transition between the

Roman-Catholic rite, the pontifical exorcism, the exorcisms from the prayer book and the extracanonical exorcisms (unwitchments) of the magicians can also be seen as seamless (de Martino, 1963: 145).

Lay unwitchers, in their turn, based a considerable part of their authority and legitimation on the bible (Kruse, 1951: 61). A cunning woman from Schleswig expressed it as follows: 'Since there have been witches and devils in former times, why should there be none today? It is God's command to fight them! Or should I become unfaithful to God?' And a witch-doctor from near Kiel argued: 'Christ exorcised the evil powers. Why should I not do it?' (Kruse, 1951: 39–40). The 'drive to act as a missionary,' Bartholdy observed, is linked to 'a strongly developed ambition for recognition and power' (1969: 42). Magical healers 'possess a very strong personality that confers a certain charisma on them, which they do not deny themselves using' (Camus, 1988: 46). This constituted the essence of the unwitcher: he had to be more powerful than the witch and in a sense also dominated the bewitched, who not only needed to follow his directives to the letter (otherwise risking failure) but were also obliged 'to tell it all' (cf. Favret-Saada, 1980: 93).

The unwitchers' power was mediated through the tales that were told about them and through their actions. Even their gender contributed to their power, as the men among them were supposed to be more powerful than their female colleagues; they had 'stronger blood' (Camus, 1988: 29). A considerable number of the tales concerned the origin of the unwitcher's might. Uncle Giuseppe, a Lucanian cunning man, was said to have bought his spells from the devil at a cemetry (de Martino, 1963: 98). The power of Croatian and Norwegian cunning women was allegedly given to them by fairies (Bošković-Stulli, 1992: 146; Mathisen, 1993: 23–4). Elsewhere unwitchers obtained their power through inheritance or vocation, from books or from teachers. As was apparent in the case of Eberling, several of these aetiological motifs could be related in combination. In a few instances we are even presented with only the stories, without any reference to the social existence of the protagonists. Today's *táltos* or *garabonciás* (the Hungarian equivalents of cunning men) are merely 'the heroes of legends', reports Dömötör (1982: 133; also Pócs, 1989a: 253). Thus the weather wizard she interviewed in 1968 and who related many details about his art was a 'normal member' of his village society (Dömötör, 1972: 381–4). These reports are nevertheless inconclusive, as Eastern European folklorists have been more interested in 'belief-systems', and in the content of the tales or the form of a custom, than in how they were situated and embedded in temporal social networks. The Croatian and Serbian *krsnik* had no meaning without his opposite witch (Bošković-Stulli, 1960: 278), yet we are told little about his role as 'witch-doctor, healer and magician' (1960: 291).

The unwitchers' actions were meant to impress both their clients and the witches. At times, they resorted to cheating and even exercised sexual power (Kruse, 1951: 64–5; de Martino, 1963:97; Favret-Saada, 1980: 31–38; Daras, 1983: 159). To overcome the witches' evil influences they engaged them in magical combat, which also showed on the physical level. As Favret-Saada depicted the 'woman from Izé': 'Her courage and willpower are clear: she is repeatedly shaken by spasms, has sleepless nights' (1980: 159). 'I delivered a woman from an evil charm and I fell ill,' a Galician unwitcher said (Lisón Tolosana, 1994: 260). Eberling referred to the 'inner strength' he needed (also in Schäfer, 1959: 113). We have also encountered a similar trait in the descriptions of Belgium clergymen, bathing in their sweat, although some of the monks themselves attributed it to the heavy habits they wore or to the physical work they had performed just before attending to their visitors (Daras, 1983: 153). Other unwitchers only provided their clients with medicines or advice, aimed more at changing their behaviour than at subduing the witch's power. An Andalusian wise woman, for instance, after diagnosing a bewitchment, made her patient lie prone on the floor, after which she pressed 'his temples roughly with calloused fingers, rubbing in more oil, while imploring the Holy Spirit three times to intercede'. The man was told to keep out of sight of his neighbour and not to show his wealth, so as not to arouse jealousy (Gilmore, 1987: 168).

A part of the unwitcher's authority stemmed from the ambivalence that sometimes surrounded him. This led to the perception that he could cast spells as well as counteract them. Some even used intimidation to develop this aspect of their image (Schöck, 1978: 145). This ambivalence was widespread. Even the clergy were said to be 'skilled in matters of salvation, but also in matters of damnation' (Mathisen, 1993: 21; cf. Juliard, 1994: 281; Rockwell, 1978: 89), as we have also seen in the Belgium legends. In Greece, 'the priest's curse may bring much harm and grief to the villagers' (Dionisopoulos-Mass, 1976: 55). Scandinavian cunning men were able to bewitch as well as to cure (Tillhagen, 1969: 134). 'Many of the wizards of the Hungarian countryside were equally at home in both white and black magic,' reported Dömötör, 'and it is fequently very difficult to determine who is the positive worker of a cure' (1982: 129). 'The same old woman,' according to a Portuguese anthropologist writing about cunning women, 'will be seen by some as virtuous and by others as wicked' (Cutileiro, 1971: 273). Occasionally, an unwitcher was even asked (by a different client) to undo his own spell (de Martino, 1963: 80; Lorint and Bernabé, 1977: 64). But this did not immediately turn every unwitcher into a witch, or imply that every accused (ascribed) witch was a practitioner of magic. In the French Bocage a distinction was made between unwitchers 'for good' and 'for evil', between those who could stop a spell and those who could return its evil influences upon the original sender. Those who were imputed as witches stood apart from these experts. Witch and unwitcher might resemble each other, but they were not equivalent (Favret-Saada and Contreras, 1981: 110). They were also socially distinct: whereas the witch was mostly a neighbour, the unwitcher usually turned out to be an outsider.

As with witchcraft legends in general, tales told about unwitchers need to be related to the position their tellers occupied within the witchcraft triangle (or outside it in the case of interested skeptics) and to their social standing to be accurately interpreted. Stories about the unwitchers' evil deeds could, after all, have been circulated by their competitors (Schäfer, 1955: 45). Alternatively, they could be more generally dependent on their proponent's place 'in the changing network of friendships and enmities that underlies village life' (Cutileiro, 1971: 273). In the final analysis, the unwitchers' range of power was determined by the opinions and deeds of their clients, rather than the other way around (Schöck, 1978: 153; de Blécourt, 1990: 257).

ACTIVE BEWITCHMENTS

Since unwitching was clearly practised (though not always discernibly so), would there not also be rituals of bewitchment? Favret-Saada repeatedly argued against the notion of active witches. 'Witches,' she wrote, 'never recognize themselves as such' (1980: 125): 'No one has ever seen a witch in action'. As far as she was aware 'there are no witches actually performing the bewitchment rituals attributed to them, or,' (she added with the ethnographer's caution) 'they are extremely rare', being performed by 'an eccentric unwitcher', for instance (Favret-Saada, 1980: 135; see also Schöck, 1978: 129). Dömötör contradicted this, although there was never any actual debate about it. Discussing image magic, defined as 'the preparation of an image of the intended victim, followed by its destruction', the Hungarian folklorist remarked: 'Of course it is performed in secret, and hence we seldom find such images in the museums' (1982: 161). 'I have no doubt at all as to the existence in Galicia of concrete maleficent practices,' the Spanish anthropologist Carmelo Lisón Tolosana admitted (1994: 276). His colleague Richard Jenkins made a similar remark about Ireland (1977: 39). Yet in 30 years of dealing with witches, Kruse never encountered a woman who was accused of witchcraft and had really tried to practise it (1951: 195; cf. Sebald, 1986: 274). Someone accused of witchcraft, concluded Favret-Saada, was nearly always 'totally innocent' (1980: 161). Conversely, people who secretly performed bewitchment rituals may not, it seems, have been accused of it.

The denials indicate that practised witchcraft has not only been an issue, but also that it exists. People could intimidate one another with bewitchments (Schäfer mentions a case in which a woman threatened to bewitch a man in order to regain the money she had lent him, whereupon he killed her; 1955: 59) and they might easily go further. As in the case of Satanic rituals, stories may have been the basis for actions, a process folklorists have termed ostention. Part of the reports on practised witchcraft may still refer to ascriptions, however. Material objects, like the clusters of feathers found in the beds of the bewitched in Germany, the Netherlands and the Basque country (Caro Baroja, 1965: 235) served to mobilize witchcraft beliefs, as they were taken as evidence of bewitchments. No one, of course, ever caught a witch producing them, not even magically. But the range was much wider. As every object could be invested with nefarious power, it was best not to exchange anything with witches (Kruse, 1951: 42). Roumanian peasants refrained from taking objects they found, as there was always a chance that they were unclean and caused bad luck (Lorint and Bernabé, 1977: 108). In themselves, 'bewitching' objects only point to a notion of the practising witch; they do not show the practice itself. They are defined by the bewitched and are not related to the intentions or the premeditations of the witch.

This subtle difference pertains equally to books of spells. Although many witches are said to possess them, their presence is sometimes elusive. Daras for one, never managed to trace a copy of the *Double Ambrosius* frequently referred to by his informants (1983: 161). Kruse only heard about a fictitious black book which had the spells printed in it in white (Baumhauer, 1984: 233) and Favret-Saada was told about grimoires with the inscription on the bottom of each page: '*Turn the page if you dare, or if you understand*'. She herself did not see such a book, nor had the bewitched who relayed the information to her (1980: 134). In contrast, one of the Dutch legend collectors never even started to look for the *Seventh Book of Moses* at all, since he was convinced that it was only a fantasy (de Blécourt, 1990: 223). Books of Moses are in fact widely distributed, as are their French equivalents, such as *Le Dragon Rouge* or the big and little *Alberts*. But their fame has exceeded their occurrence: suspicion of their possession can suffice to make someone into a witch (Schöck, 1978: 102). On one occasion, ownership of a copy of the *Book of St. Cyprian* was denied, for admitting it 'would automatically imply (. . .) the intention of using it' (De Pina-Cabral, 1986: 178). Apart from northern Portugal this book has also been found in Denmark where it figures in tales about compulsive reading (Rockwell, 1978: 91; cf. Henningsen, 1982: 131). In Greece, the possession of texts with spells has been said to cause madness (du Boulay, 1974: 67). The meaning attached to these books can be of more importance than their actual content (Hauschild, 1980: 143, 1981: 543; cf.

Gaboriau, 1987: 130–3). The professional witches (or 'excentric unwitchers') interrogated by Camus certainly acquired their spells and rituals from written tradition. For them books of spells were only a means and it depended on the witches' power, on their 'gift', whether the prescriptions would work (Camus, 1988: 57).

One of the other Hungarian folklorists, Éva Pócs, has made a special study of magic knots. In it, she concluded that for her informants the distinction between 'active and passive ligatures' (i.e. between performed and ascribed bewitchments) was irrelevant (1967: 109). As far as the people she questioned can be classed as the bewitched, the observation carries weight. For the witch, however, the distinction would have been vital. Objects, whether photographs, puppets, knots or books, stand out in any argument about active bewitchments, precisely because they tie the witch to the bewitched and because they are 'destined to create a link between the sorcerer and his victim' (Camus, 1988: 100). To be recognized as an acting witch, one has to make magic. (As will become apparent in the next section, the material creation of bewitchments is also defined in opposition to the evil eye, which can be involuntary). In Latin languages this is articulated as *feitiço* (Portugese), *feitizo* (Spanish), *fattura* (Italian) or *făcătură* (Roumanian): something that is made and will contiunue to make. It includes the enchantment, its effects and the object enchanted (Guggino, 1994: 640; cf. Appel, 1976: 17) – in short, a fetish.

The most prominent kind of active bewitchment is love magic (see D1355 and D1900 in the motif indexes). It is occasionally found in Northern Europe (Tillhagen, 1969: 136) and in Germany (Hauschild 1980: 150). In 1952 a court in Kiel dealt with a woman who thought she could make her husband return to her by administering him two drops of her menstrual blood in a cup of milk (Schäfer, 1959: 106; Bartholdy, 1969: 38). But most reports stem from southern and eastern areas. As something to perform, texts about love magic often take the form of a recipe: To bind a man, you need nine nuts, his belt, a woollen thread as long as his waist, a key and a bolt. His sperm should be put into the nuts and everything should be tied into a white handkerchief and be hidden somewhere, while a binding charm is recited (Lorint and Bernabé, 1977: 104–5). A Hungarian fetish is made from nine knots and tied into a thread from a man's dirty underpants (Pócs, 1967: 85). 'When a woman wants to seduce a man, or seeks revenge on him, or just wants to hurt him, she urinates before his door, or she gives him a cup of coffee or a liqueur with some drops of her menstrual blood mixed in it,' says a statement from Galicia (Lisón Tolosana, 1994: 144). A woman can also mix some drops of menstrual blood with the ashes of her pubic hair and the hairs from her armpit. She should turn this into a powder and take it to church, then pronounce the following charm during the substantiation: 'Blood of

Christ, Demon, tie me to him, you have to tie him to me, so he will not forget me' (de Martino, 1963: 24). Of course, the rag doll makes its appearance as well (Bouteiller, 1958: 106), for example in a spell to get rid of rivals in love, according to which the doll should be buried in an 'impure spot', sometimes pierced with a needle (Lorint and Bernabé, 1977: 116), or put on a train to make the enchanted person go away (Andreesco-Miereanu, 1982: 255). Love magic is not always clearly distinct from magical murder (D 2061). In Greece, a midwife cited a case 'in which a sorcerer tried to kill four people by burying their pictures in the graveyard after piercing the portraits' eyes with needles and writing curses on the paper' (Blum and Blum, 1965: 150). While magic potions have to be consumed, the way for other fetishes to operate is for them to be hidden out of reach of the bewitched, not only in impure spots, but also, for instance, in a buried coffin (Risso and Böker, 1964: 18). These instances of the material aspects of practised witchcraft make it tangible. They are also very anecdotal and verging on the sensational, without revealing much of their rareness or popularity. At this stage, analysis is therefore only possible on a general symbolic level.

The general principles of the workings of magic have been known since Frazer formulated them at the end of the nineteenth century. What has been in physical contact with someone is still connected with that person and can hence be used as a channel to influence him (contagious magic). Like produces or substitutes like (homoeopathic or imitative magic). To this may be added a third principle, namely, that a part refers to the whole (synechdotal magic). Thus a lock and a bolt represent the closing off of a man's affections for other women (at least in the above context). A knot (or a nut) tied into a thread of a man's underpants ties him. A photograph pierced causes pain to the one depicted. The above examples, however, also point to more specific rules. Love magic is used primarily by (or attributed to) women. 'Love potions (. . .) are used extensively by young unmarried women and married women alike, both to win the love of young men and to preserve that of their husbands' (de Pina-Cabral, 1986: 178). Men only seldom resort to it (Risso and Böker, 1964: 21). Most of the men involved in the practice of maleficent magic seem to be professionals (sometimes called sorcerers). But only women use parts of their own body. This concerns not just any bodily refuse such as skin, hairs or nails, but pieces from private parts and a substance only women can produce. In love magic the part not only refers to the whole, but also to the specific role that the witch hopes her victim will fulfil. Although the blood and the hair symbolize sexuality, they rather add to its power than substitute for it. The menstrual blood also has to be drunk by the intended lover (or husband), presumably unwittingly. In this way the woman's body and her sexuality are incorporated into the man's on a intuitive level. Other fetishes, on the other hand, are not meant for consumption and have to be kept away from the victim as far as possible. Made from bodily waste or pieces of clothing from the bewitched, they work at a distance from both witch and bewitched. They are not so much binding as manipulating or dominating. They can even destroy and are used by women as well as by men. The dividing line, it turns out, does not run between love magic and death magic, but between fetishes hidden within the victims body and those hidden outside it. The question remains whether, apart from gender, these symbolic differences correspond to other social differences within the societies of the people involved.

At this point it may be possible to attempt an explanation of the Naples case cited at the beginning of this essay. The old woman was probably a cunning woman, caught in performing love magic, the lamb's head functioning as a *fattura*. The nails can only point to nailing, but the 'kind of steel comb', since it is not very accurately described, remains unclear to me. My guess is that the contraption was aimed at binding a female client, represented by her hair, to a young, sexually innocent man (the lamb). The number of nails could have reflected the client's age. But I will gladly exchange this interpretation for a more locally informed one.

The material components of active bewitchments may have been more durable and thus better noticeable, but the charms and prayers sometimes pronounced also filled an object with magical power. Apart from that, cursing is a way of acting like a witch. 'One "casts" a malediction, just as one casts a spell' (Lorint and Bernabé, 1977: 109). Wishes work just as well. For example, a French medium was convinced that her wish had released the evil forces that had killed a motorist (Camus, 1988: 45).

THE EVIL EYE

Within the witchcraft discourse harmful powers are thought to emanate from the witch in several ways. In Scandinavia evil eye, evil intent, evil tongue, evil hand and evil foot have all been distinguished (Tillhagen, 1969: 139; Alver, 1989: 118). In Germany, Belgium and the Netherlands terms are to be found for the evil eye and the evil hand (Wittmann, 1933: 58–59), although sometimes more as a synonym for bewitchments than immediately referring to a form of transmission of evil influences. The terms nevertheless do indicate the specific kinds of bodily language the witchcraft discourse also includes, for the acts of looking, touching and speaking are central to it, even without being named specifically (Bouteiller, 1958: 89–93). They provide a focal point in the process of attribution; the bewitched take specific words, behaviour, or a mere glance as the defining moment of a bewitchment. Once someone is identified as the perpetrator, then all her subsequent comings and goings only reinforce the suspicion (Schöck, 1978: 114). And to prevent further trouble all contact between bewitched and witch, whether by eye, touch or speech, has to be avoided (Favret-Saada, 1980: 111–7).

Probably for reasons of differences in proxemics, bodily bewitching faculties become fewer the more southerly one gets; in southern countries only the evil eye seems to have survived, although concepts akin to the evil tongue occur in Greece (Dionisopoulos-Mass, 1976: 53; Stewart, 1991: 233) and Portugal (Cole, 1991: 114). (The corresponding motifs for the evil eye are D2071, D2064.4 and G265.11* 'person or animal admired by witch becomes ill', which once again underlines the peculiar logic of the indexes). This section will be devoted to the evil eye, mainly because some authors distinguish it from witchcraft. Garrison and Arensberg, for instance, situate the evil eye in 'complex societies having superordinate authorities' and witchcraft in 'less complex societies' (1976: 322; cf. Galt, 1982: 665–8). The evil eye discourse is seen as a 'closed symbolic system' (Hauschild, 1982: 91–2), or as 'a fairly consistent and uniform folk belief complex' (Dundes, 1992: 258). It is even considered as a special species within the family of superstitions, analogous to plants (Vuorela, 1967: 9–10). Moreover, the evil eye has attracted its own body of literature and an attempt has been undertaken to devise an outline for an 'exhaustive description' of it (Lykiardopoulos, 1981: 229). It has a different, seemingly autonomous history attached to it, going back to Old Testament and classical times while skipping the witch trials (Dundes, 1992: 259–62; cf. Hauschild, 1982: 20–1). Within the context of European witchcraft, however, the isolation and reification of the evil eye is untenable, a result of an outsider's approach (cf. Jenkins, 1977: 36). It will thus be no surprise that most publications about the evil eye are only descriptive and superficial. They 'consist soley of anecdotal reportings of various incidents' (Dundes, 1992: 262). Disdain is present also; as a reporter noted in 1923: 'there seems nothing more of scientific value in these spells. The words are generally a pattern of mere nonsense' (Hardie, 1992: 122). Those who believe in the evil eye are 'persons in whom suggestibility is irresistible'. They are 'uneducated' and possess an 'unscientific mind' (Zammit-Maempel, 1968: 1, 6).

If I present Greek discourse on the evil eye as an example here, it is with a certain feeling of caution, as this may evoke the same kinds of problem that we encountered in the descriptions of bewitchments and unwitchments in West-European regional folklore publications. On the one hand, texts are not localized and situated as to participants, gender or belief. On the other, the evil eye concerns only one way of bewitchment, and descriptions consist of 'overlapping images formed from a common repository of cultural representations' (Stewart, 1991: 237). In Greece, the suggestion of the evil eye can be made 'if a person feels listless, exhausted, or has a persistent headache or fever. The special symptoms of the evil eye can vary from person to person' (Stewart, 1991: 232). A cunning woman explained it as follows: 'The effects of the evil eye become "knots" and they move far inside you. When you are first bewitched you have the headache; later your bones are affected and they hurt; then your heart becomes involved, and you may have diarrhoea and vomiting. Your stomach becomes like a ball of thread, (Blum and Blum, 1965: 185). To counteract or prevent the evil eye an enormous amount of amulets are on hand. New mothers, who with their young children are especially prone to catch the eye, have 'a variety of prophylactics under their pillow or on their head, such as a red string, incense, bread, salt, garlic, indigo blue, a nail, gunpowder, a black and white thread, a ring, a pair of silver buckles' (Hardie, 1992: 110). Prayers or spells are also abundantly present. A fairly common ritual of detection is to drop oil in a cup of water. If it disappears the illness in question is a result of the evil eye; if it stays afloat in the water there is no evil eye involved. Next the water can be drunk or used to sprinkle the victim with (Blum and Blum, 1965: 68). The boundaries between diagnosis and cure are blurred. 'If during diagnosis it is deter-mined that the person was afflicted by the eye, he is instantly cured, the evil being dissolved' (Dionisopoulos–Mass, 1976: 45); the cure follows naturally from the diagnosis (Herzfeld, 1986: 110; Stewart, 1991: 234). It does not usually involve the witch herself.

What seems to distinguish the evil eye concept from other kinds of witchcraft is its 'random pervasiveness' (Gilmore, 1987: 169). Anyone can have it, whether voluntarily or involuntarily (Hardie, 1992: 109), although women and especially menstruating women (Campbell, 1964: 390; Stew-art, 1991: 233) are often singled out. The evil eye has been considered as 'a form of witchcraft in which the bewitching person may not be aware of his own power and may have no evil intent' (Blum and Blum, 1965: 124). For this a simple remedy is available. 'If the admirer himself is conscious of his power and wants to forestall it in some situation where he genuinely wishes no harm, he will perform a ritual of riddance upon himself, spitting and publicly imputing the worthlessness of that which he admires in order to protect it from the spell he might otherwise cast upon it' (Blum and Blum, 1965: 40; cf. 186). Other authors report the same (Campbell, 1964: 338; Lykiardopoulos, 1981: 226), but the prescriptive forms of these reports (Stewart, 1991: 233 has 'one must spit') makes them seem detached from social practice.

The Greek evil eye discourse is probably internally differentiated, according to gender, genre and narrative mode, to different social or age groups, and to region. It is hardly possible to make these distinctions on the basis of the 'sketchy and sporadic' data provided (Herzfeld, 1981: 562), since they are not related to the tellers. Something of the possible differences is noticeable in the tales of the cunning women quoted above whose 'concepts of the evil eye and its treatment are much more elaborate than those of the other villagers' (Blum and Blum, 1965: 187). Situating the discourse becomes the more urgent if we are to judge its social aspects. The notion of the unintentional witch, for example, is dependent on the position of the speaker within the witchcraft triangle; it can only be uttered by the bewitched or the unwitcher. Yet this is hardly commented upon in the literature (the notion may have derived from religious teaching). The witch herself remains obscure, and the unwitching rituals seem to confirm this. Only in a few instances have I found rites of identification. Names of suspected witches are written on a piece of wood carbon and these are dropped into water one by one. If the carbon sinks, the person whose name it carries is presumed guilty (Campbell, 1964: 339). The other method involves burning cloves. When they split open, this is considered a positive answer to a question about the afflictor's identity (Dionisopoulos–Mass, 1976: 47). Bearers of the evil eye are designated, but apparently not always to the researchers. 'The most difficult information to glean is that concerning those who can give (. . .) the evil eye,' reported a British army-man from Athens (Gubbins, 1946: 197). In another case the cunning woman 'was unwilling to tell us who in the village has the evil eye' (Blum and Blum, 1965: 186). This may be more generally the case in the Mediterranean countries. 'We don't believe in witches,' a woman in San Sebastian told anthropologist William Christian. 'And if we do, we don't talk about them'. It is considered sinful (1972: 194, 192). His German colleague Thomas Hauschild noticed a similar reluctance in the literature on the South-Italian evil eye (1982: 96). People who were willing to talk apparently did not tell everything and most of the researchers were satisfied with what they got. This dearth of research is concealed by the remarks about the evil eye's autonomy and yet there has been no lack of speculations and explanations.

Undoubtedly the most sophisticated explanation of the evil eye has been put forward by the Californian folklorist Alan Dundes. In order to understand the evil eye complex in its totality, that is, to solve the problem of why the evil eye manifests itself 'precisely in the form that it does' and 'to account for most, if not all of the elements in the complex, including the manifestly male and female components' (Dundes, 1992: 265), he constructed a set of four 'theoretical underlying principles'. Abbreviated, they are as follows: (1) Life depends on bodily fluids, of which (2) there is only a limited amount. (3) These fluids should be equally divided among members of a community. (4) Eyes are symbolically equivalent to live-giving, liquid-producing organs (1992: 266–7). In Dundes' interpretation the evil eye symbolizes the lack of fluids; its 'most common effect' is 'a *drying up* process'. It is envy 'expressed in liquid terms'. 'The have-nots envy the haves and desire their various liquids.' Dundes exemplifies: 'Whether it is the dead who envy the living (. . .), the old who envy the young, or the barren who envy those with children, it is the blood, sap or vitality of youth, the maternal milk, or masculine semen that is coveted' (1992: 274). This explains, among other things, why spitting mitigates praise (1992: 276) and why menstruating women are so much feared. 'Clearly, a woman who was losing blood, a life fluid, would represent a threat to the life fluids possessed by others (potential victims of the evil eye). According to a limited-good worldview, the loss of menstrual blood would require making up the liquid deficit – at someone else's expense' (1992: 285).

Despite the attractiveness of Dundes' theory, it may need revisions in several places. The theory of the limited good, for one, presupposes a closed society and ignores the more complex relations of interdependence current in Europe (cf. Hauschild, 1982: 67; Alver and Selberg, 1988: 29–30). Rather than an egalitarian society, it is probably more an 'egalitarian ideology' (de Pina-Cabral, 1986: 186) within a stratified society, that prompts ill feelings. Dundes could also have been more forthcoming on the symbolic articulation of the gender relations within the complex, as the penis usually plays the part of the good eye by protecting against female evil (Hauschild, 1982: 117; de Pina-Cabral, 1986: 181; Lisón Tolosana, 1994: 142–3). The myopic folklore accounts on which Dundes built most of his argument were produced for certain reasons. The evil eye was easy to research because of the tangibility of its counter charms. 'On markets in Italy today,' wrote Dömötör, 'it is still possible to buy amulets designed to offer protection against the evil eye' (1982: 171). This material component promoted collecting and interpreting. Listening to the people involved was only necessary to some extent; it could also be confusing. Maltese farmers, for instance, were reported to have smiled when asked about the meaning of the cattle horns which adorned their abodes, 'though inwardly full of fear of the dreaded "eye",' they 'evaded the question by saying that the horns on their farm had been set up by their ancestors' (Zammit-Maempel, 1968: 8). Another man 'stated that his intention was to show his great love for cattle and to indicate that he reared cattle in that place' (1968: 4). To publish on the evil eye was thus to stress the social and cultural distance between researcher and researched (Argyrou, 1993: 256–9). It provided an excuse to dabble with the exotic and to play with phalli.

There is little in the descriptions of the evil eye that justifies its separation from witchcraft in general. On a practical level bewitchments and the casting of the evil eye cannot but be treated as synonymous, as is shown, for example, by Vuorela's (1967) endless enumerations of Finnish motifs. Although Dundes mentions witchcraft only once, he does so in a comparative sense, observing that 'accusations of possessing the evil eye give social sanction to ostracizing an individual, often transforming him into a pariah' (Dundes, 1992: 294). More probing research should, in addition, recognize the evil eye and fetishes as the two main categories of bewitchments (De Martino, 1963: 81; Risso and Böker, 1964: 17; cf. Dionisopoulos-Mass, 1976) and the defining link between them. This requires anthropological training to supplement folkloristic curiosity.

MAYENNE, 1970

Anthropologists produce their own sources by writing fieldwork diaries. Most of the time they keep these notes to themselves and only present their readers with highly edited selections so as to illustrate their overall argument. Because anthropologists focus on a particular village, witchcraft is usually not one of their main preoccupations. The French anthropologist Jeanne Favret-Saada was one of the few to study witchcraft almost exclusively. From July 1969 to September 1971 she lived in 'Saint-Auvieux', a village in the Bocage (hedge country) of Mayenne. In 1972 she spent eight months there and in the following years another two or three months a year, until 1975 (1980: 31). During the first period, she produced 2,600 typed pages of field notes. These she edited and partly published, with the help of the therapist Josée Contreras (Favret-Saada and Contreras, 1981). Among other things they reveal the chain of events that turned her from an outside researcher into an insider by initiating her in the witchcraft triangle. This story she only hinted at in her witchcraft monograph and her English publications although it constitutes her most important contribution to witchcraft research. 'My progression through witchcraft had taken a distinct turn,' she wrote in her book, 'ever since an old bewitched man, père Séquard, had acted as my annunciator and had brought me to his unwitcher, Madame Flora' (Favret-Saada, 1980: 175; her names are also pseudonyms).

In early January 1970 Favret (as she was called then) first heard about the village of Pouancé. Brice Houdemont, one of the doctors she spoke to (she started her research by interrogating doctors and priests), had been told by his mother that people there had called in an unwitcher. The man had 'predicted that, when he put his hand on the house of the witch, all the lights would go on inside. And really . . .' (Favret-Saada and Contreras, 1981: 98; cf. 200). A month later the doctor mentioned the case again. He suggested that they visit his parents. His mother, Madame Houdemont, turned out to be an especially key informant. She took care of Favret and brought her into contact with some of the bewitched and with clairvoyants operating in the region. Then, during the first weeks of spring, the story slowly unfolded. It had several layers and it remained incomplete because a number of the people involved did not want to discuss it (and the researcher did not pursue all its aspects). The more people she spoke to, the more complicated the story became. There was, for instance, a political interpretation which served as a public justification. According to the doctor, Pouancé was divided in two factions of 'eighteen (male) witches who declared themselves as such, [and] eighteen bewitched and their unwitchers.' The troubles had started after the bewitched had won the last municipal elections, four years previous (1981: 158). One of the 'witches', who had taken one of the bewitched to court for slander, explained it in the same fashion.

'It's all political, the whole story. It's politics, from A to Z!' Arnoult considers the 'so-called victims' as mad, as evil doers who treat anybody as a witch. They even accused the chemist, pour old thing, and as a consequence he suffers from depression. He withdrew from the committee for the celebrations. 'That doesn't exist, it's false and idiotic!' (1981: 209–10).

Yet the local butcher disagreed. The bewitched were divided among themselves. 'It's not a story about rivalry between business men, everybody has lost clients, people are frightened to have to choose between the two camps and they shop at Mortain' (1981: 218). Also père Houdemont contradicted his son. People never called themselves witches. 'How do you want them to say it, . . . these people, they never admit it!' The police had held an inquest. 'The bewitched spoke, but only they' (1981: 176).

The court cases had been started by a farmer who had lost 95 fat pigs through bewitchment and had made a complaint about toxication. The Houdemonts already mentioned him several times in early March (1981: 176, 177) and a month later the butcher added a picture of a man who was upset so much 'that he was roaming the whole night around his land, armed with a gun' (1981: 219). 'I am the municipal councillor,' the butcher explained, 'therefore, obviously, they speak to me. I don't say anything. I don't talk about other people's affairs! All you have to do is to ask Jules Séquard, he will speak, it happened to him' (1981: 218). Thereupon Madame Houdemont suggested that they pay Séquard a visit, since 'they are friends' (1981: 220). She filled Favret in on the farmer's background. 'He used to castrate bulls, like his father, and he was a butcher, like his father-in-law. About five years ago he left it all, he bought a farm on which he works alone. You will see, this is a man of character' (1981: 230). But the first visit turned into a failure:

A little fat man, quick tempered. His right hand is paralysed. He apologizes slightly. He complains that he has to do everything, his farmhands are drunkards. (. . .) 'What is it about?' I don't tell it again, he knows it. Prone to quarrelling: 'Your professional identity card!' I don't have it. 'Then I won't say anything to you, even if you have come with Madame Houdemont!' I propose to show him my papers the next time, he agrees to see me on Thursday morning. Madame Houdemont tries to appease him, talks about things, tells about certain cows that have aborted. In all innocence, I ask if it concerns brucellose. Séquard: 'Ah, you're very well informed.' In covered terms, he relates the illness of his own cows – I ignore it. He answers roughly: 'I don't talk anymore, first your papers!' I am looking up at him and I smile. He threatens: 'Don't try to cut corners!' I have understood. He sees in me a representative of the 'administration', the rubbish bin where he puts all the cops, the judges, the tax agents and the employees of the agrarian Bank. His life seems to be a perpetual act of defiance against the 'administration' (1981: 231–2).

Six days later Séquard was quite willing to speak. They discussed his past, his trade and the recent events in Pouancé. The anthropologist let her interlocutor determine the course of the conversation. Her questions provided him mainly with room for his elaborations. Talking about his recent troubles, he mentioned that a card layer, a certain woman from Taron, had predicted that people would try to trap him. 'She is very strong, she uses all the decks', he declared. 'But it is impossible to just visit her, you need an intercessor'. Séquard then embarked upon his 'famous' yarn about the 95 fat pigs. First 10 died, then 3 more, then 13, 25 and five. When he finally thought he had found the cause he bought 40 new pigs. Again there was a catastrophe. They all died at the same time. 'I did all that was necessary, I didn't make any mistake and I lost 95 pigs altogether. That's seven million!' 'Thus there was someone who poisoned the animals?' Favret asked. 'No,' answered the farmer, 'it's witchcraft' (1981: 241).

> I didn't believe in it at all before I was caught. Even in the obvious case, I didn't believe in it at all. I knew well peasants, who when their animals died said, 'O God, they are bewitched!' The first time, the farmers heard something in their barn: pans, empty tins, a damned sabbat! Then one day, they didn't speak about it. I asked why, they said to me: 'Well, the priest has come . . .' But I didn't believe it.

He explained that he himself had cured animals since he was 10. As long as his cures worked he did not consider witchcraft an option. But in the recent case unbelievable things had happened. He had produced a terrible stench that was only detectable to himself and his family. His friends had not smelled anything. 'Did he understand himself that he was bewitched?' Favret asked. 'No, it was a farmer who told me that, an old client of mine who also had misfortunes' (1981: 242). At first, he was even suspected himself. As a castrator, he possessed medical books, which sufficed to surround him with the aura of witchcraft. Bit by bit, he convinced his fellow villagers that he himself was the victim. After all, he had lost 95 fat pigs. The woman from Taron, to whom he was brought by his annunciator, gave him holy water and a formula. These cured his animals where the vaccinations of the veterinarian had failed. When the story was finished the Séquards asked Favret how she coped with her work. 'Badly,' she replied.

> 'Well, one can see that it shakes you . . . when you were told about the pigs, your hands were shaking!" They find that I look haggard, they suppose that I suffer from insomnia, and then all those car accidents, 'that's not normal'. He, determinedly: 'You cannot go on like this! You'll have to go to the woman of Taron' (1981: 244).

By implying that the anthropologist was bewitched herself, Séquard reversed the roles of interviewer and interviewee. It also appeared that words did not convey everything. Verbal communication, Favret-Saada reflected later, 'constitutes one of the poorest varieties of human communication'. Involuntary communications which carried the 'affective intensity' of the moment were much more central to the anthropologist's experience (1990: 195). This obviously also occurred during her consultation with madame Flora, the woman from Taron. In the descriptions, the researcher's aversion stands out. 'I have to force myself to write down this consultation, with the greatest reluctance,' runs the beginning of her entry about her first visit to her unwitcher (Favret-Saada and Contreras, 1981: 259). Everything conspired to keep her from reaching the fortune-teller: she had a car accident, problems with the directions, and a lack of sleep. Reporting the event in her diary took several days. 'The consultation had lasted for two and a half hours. The clairvoyant wanted to surprise me either by explaining or by asking questions at the speed of a submachine gun,' Favret wrote. 'Certain themes came up so frequently that I forgot when she had said what. Her interpretations – and she has given me at least 300 of them – changed considerably from one to another: an adjective, an intonation' (1981: 261). Only after three days could the researcher bring herself to note down the parts about her own bewitchment.

> At the beginning, madame Flora has 'seen' that I do my job passionately, that I see the obstacles – among others my husband – but that I

overcome them cheerfully enough. 'If you want to get at something, you'll really get it!' Very quickly the bad cards began to pour down: 'But there is an obstacle . . . something worries you . . . frightens you . . . very much!' (Among others, to let an unwitcher see my life). Luckily, a joker appeared: 'Complete success in your endeavour'. The next round is devoted to the reasons for my fear. 'Somebody resents you very much, it is linked to your job . . . And at this moment, you're so nervous about it that you must be careful . . ., you must take your life into your own hands my poor lady, otherwise there will be doom' (1981: 268–69).

Favret explained that she worked on witchcraft. The fortuneteller was interested and took out her major tarots. 'You are right to study that, because people are not sufficiently suspicious and one ought to prevent them,' she said. (It was later suggested that madame Flora thought a book would reveal the secrets of her competitors; Favret-Saada, 1980: 175). She offered to inform her client about a court case she was involved in, but Favret declined.

Looking into the great tarots, she suddenly sees the sign of my death, a woman who they pull by their legs. 'That's you! There's someone who wishes you evil . . . They want your skin, you see, a tomb.' Several horrible cards. Madame Flora seems very worried. Her reading of the cards has become even faster, so that one can hardly understand her. She throws at me a whole series of verbs, which describe me as being dead or in great danger. A long moment passes, which I cannot quite remember (Favret-Saada and Contreras, 1981: 270).

The unwitcher next told the researcher that she could take care of it. Did she want to be unwitched? 'Yes,' Favret replied (1981: 270). Thus started a long collaboration between the anthropologist and the fortuneteller. First, however, Favret had to overcome her anxiety, the 'fear which sometimes paralysed me for weeks' (1980: 175). She had to accept that her subjects had turned the tables on her and she had to get used to having her private and social life dissected, among other things in terms of death. 'For the moral of the story is that no one escapes violence: he who does not attack automatically becomes the victim; he who does not kill, dies' (1980: 122). From the safe distance of two decades later, however, Favret-Saada admitted: 'Of course, I never took it to be a true proposition that a witch could harm me by casting spells or pronouncing incantations. But I also doubt that the peasants themselves took it to be so' (1990: 192). Other anthropologists working on Europe have never immersed themselves so deeply in local witchcraft discourses and never reached Favret-

Saada's level of communication and sophistication. But they have looked at witchcraft from a wider perspective.

SPATIAL DIMENSIONS

Actual witchcraft discourse takes place in concrete situations. It is also part of larger contexts: spatial, cultural, social and temporal. Although most of the transmitted witchcraft texts scarcely divulge anything about the specific sequence of the settings in which they are produced (from the original event to the moment of recording), we can at least pay attention to these wider contexts, if only in a fragmentary way. Starting with the geography of witchcraft here, we will in the next sections dwell on the particular cultural categories that inform and shape the discourse, on the social dimension and, finally, on the questions of continuity and change.

The divide between town and countryside stands out as the most striking geographical feature of the discourse. While there is no description of cases from towns (both folklorists and anthropologists have stayed far away from them), researchers are not unanimous about the prevalence of the discourse in the countryside. Schäfer, working from court cases, placed witchcraft accusations exclusively among the inhabitants of the country-side. The interhuman, neighbourly relationships, which determined life in the villages, were, after all, missing from the towns (1959: 67; but cf. Schöck, 1978: 231–2). The German cases of the 1950s all happened in a 'social environment of farmers' (Baumhauer, 1984: 205). Similarly, Favret-Saada's main informants wondered about urban witchcraft; 'they cannot understand on what pretext city-dwellers would mutually bewitch each other, since there is no real contact (. . .) or acquaintanceship' (1980: 81). The German surveys did not register any significant difference between village and city (Schöck, 1978: 158–9), nor did they inquire about concrete accusations. In cities, it has been suggested, a different kind of witchcraft is present. 'If, in the country, one fears the destruction of crops or animals by the evil eye, in the town one fears that the *mal ochio* will cause a son to fail an examination at a professional school or ruin a daughter's chances for a good marriage' (Romanucci-Ross, 1991: 7). Moreover, the urban eye is related to specific people, whereas in the countryside it is more situational, at least in Southern Italy (Hauschild, 1982: 206). According to Camus' informants urban witchcraft is of a more violent kind (1988: 79). Certainly, towns accommodate professional for-tunetellers (Galt, 1982: 673; Hauschild, 1982: 209; cf. Davies, 1997a: 611) who can deal in unwitching and fetishes. Recent Dutch advertisements from Amsterdam, Rotterdam and The Hague, for instance, offer 'protec-tion' and *bewerkingen* (the Dutch equivalent for fetishes, derived from a verb meaning 'to influence' or 'to bring about'). On the whole, this is a highly under-researched area (cf. Röll, 1991; Juliard, 1994: 276–7). It is also an area in which immigrants are active.

Further geographical differentiation concerns the countryside itself. The mapping of motifs was one of the ways in which folklorists hoped to trace prehistoric beliefs and practices. After this academic custom fell into disuse, mapping survived as a method which at least showed the places where some kind of research had been carried out and where it was still lacking. As such it promoted notions of systematic research. In witchcraft studies, however, mapping has hardly resulted in substantial conclusions. It is known, for instance, that within the German-speaking areas weather witches used to be concentrated in the south (Wittmann, 1933: 77–8). Or that the curious custom of unwitching children by blowing water on them has been restricted within Finland to South Karelia and Ingermanland (Vuorela, 1967: 76). But how this is to be explained culturally remains an enigma (Wittmann points to the weather conditions in the mountains). Folklore atlasses only display maps (cf. Lehnert-Leven, 1995: 141) and the accompanying comments merely describe those maps.

Mapping is only a research tool. It requires extensive knowledge about the distribution of other phenomena to be viable. For only in comparison with other maps may hypothetical connections become apparent. Traditions concerning the Hungarian *táltos*, to mention one of the few available instances where mapping has proved helpful, functioned the longest in areas were rinderpest raged (Kovács, 1977: 267). *Táltos* seem to have specialized in unwitching cattle and not adapted to changing circumstances. Another example of the possible advantages of mapping concerns the relation between violent techniques for identifying witches and orthodox calvinism in the Netherlands. Their occupation of the same geographical space has contributed to the argument about the scope for unwitching actions available within calvinist ideology (de Blécourt, 1996: 349–351). The combined distribution of motifs, such as those dealing with fetishes and the evil eye, may equally point to a religious, in this case Catholic, connection. A geographical overview of motifs may also help to provide insights into their distribution and derivation. In all these areas, however, it should be taken into account that the meaning of particular motifs may change in the course of their journeys. As we have already seen, differences can occur with respect to gender or genre and ignoring this can be counterproductive, especially in a search for wider relationships.

Mapping can also reveal spheres of influence of witches and cunning folk. Applied to a well researched area with a high density of unwitchers, such as the east of the Dutch province of Frisia during the decades around 1900, it shows that consultations were not random but followed a pattern (de Blécourt, 1988). It is possible to discern categories of popularity (local, regional and super-regional), as well as geographical delineations within the different categories. People from one particular place either consulted a local witch-doctor or a more famous one farther away. As a rule one did not visit an unwitcher from outside his territory. Corresponding or contrasting patterns may be found in other regions (cf. Schöck, 1978: 133–5). The Rendsburg cunning man Christian Piehl certainly had superregional status, since he received letters from all over Germany (Kruse, 1951: 66; Baumhauer, 1984: 240). The *maghos* of Paphos was visited by Greeks from all over the world (Argyrou, 1993: 260). The inhabitants of Albano in southern Italy, to name one of the other scarce examples, 'consult cunning men and women from other, more or less removed villages such as Tricano, Oppido and Genzano, but the magic life of Albano is dominated by *uncle Giuseppe*' (de Martino, 1963: 79). This points to categories of popularity, but we need to know more, both about unwitchers in other villages and about possible specializations, to arrive at relevant conclusions.

Witches also exercise their influence within specific territories. When several witches are designated in one village (as in Sarzbüttel), they are usually neighbours of the bewitched. In a small community there is probably only one well-known witch, apart from others who are only labelled as such within a small circle (see Schöck, 1978: 234–5; van Eyen, 1989a: 143–4). Alle Tet from Frisian Harkema offers an example of how distance influences the image of the village witch. In the stories told by her neighbours her bewitchments were deadly, whereas in other parts of her village her victims recovered. Outside informants merely related tales about her power, without mentioning bewitchments. 'Witches who live nearby are the most dangerous,' concluded Wytzes (1995: 89). This indicates that space should not only be understood in terms of physical distance (and obstructions), but also as something to which meaning is attached. Thus the letters Piehl showed to Kruse indicated more than just the places where his clients came from. By expressing his power geographically, they signalled the unwitcher's wide reputation.

The notion of meaningful, magical space does not immediately tie every witch to crossroads or graveyards. There are functional distinctions. While active magic may gain in power by being performed in some numinous spot, in warnings addressed to children we find a slightly different demarcation. The threatening witch figure serves to keep youngsters away from orchards, cornfields or 'dangerous or forbidden places' (Widdowson, 1973: 216) in general. In Roumania, she appears as the old woman of the wood, the mother of the trees who can cast the evil eye on you (Andreesco-Miereanu, 1982: 254). But whether a threatening witch with fairy-tale-like appearance turns into an accused witch remains to be seen. Bewitched space does not usually belong to the categories of outside and removed, as in the case of a wood, but to inside and nearby, as in the case of one's property (Favret-Saada, 1980: 127) or one's body being attacked. Protection against bewitchments is secured by having a priest perambulate and sanctify one's land, in hanging blessed objects and amulets at the windows and doors of one's house, or in burying them under the threshold. Unwitchers walk around houses and pay special attention to thresholds and openings (Favret-Saada, 1989: 45). Before starting an unwitching ritual, all doors, windows and keyholes have to be closed off (Kaufmann, 1960: 89). Eberling advised a client to stuff the keyhole with a wad of cotton with three needles stuck into it (Baumhauer, 1984: 262). Witches are supposed to bury toads in front of a house or to hammer steel nails into walls (Favret-Saada, 1980: 135). Knots that supposedly cause impotence are found hidden under the threshold (Pócs, 1967: 114). Legend texts are teeming with similar incidents, yet they have hardly been a thematized issue in the literature. What characterizes the witch is her transgression of boundaries, her intrusion into someone else's domain, not only culturally and socially (Herzfeld, 1981), but also spatially. As the anthropologist Joâo de Pina-Cabral expresses it: 'sanctified space has gaps in it' (1986: 185) and through those gaps witches strike.

CULTURES OF WITCHCRAFT

The articulation and symbolization of social and cultural boundaries by the witchcraft discourse connect it to dominant local value systems, or at least to 'a much wider complex of ideas' (Herzfeld, 1981: 571) in general. Indeed, social norms and values are defined by their limits and when the discourse marks their transgression (to the bewitched bewitching is a criminal activity), it is, in turn, also conditioned by them. Anthropologists working within Europe have denoted different categories that encapsulate witchcraft. Some stress the importance of religion, others pay more attention to notions of honour or envy.

In social evolutionistic thinking magic (and witchcraft) preceded science and religion in time. Even when overt evolutionism was abandoned as discriminatory, it remained hard not to regard magic as a separate category, or even system of behaviour, in opposition to official institutions. But if the Church or the Academy uses discourses that are alien to witchcraft, this does not imply irrational or irreligious believers. We have seen above how unwitchers, Eberling among them, considered themselves devout Christians. 'Juana is insistent upon her orthodoxy and devotion,' anthropologist Julian Pitt-Rivers wrote about an Andalusian wise woman (1971: 191; cf. Argyrou, 1993: 260). Moreover, fetishes were blessed in church and charms made there. In Greece, homemade *phylactos* 'must be kept at a church for forty days and blessed to acquire power' (Dionisoupolos-Mass, 1976: 47). In addition, means of protection and unwitching are fetched from monasteries and many 'therapeutic instruments are objects which form part of orthodox Catholic ceremonial and which refer either to the passion of Christ or to his transubstantiation in the Eucharist' (de Pina-Cabral, 1986: 184). The Greek church has an official spell against the evil eye, mainly to promote ecclesiastical authority (Stewart, 1991: 235). Villagers and local priests are in all likelihood 'unable to tell the difference between Orthodox and supposedly superstitious practices' (1991: 243). Magical words have physical effects because 'the body is made of syllables', according to a Sicilian cunning woman in reference to John 1:1 (Guggino, 1994: 639). Thus, official religion has provided a justification for thinking and acting in terms of witchcraft. As a Greek physician said about his fellow villagers: 'They do, of course, believe in the evil eye. I don't; they do because it is in the Gospel, where St. Paul speaks of it, and the majority think it exists' (Blum and Blum, 1965: 141).

The relationship between witchcraft and religion is probably even more profound than these examples suggest, although there has been little systematic research on the subject, as Schöck has stressed. She found the witchcraft discourse especially vigorous among people with a 'pronounced religious disposition' (1978: 164). Of the Protestants in the Netherlands and adjacent Germany it has been the more orthodox who have adhered to the discourse the longest (Kaufmann, 1960: 84; De Blécourt, 1996). This would indicate that the decisive factor connecting witchcraft discourse to the creed is not adherence to the main Christian denominations, but the degree of religiosity itself. Moreover, different kinds of witchcraft are possibly founded on different kinds of orthodoxy and different creeds allow different reactions to bewitchments. Calvinists have threatened their witches more violently, for instance, while Catholics have shown a greater proclivity towards practising the craft (de Blécourt, 1990: 223).

Envy is one of the other concepts frequently cited as governing witchcraft and more specifically the evil eye. Norwegian ethnographers formulate it as follows: 'The concept of the ability to cast spells has as a precondition a concept of an evil mind, which often may be seen as envy' (Alver and Selberg, 1988: 28; cf. Laplantine, 1978: 106–10; Juliard, 1994: 279–80). 'When a child falls victim to the evil eye,' reports a Portugese anthropologist, 'an immediate review of neighbourly relations takes place: the recent past is scrutinized and manifestations of envy on the part of some neighbour are soon discovered' (Cutileiro, 1971: 275). Envy, however, is not just an emotion. The Portugese *inveja*, 'one of the central concepts of the peasant worldview,' refers not just to envy, but also to 'harm caused by envy'. It is one of the major causes of misfortune (cf.

Herzfeld, 1981: 564) and incorporates a wide range of behaviour, including gossip, sorcery and the evil eye (Cole, 1991: 114). According to De Pina-Cabral *inveja* is 'harmful and is related to awareness of differences in wealth and fortune' (1986: 176). In this sense envy points to social relationships between the individual and community (Gilmore, 1987: 164) and between households. It is a 'metaphor for talking about political relations within the community, especially relations among women' (Cole, 1991: 122; cf. Lisón Tolosana, 1994: 229). Where envy is indicated as the category covering witchcraft, honour is usually not mentioned, and vice versa. The two concepts seem to represent corresponding processes, only approached from a different angle. Honour, and precisely its material aspects, breeds envy (Campbell, 1964: 340).

An accusation of witchcraft is an infringement of the accused's honour and, as in the previously mentioned case of the Holstein labourer whose wife was taken for a witch, of the honour of the family represented by the male head. The South-Italian notion of honour resembles this German instance: the family is considered as an extension of its male master (Hauschild, 1982: 120). In the French Bocage the same principle can be found in the witchcraft discourse, as the head of the family is the target of bewitchments, even if only his wife and children suffer from the consequences, 'since the goods and the people who bear his name are one with him' (Favret-Saada, 1980: 117; 1989: 43). Apparently this is not so in southern Italy, where mainly women are involved in the bewitchment of children and breast milk. Hauschild therefore concluded that the evil eye also involved an inversion of social and psychical reality (1982: 124), that is to say: witchcraft expressed the manipulation of female honour within a patriarchal system. In that way it coincided with envy.

The relation between witchcraft and female honour is illustrated in a Greek (Cypriot) case about a girl who married above her status. As there are two versions of this story, we can use the one to comment on the other. The boy's family, of course, distrusted the union. They said the girl 'took his mind away' (Argyrou, 1993: 263), or that the girl's mother 'must have put a love potion in his food' (Dionisopoulos-Mass, 1976: 58). It did not deter the couple from marrying. Soon afterwards, things went wrong. The groom went into military service and rumours started about his wife's infidelity (1976: 59). In the other version of the story the couple began to quarrel. The girl's reputation was damaged in both versions, because she was considered as either quarrelsome or unfaithful. This provoked reactions. The girl's mother (in the quarrel version) suddenly found an object under the conjugal bed. 'It was a white piece of cloth tied into a knot and covered with hair' (Argyrou, 1993: 261). Since this was a clear sign of bewitchment, the communal gossip shifted from the girl to the boy's mother who was seen as the producer of the fetish. The same shift occurred in the infidelity version, but here the 'evil tongue' was used in retaliation, as it was rumoured that the boy had been impotent (Dioniso-poulos-Mass, 1976: 59). These forms of witchcraft accusations served as attempts to rebalance the social inequality that had started with the 'dishonourable' wedding. They were used as a strategy to 'resolve intrac-table social problems' (Argyrou, 1993: 267) and could be seen as 'face-saving devices' (Dionisopoulos-Mass, 1976: 60). The results, however, could be detrimental and lead to 'total village disharmony' (1976: 61).

It was no coincidence for the witchcraft discourse to have materialized around the time of the wedding. 'A new mother and child (especially a baby boy and his new parents), a newly engaged couple, or newlyweds must be especially careful, since the whole village is full of envious, barren women, sterile men, envious unmarried maidens and youths, and envious parents of unmarried children.' Vulnerability to witchcraft is high 'at times of rites de passage' (Campbell, 1964: 62, 120; cf. Blum and Blum, 1965: 127–8; Vuorela, 1967: 19; Dionisopoulos-Mass, 1976: 44). Stories about witchcraft 'originate at the particularly dangerous moment in which, in the space of a few months, a son buries his father, takes over the tenancy in his own name, gets into debt for a quarter of a century with the credit banks and takes a wife to help him in his tasks (Favret-Saada, 1980: 137). Unwitchers probe specifically into these events (Favret-Saada, 1989: 45). Everywhere bewitchments happen when people are in transition between one social status and another, during temporal gaps and in the liminal position when a person's place in society is in flux. While in these moments the witchcraft discourse can be instrumental in redefining a person in relation to others, religiosity, honour and envy provide the (relatively) stable values against which this is accomplished.

WITCHCRAFT CONFLICTS

In contrast to fairy-tales, where the witch resides in a wood (Vordemfelde, 1924; Wittmann, 1933: 96), the witch of everyday life lives in one's own village. The social function of witchcraft discourse within a village has usually been conceived of in terms of social control. Witchcraft is a stabilizing safety-valve that preserves social norms. As a marxist anthropol-ogist expressed it: 'fear of the evil eye enforces social conformity in a community where the values of individualism and competition are firmly anchored' (Appel, 1977: 76). Yet it is Herzfeld's view that 'social control is inadequate as an explanation of the phenomena in question' (1981: 562). Possible disruptive effects were hardly studied by functionalists, mainly because researchers seldom occupied the witch's position (if they allowed themself to participate in the triangle at all).

Most of the time bewitchments are ascribed to someone. This almost automatically produces conflicts since the label 'witch' is invariably contested by its carrier. Establishing a link between a bewitchment (or a series of bewitchments) and its perceived origin causes social tension, 'the price to pay for intense social interaction' (Jenkins, 1977: 51). And because at the time of the diagnosis of a bewitchment the identity of the 'witch' is usually unknown to the bewitched (even when there are known witches around), identification techniques are a crucial step in the labelling process. 'In all cases of evil eye there is considerable speculation among the victim's relatives as to the identity of the guilty party' (Cutileiro, 1971: 275; cf. Dömötör, 1982: 168). The range of identification rituals, some of which have already been mentioned earlier in this essay, is vast. The outcome, however, is rather circumscribed. The typical witch is someone who is already known to the bewitched (Camus, 1988: 107), if not in the capacity of 'witch'. She is someone who lives in the neighbourhood and a woman. Further modifications depend on the 'witch's' reputation. Those who are able to mobilize support against their accusers find the accusation comparatively insignificant. The label sticks more easily to someone who already occupies a low status within the village and whose conduct is already under scrutiny. As Schäfer expresses it: 'Everyone, who deviates outwardly from the average country dweller, is in danger to be reputed as a "witch"' (1955: 34). She is 'an enemy of the collectivity' (Juliard, 1994: 285). The labelling can also be random; the 'chance witch' may not have been suspected before. But the persuasiveness of the witchcraft discourse is such that the surprise eclipses possible doubt. 'The witch's family background might have been "a little odd"; or the suspected woman appeared generally strange; "she interfered in other people's business", "spoke her mind", was not able to "keep anything to herself"; was impertinent; she was "simply weird"; she was "a real rascal"' (Schöck, 1978: 235; see also de Pina-Cabral, 1986: 181). Such, at least has been the picture in those areas where labelling has been a public process involving the whole community, even when it has started on a more modest scale. In Sarzbüttel the confrontation between the supporters of Eberling on the one side and the suspected witches and some enlightened people on the other disrupted the whole village (Baumhauer, 1984: 215). As has been written about Greece: 'Sorcerers are those who have created a tense situation of hostility and unhappiness in the society, which would include the relatives of the two families involved, and therefore nearly the whole village may be brought into play' (Dionisopoulos-Mass, 1976: 55). There seems to be no reason why this image of the village witch should not be extended to the whole of Europe. At the very least deviations from it may provoke an interesting line of argument.

Removing the enmity against the witch by use of witchcraft is impossible. If nothing was done, conflicts end with the death of the witch or her leaving the community. Otherwise the accuser has to be taken to court, to be forced to revoke the insults and to ask the 'witch' for forgiveness. This form of legal proceedure has existed since the seventeenth century (de Blécourt, 1990: 75–9) but traces of it have remained in twentieth-century local customs (Kaufmann, 1960: 99; Sebald, 1986: 276–7). As is apparent from Kruse's observations, confidence in the effects of legal intervention had subsided by the twentieth century (cf. Favret-Saada, 1971: 880). There were, however, other ways of circumventing conflicts or of tempering them. Partly, this was up to the witch herself, who could sometimes manipulate accusations for her own benefit (Dömötör, 1973: 179; Dekker, 1991: 194) and thereby strengthen her position within the community instead of weakening it (Jenkins, 1977: 38). In the Dalmatian coastal area a witch is believed to stop being a witch when she goes to confession (Bošković-Stulli, 1992: 153). Elsewhere, believers have taken the initiative. In the words of a Norwegian informant: 'The best way to avoid people who spread evil is to be kind to them' (Alver and Selberg, 1988: 29). This would confuse the witch, as would insulting her (Vuorela, 1967: 93). 'Persons capable of *vascania* are simultaneously mistrusted and kindly treated, as no one wants to bring down this type of wrath on himself' (Dionisopoulos-Mass, 1976: 52). Or, as an anthropologist noted in an Iberian context: 'if a woman is accused of being a witch, she should not be antagonized because witches kill those whom they "envy"'(De Pina-Cabral, 1986: 177). The 'notion counselled caution in personal dealings', one of his colleagues observed, 'but did not appear to affect seriously the social personality or relationships of the alleged witch' (Freeman, 1979: 120). These last remarks may very well allude to situations where witches are discussed without reference to recent bewitchments. Presumably conflicts do not have to come to a head everywhere and can also fade out.

The concept of the unintentional witch, as it occurs in some forms of the evil eye, presents another witch-figure without the social sting. According to anthropologist Campbell, one of the few authors to proble-matize this issue, 'the question whether the evil eye of any person is to be attributed to unconscious witchcraft or intentional sorcery depends upon his relationship to the victim'. He regards bewitchments between kinsmen and affines (especially brothers' wives) as unconscious. Unrelated bewitch-ers, on the other hand, are ascribed 'more conscious motives' (1964: 340). The appeal of this social functionalist interpretation is that it links different forms of witchcraft to different social constellations, but one of its flaws is the disregard of gender. Accusations within the family group are addressed from women to women. This raises the question: are men more involved in outside bewitchments?

Witchcraft without witches is, of course, even less socially disruptive. 'I never say who it is because it leads to hatred' a French cunning woman is reputed to have said (Favret-Saada, 1980: 158). Protective measures and unwitching techniques in which identification is absent focus equally on the process of healing and the relationship between bewitched and unwitcher. At the island of Pantelleria there is a 'lack of interest or concern about the specific identity of gazers' (Galt, 1982: 673). Likewise, in Greece, 'there is no person category corresponding to "witch" or "one who casts the evil eye"'' (Herzfeld, 1981: 564). As mentioned before, it is uncertain whether this is an accurate picture or merely the result of superficial research. Informants may be unwilling to discuss actual witches. They may practise avoidance in such a way that they are unfamiliar with their witches (cf. Hauschild, 1982: 165). Or witches are indeed absent. This brings us back to the issue of the researcher merging into the witchcraft discourse. Apparently anthropologists mainly interrogate witches' enemies, the bewitched and unwitchers (but do they talk to men or to women?), even when witches do appear in their narratives. Do they consider their choice justified because Mediterranean witches are, in comparison to those in northern Europe, less oppressed and isolated? On the whole, anthropologists hardly evaluate their human (and in the case of Hauschild, written) sources critically. Even apart from the possible lacuna in their assessment of the evil eye, there is still the neglect of fetish witchcraft, which, by definition, has a perpetrator.

Favret-Saada's decision to side with the bewitched and unwitchers was certainly facilitated by the isolation the bewitched suffer from during the process of unwitching, not least because the discourse forces them into it. Although in the Bocage the 'witch' has to be known in order to avoid communication with him, there is no village witch: 'witchcraft is always a matter of a dual relationship between two families only' (1980: 165). The witch's identity is only known to the unwitcher and the bewitched. 'The characterization as a witch, as such, cannot in any circumstances be made public; one can laugh and call him a "*filthy bastard*" but one never explicitly states that he is witch' (1980: 166). Whereas elsewhere witches are women, in the Bocage, by some twist of fate, witches and bewitched are men.

The peasant society in which witchcraft thrives has been characterized as public. 'One's every action is easily observed by one's neighbors, and privacy is almost unknown' (Dionisopoulos-Mass, 1976: 43; see also Favret-Saada, 1980: 53–4; Favret-Saada and Contreras, 1981: 248–9; Galt, 1982: 674; Lisón Tolosana, 1994: 229). It concerns 'a community that was relatively restricted geographically, economically and socially, closed and integrated, in which witchcraft formed specifically one of the possible regulation mechanisms' (Laplantine 1978: 98). In this kind of society women occupy a specific place. They are 'primarily responsible for making a marriage work and for maintaining household harmony' (Argyrou, 1993: 262). 'Still today she has no say in public life (. . .) outside the family she enjoys few rights and as a wife she is often treated brutally' (Risso and Böker, 1964: 23). Thus they are subjected to the 'tension between the dominant husband/submissive wife ideal and the reality in which the wife was perhaps the most important of the two *within the household*' (Jenkins, 1977: 52). Women are considered as 'sources of uncertainty' (Christian, 1972: 192) and female sexuality is an 'anti-social force' (Pitt-Rivers, 1971: 197; cf. Lisón Tolosana, 1994: 145). Within these patriarchal face-to-face societies all women are potential witches and in danger of loosing their feminity. This is best described in Ukrainian legends in which witches are depicted as non-feminine, for wearing beards, and as non-human because they are equipped with tails (Kovács, 1977: 247, 257, 278).

THE END OF WITCHCRAFT?

The continued existence of the witchcraft discourse has been attributed to several causes. Some authors, taking a vulgar rationalistic approach, have considered witchcraft to be an obsolete, old-fashioned way of thinking and have explained its presence accordingly. 'The delay in technology was matched by delay in the modern medical viewpoint and hence preserved an unscientific understanding of diseases and of death,' says an American sociologist (Sebald, 1986: 270; cf. Dekker, 1991: 195). The discourse was superseded by 'an alternative set of aetiological categories' that 'perhaps held out greater hopes of successful treatment' (Jenkins, 1977: 52). Within this modernist frame the disappearance of witches is seen as the product of such things as the entry of the workforce into a new era: roadbuilding and the tourist trade do not seem to be compatible with explanations in terms of witchcraft (Varga, 1939: 130–1). This supposedly happens during the transmission of the discourse from one generation to the next (1939:132). As Dömötör remarks about love magic: 'younger people no longer have any faith in such practices but older people still recall them' (1982: 189). 'The young tend to be slightly more sceptical than the old, men tend to be much more sceptical than women,' observes a British anthropologist on Andalusia (Pitt-Rivers, 1971: 199).

The problem with the rationalistic views of witchcraft is their presupposed narcissistic hegemony. This is supposed to lead simply to the erasure of all other modes of thought, especially among men and the more impressionable young. The effects of what has also been termed 'a symbolic class struggle to impose a particular [modernist] worldview on the rest of society' (Argyrou, 1993: 257) have been the subject of hardly any research. Irrational people are supposed to have reacted passively to the new developments, not acted on their own account. Although many reports about witchcraft have been instigated by attempts to civilize the 'superstitious', in fact they also show their failure. Kruse, whose writings display another version of the same rationalist way of thinking, represents an extreme example of this. When he criticized the State, the Church and the Academy as the main institutions that supported the continuation of witchcraft, he was not suggesting that they adhered to a similar kind of irrationality to that found in witchcraft accusations. He was rather deploring their lack of interest in teaching a rationalistic worldview and their ignorance of the grief witchcraft caused the accused (Baumhauer, 1984: 78). As long as neighbours and relatives could act as annunciators, apothecaries sold anti-bewitchment drugs (as *Asa Foetida*) and witch-doctors kept indicating the human culprits of bewitchments, the belief would never be erased (cf. Dekker, 1991: 187). Next in importance to the professional unwitchers Kruse blamed publications about witchcraft, not only the nefarious *Sixth and Seventh Books of Moses* (Hauschild, 1981; Baumhauer, 1984: 83–97), but also collections of folk-narratives and even fairy-tales. 'Popular literacy, rather than dispelling popular "credulity", may have actually helped sustain and even promote superstitious beliefs and practices', Davies agreed (1995: conclusion).

Witchcraft, as we have seen, has provided another kind of rationality. 'The Galicians doubted their beliefs, submitted them to a rational critique, looked for arguments and verified situations which, according to their point of view, could demonstrate the existence or inexistence' (of those beliefs), Lisón Tolosana wrote. 'The enterprise is, to all evidence, particularly rational' (1994: 316; see also Favret-Saada, 1980: 193). People are able to switch from one rational discourse to another. Séquard, for one, only resorted to the witchcraft discourse after both he and the veterinarian were at their wits end, and Eberling's clients had consulted doctors in vain before they called on him. 'With magical models of interpretation domains are covered, which are not satisfactory explained with positivist and rational explanations,' concludes a German folklorist (Paul, 1993: 116). Different discourses can exist simultaneously and which one is actually applied depends on the people and the situation. If we want to gain a better understanding of the perseverance of the witchcraft discourse, we need to define the (changing) contexts in which it is used more presicely and to take into account, for instance, that they can influence men and women differently.

Weiser-Aall's article in the *Handwörterbuch des deutschen Aberglaubens*, which is paradigmatic for many of the folklore surveys of witchcraft, 'suggests a universal German witch belief, that is shared by all people to the same degree in many regions' (Baumhauer, 1984: 209). This does not correspond with actual findings. The discourse may have been mainly operative in face-to-face societies where women have occupied a subordinate position, but even there it does not need to have been always at the forefront of people's thoughts. In the Vendée it was 'marginal and in the minority' (Gaboriau, 1986: 177). In northern Spain it was 'not a major preoccupation' (Christian, 1972: 193); 'witches are quite peripheral to questions of harmony and disharmony in the community at large' (Freeman, 1979: 119). These statements could, of course, refer mainly to the researchers' failures to enter the witchcraft triangle (they are somewhat contradicted by the research of respectively Favret-Saada and Lisón Tolosana, although these ignored questions about the relative importance of witchcraft), but they nevertheless indicate the possibility of marginality within village life. A more general marginality appears from the pattern revealed by witchcraft's uneven geographical distribution. Danish accusations have been restricted to 'a few remote corners of the country' (Henningsen, 1982: 137). Bewitchments in twentieth-century Drenthe (mainly of children) have occurred exclusively in the poor, peat-digging areas with higher birth rates than elsewhere in the province (de Blécourt, 1990: 207–25, 255–6). Southern Italy with its evil eye scares is 'a part of the Third World within Europe' (Hauschild, 1982: 137). The evil eye has been mainly found in 'small villages and remote places of southern Europe' (Gilmore, 1987: 168). This (provisional) geographical picture is matched by the (also rather sparse) temporal testimony.

The rise of German witchcraft cases during the 1950s has been attributed to the influx of single women into village communities after the war (Pintschovius, 1991: 81). Baumhauer characterized the period more generally as the one that followed the overthrow of the Nazi regime (1984: 66, 201). This, however, would only have been one of the causes for the increase. Cases of bewitchments also acquired a momentum of their own and were possibly copied from each other; in 1954, for example, a Danish case occurred just accross the German border (Henningsen, 1989: 129–30). Alternatively, they were related to economic crises or even to prosperity. In the 1960s the Bocage of Mayenne was a 'conservative region with structural crises' where witchcraft accusations were more frequent than in economically stable areas (Jonas, 1993: 57). In the Portugese coastal community studied by anthropologist Sally Cole there is evidence 'that increasing commoditization and industrialization have introduced new divisions and intensified competition among maritime women' and thus more opportunities for *inveja* to develop (1991: 122–3).

The discourse indubitably carries its own power. Several of the bewitched in Oberschwaben declared that they 'had not "believed in it" formerly', but that events had left them no other choice than to be persuaded (Paul, 1993: 110). We have already encountered a similar remark from Jules Séquard. Once inside the discourse, escaping it is difficult. Belgian bewitched women 'always associated certain events with meeting the suspected person or with her power operating at a distance and this strengthened their opinions even more' (van Eyen, 1989b: 75). A witch is suspect whether or not she adheres to communal norms. Showing piety, for instance, is just a way to fool her victims (Schöck, 1978: 126).

A few scattered reports indicate that different kinds of witchcraft or different aspects of the witchcraft discourse are subject to different trends and fluctuations. German love magic, for example, is mainly found in the older (nineteenth-century) legend texts (Wittmann, 1933: 65). In Denmark, interference with butter making is the 'most troublesome and persistent form of witchcraft' (Rockwell, 1978: 93). In France it has been suggested that there has even been an increase in active bewitchments recently (Juliard, 1994: 274), a change which the newest kind of German accusation seems to support (Pintschovius, 1991: 83–4). Only the precise transition from the more traditional kinds of witchcraft is questionable, as there may have been breaches in the chain of transmission. Tracing changes can be difficult, especially if all the diverse social and cultural aspects are to be taken into account. In one of her later papers Favret-Saada compared a portion of her fieldwork results to the notes of a nineteenth-century folklorist from Normandy who had collected a few male anecdotes and read some *grimoires*. By any reckoning this is a poor basis for conclusions about change, partly because we have to guess at what the folklorist did not collect, but also because of the absence of intermittent reports. (Yet it provides a better basis for conclusions about change than when Favret-Saada's findings are projected onto one nineteenth-century folklore text, see: Liu, 1994: 22). Still it seems that by the time of Favret-Saada's research weather magic had disappeared in western France and that both the influence of priests and self-help had declined, thus leaving a bigger part for the professional unwitchers (Favret-Saada, 1986: 41, 44).

The traces of the discourse found in twentieth-century sources may also represent its last vestiges. Folklore fieldwork carried out in Yorkshire in 1974 uncovered 'evidence that belief in the witch hare and the witch cat still survives' (Smith, 1978: 100). The exact relation between tales, belief, and actual occurrence of accusations is not totally transparent, however. My conclusions for Drenthe were that the places where only tales were told had experienced cases of bewitchment about half a century earlier (de Blécourt, 1990: 208, 214). In stories about the witch's transformation into a hare or a cat she may have become anonymous, a mere woman who was seen the next day with a bandage around the afflicted wound. This is one of the instances in which witchcraft has become depersonalized, in which the human cause of bewitchments has been disappearing from view. Depersonalizations are also to be found in the advice of Frisian witch-doctors which progressed from suggestions that could lead to identifying the witch to warnings concerning the medicine bottles (1990: 246). The reports about bewitched butter churns that could be unwitched without involving the witch and some of those about the evil eye may present other examples – provided they show the state of the discourse rather than the researcher's poor assessment of it.

If the disappearance of the discourse has involved the blurring of the witch image, it would explain why in the last stages men have also been accused of bewitchments, whereas before witchcraft was a female prerogative (1990: 218, 221; see also Henningsen, 1989: 127, 129, 138). This may have been the case in Mayenne in the 1960s. Indeed, the growing influence of unwitchers may have contributed to the acceptance of maleficent male witches. If these speculations have some bearing on historical processes, they would imply that male honour usurped female honour at some point. Unwitching procedures in Mayenne were, after all, strangely feminine. They involved men conceding parts of their honour to their wives. They made the bewitched man perform tasks that were 'similar to domestic work'. Protective measures were 'of exactly the same nature as the ones usually recommended to women in avoiding male violence' and the bewitched had to submit himself to the unwitcher in a way 'usually expected from wives' (Favret-Saada, 1989: 49–50). Favret-Saada's exceptional and exacting immersion in the discourse brought her into contact with a gendering of witchcraft that so far seems to have been unique in the European context.

FUTURE RESEARCH

Favret-Saada's book *Les mots, la mort, les sorts* (*Deadly Words*) not only ends with 'mid-way speculations', it also lists a series of issues that are referred to a 'forthcoming volume'. This second book should have contained the mechanisms of imputation (1980: 21, 50), a lengthy case describing the unwitching of a female interlocutor (1980: 185), and the workings of an unwitching cure (1980: 160). Furthermore, it should have dealt with the issues of witchcraft and madness (1980: 33) and the historical–economic determinations of the witchcraft discourse (ibid. 113). Although Favret-Saada addressed some of these issues in later articles, she never wrote the advertised book. Instead she turned psychiatrist, an academic unwitcher applying the 'technique of symbolic reparation' (1986: 36). Earlier she had already dismissed a sociological approach as unfeasible since the bewitchments she came across had taken place outside 'Saint-Auvieux', the village she lived in, and it was hard to uncover the social positions of people elsewhere (1971: 879). This leaves several requirements for future research into twentieth-century witchcraft, as indeed do most of the issues that have been reviewed in this essay. Otherwise, the economic and political aspects of witchcraft have hardly been addressed in the literature on Europe. We are still unaware of the role witchcraft may have played in local power struggles, or how international market forces may have influenced witchcraft accusations or have been expressed by them.

Twentieth-century European witchcraft research has been extremely parochial. There has been hardly any communication between the several researchers. Most of them have used their own kind of sources, asked their own questions and refrained from discussing other authors. This has not only happened between disciplines, but also within them. Language barriers are only partially to blame. French research, for instance, has not built on the accomplishments of Favret-Saada (on the whole she has been taken more seriously by anthropologists discussing the crisis of their profession than by European witchcraft researchers). Neither have different sorts of sources been combined. Of all the researchers presented in this essay only Schöck made use of oral as well as written material. Favret-Saada did not collect any legends and in striving to disassociate herself from the police and the justiciary she remained aloof from police files and trial records. She may have wanted to aim her research at the core of the regional witchcraft discourse rather than to explore its edges (where she would have situated the investigations by the authorities). But a meticulous analysis of other records than her own would have provided different angles on cases and therefore a fuller picture. On the other hand, other anthropologists have not even begun to reach the depth of Favret-Saada's research, let alone used other sources.

Legend texts may have been easily derided, especially by authors who have had access to more extended case material. Yet as I hope to have shown, despite the bias of their collectors, legends do offer fascinating prospects, even if within the scope of this essay it was only possible to indicate a few directions of possibly fruitful analysis by considering repertoires, genre, gender and geography. The enormous amount of legend texts in the folklore archives may now be lying idle but there may very well be times and places for which no other sources on witchcraft are available. And as long as names (of narrators, of bewitched, of witches and of unwitchers) have been transmitted, there is also the possibility of discovering more about contexts in other, oral as well as written, sources. Finding new trial records and newspaper reports demands a special approach, as it is pointless just to leaf through files and ledgers without any clues (only a few newspapers are indexed). These may be provided by letters or newspaper reports collected by folklorists. Kruse's archive can still be consulted in Hamburg, for instance.

To those researchers who do not want to become too personally involved in the witchcraft discourse, written sources may even be preferable. As we have seen earlier in this essay, undertaking extensive fieldwork is hazardous. The German ethnographer Cornelia Paul, to mention yet another example, was so impressed by what she was told by some of her fellow villagers, that she did not want to pursue the matter any further (1993: 109). 'To accept being affected, however, supposes that one takes the risk of seeing one's ethnographic project vanish,' Favret-Saada warned (1990: 195). Participating in the discourse and occupying the position of bewitched within the witchcraft triangle remains, of course, the most explicit way to commit oneself to witchcraft and the people directly involved. At best the researcher becomes an accomplice and thereby not only signals that she has taken sides, but also admits that the people researched have a hold on her. This may sometimes be absolutely necessary; at least, Favret-Saada stated that she did not have any other choice (1971: 879; 1990: 189). 'Between people who are equally affected because they occupy one or another of the witchcraft positions, something can happen which an ethnographer can never witness, things are said that ethnographies never mention, or things are not said,' she remarked in her defence of 'involuntary participation' (1990: 194–5). On the other hand deep involvement may be unwarranted in other situations and it does not always seem to be a prerogative. Favret-Saada claims to have discovered unwitching therapies that would have remained hidden to her had she only followed the more distant approach. This would not have applied to cases where only one advice from an unwitcher sufficed to start the whole process of unwitching. In the case of public witches, involuntary participation may very well necessitate that the researcher becomes a (passive, ascribed) witch.

In the field the option to switch discourses does not have to be a realistic one, as a change in discourse may demonstrate a change in allegiances. Talking to witches may betray the confidence of the bewitched and vice versa. Using a scientific discourse towards the bewitched can jeopardize research as easily as becoming 'caught'. There is thus no clear-cut solution to the problem of which position in the witchcraft triangle the researcher should occupy. It depends, among other things, on the degree to which accusations become public, on the gender of the witches and the researcher, and on her or his zeal and involvement. Whatever decision is taken, ignoring the problem amounts to insufficient and even poor research. In witchcraft research the position of the researcher and the processes of text production always have to be taken into account, even when there is no direct communication between author and subjects (as is the case of this essay).

Witchcraft discourse can be seen as an expression of social conflicts, as the transgression of all kinds of boundaries and as a way of articulating the submission to interpersonal power. While these analyses require profound investigation, symbolic interpretations of the discourse can already be suggested on the basis of superficial material. This is not to belittle the value of the symbolic. But it will gain in relevance only when more is known about the gender of the participants, their age, their social position and other contextual details. We also do not always perceive why a specific symbol is favoured in one situation and not in another (not every symbol can be meaningfully reduced to liquid). If there is a general theme in European witchcraft in the twentieth century, it can be summarized as liminality. This applies literally to the importance of the threshold in bewitchment, identification and unwitchment. It is equally manifest in the other spatial and in the social and temporal aspects of witchcraft. Not only are witches liminal figures, the bewitched are also in a state of liminality, vulnerable to evil influences because they are moving from one life-stage to the next. Bewitchments, we can conclude, are especially apt to occur when the bewitched enters the liminal dimension where the witch abides. Conversely, someone is placed in the liminal position of witch because the bewitched experiences misfortune from their own liminality. This general outline is specified in local discourse.

The more a researcher participates in the witchcraft discourse, the more unique its local manifestations seem to become. The witchcraft of Mayenne 'is the product of an authentic cultural "labour" of the local community, the product of an incessant negotiation conducted with the dominant national culture,' writes Favret-Saada (1986: 29). Local witchcraft discourses are accentuated and even defined by the locally current value systems. Seen from this angle, local witchcraft discourses are distinctive, comparable to other discourses but dissimilar from them. However, the tension between general themes and local (or regional) particularities is above all a function of the distance between whatever academic approach is adopted and local communication. On the practical level there is no generalized and abstract discourse; at the most, people have heard about witchcraft discourses different from their own. As anthropologist Anthony Galt has remarked: 'In the Mediterranean area we are dealing with peoples who have a long history of movement and contact and therefore of such conversations [about the evil eye], or at least awareness of each other's belief systems' (1982: 668). The regions discussed in this essay are not isolated islands and any future general theory on traditional European witchcraft will need to be supported by evidence about communication across their permeable boundaries. My opening example illustrates this point as well, since the old woman had to pass the customs and thus cross boundaries literally.

Bibliography

Aarne, A. and Thompson, S. (1973) *The Types of the Folktale: A Classification and Bibliography* (Helsinki).

Ackerman, R. (1987) *J.G. Frazer, His Life and Work* (Cambridge).

Adler, M. (1986) *Drawing Down the Moon*, 2nd edn (Boston).

Adshead, G. (1994) 'Looking for clues: a review of the literature on false allegations of sexual abuse in childhood', in Sinason, V., ed. (1994): 57–65.

Alderman, C. (1973) *A Cauldron of Witches* (Folkstone).

Alfred, R. H. (1976) 'The Church of Satan', in C. Glock and R. Bellah, eds *The New Religious Consciousness* (Berkeley): 180–202.

Alver, B. G. (1989) 'Concepts of the soul in Norwegian tradition', in R. Kvideland and H. K. Sehmsdorf, eds *Nordic Folklore* (Bloomington and Indianapolis): 110–27.

Alver, B. G. and Selberg, T. (1988) 'Folk medicine as part of a larger concept complex', *Arv. Scandinavian Yearbook of Folklore 1987*, 43: 21–44.

Andreesco-Miereanu, I. (1982) 'Espace et temps de la magie dans un village Romain actuel', *Cahiers Internationaux de Sociologie*, 73: 251–66.

Appel, W. (1976) 'The Myth of the *Jettatura*', in C. Maloney, ed. *The Evil Eye* (New York): 16–27.

Appel, W. (1977) 'Idioms of power in southern Italy', *Dialectical Anthropology*, 2: 74–80.

Aquino, M. (1975) *The Book of Coming Forth By Night* (San Francisco).

Aquino, M. (1992) *Black Magic in Theory and Practice* (San Francisco).

Argyrou, V. (1993) 'Under a spell: the strategic use of magic in Greek Cypriot society', *American Ethnologist*, 20: 256–71.

Armstrong, L. (1978) *Kiss Daddy Goodnight: A Speakout on Incest* (New York).

Auhofer, H. (1960) *Aberglaube und Hexenwahn heute: Aus der Unterwelt unserer Zivilisation* (Freiburg, Basel and Vienna).

Bainbridge, W. S. (1978) *Satan's Power: A Deviant Psychotherapy Cult* (Berkeley).

Bainbridge, W. S. (1991) 'Social construction from within: Satan's process', in J. T. Richardson *et al.*, eds (1991): 297–310.

Barker, E. (1989) *New Religious Movements: A Practical Introduction* (London).

Barker, E. (1994) 'New religious movements in Europe', in S. Gill, G. D'Costa and U. King, eds *Religion in Europe: Contemporary Perspectives* (Kampen): 120–40.

Barnard, E. (1937) *Shelley's Religion* (Minneapolis).

Barry, W. (1891) 'Neo-paganism', *The Quarterly Review*, 172: 273–304.

Bartholdy, R. (1969) *Zauberer und Recht: Untersuchungen zur rechtlichen Volkskunde in Schleswig-Holstein*, inaugural dissertation, Christian Albrechts Universität (Kiel).

Barton, B. (1990) *The Church of Satan* (New York: Hell's Kitchen Productions).

Baughman, E. W. (1966) *Type and Motif Index of the Folktales of England and North America* (The Hague).

Baumhauer, J. F. (1984) *Johann Kruse und der 'neuzeitliche Hexenwahn': Zur Situation eines norddeutschen Aufklärers und einer Glaubensvorstellung im 20. Jahrhundert untersucht anhand von Vorgängen in Dithmarschen* (Neumünster).

Beard, M. (1992) 'Frazer, Leach and Virgil', *Comparative Studies in Society and History*, 34: 203–24.

Beck-Braach, H. (1993) 'Magie und Vorurteil: Protokol einer Feldforschung', *Kea. Zeitschrift für Kulturwissenschaften*, 5: 71–86.

Beckman, J. (1987) 'Vindicte populaire et sorcellerie en Wallonie', *Tradition Wallone*, 4: 65–78.

Bennett, G. (1993) 'Folklore studies and the English rural myth', *Rural History*, 4: 77–91.

Bennett, G. (1994) 'Geologists and folklorists', *Folklore*, 105: 25–37.

Berg, M. van den (1960) 'Onderzoek naar de sagenmotieven in de polders van Antwerpen', *Volkskunde*, 61: 26–33.

Beth, R. (1990) *Hedge Witch* (London).

Black Flame, The

Black Lily, The

Blavatsky, H. (1877) *Isis Unveiled* (London).

Blécourt, W. de (1981) 'De volksverhalen van J. R. W. Sinninghe', *Volkskundig bulletin*, 7: 162–93.

Blécourt, W. de (1988) 'Duivelbanners in de Noordelijke Friese Wouden, 1860–1930', *Volkskundig bulletin*, 14: 159–87.

Blécourt, W. de (1989) 'Heksengeloof: toverij en religie in Nederland tussen 1890 en 1940', *Sociologische gids*, 36: 245–66.

Blécourt, W. de (1990) *Termen van toverij. De veranderende betekenis van toverij in Noordoost-Nederland tussen de 16de en 20ste eeuw* (Nijmegen).

Blécourt, W. de (1991) 'Four centuries of Frisian witch doctors', in M. Gijswijt-Hofstra and W. Frijhoff, eds (1991): 157–66.

Blécourt, W. de (1994) 'Witch doctors, soothsayers and priests: on cunning folk in European historiography and tradition', *Social History*, 19: 285–303.

Blécourt, W. de (1996) 'On the continuation of witchcraft', in J. Barry, M. Hester and G. Roberts, eds *Witchcraft in Early Modern Europe: Studies in Culture and Belief* (Cambridge): 335–52.

Blum, R. and Blum, E. (1965) *Health and Healing in Rural Greece: A Study of Three Communities* (Stanford).

Bonewits, I. (1972) *Real Magic* (New York).

Bošković-Stulli, M. (1960) 'Kresnik-Krsnik, ein Wesen aus der kroatischen und slovenischen Volksüberlieferung', *Fabula*, 3: 275–98.

Bošković-Stulli, M. (1973) 'Witchcult: fact or fancy?' *Gnostica*, 3.4: n.p.

Bošković-Stulli, M. (1992) 'Hexensagen und Hexenprozesse in Kroatien', *Acta Ethnografica Hungarica*, 37: 143–171.

Bostridge, I. (1997) *Witchcraft and its Transformations c. 1650–c. 1750* (Oxford).

Bottoms, B., Shaver, P. and Goodman, G. (1996) 'An analysis of ritualistic and religion-related child abuse allegations', *Law and Human Behaviour*, 20: 1.

Bottrell, W. (1870) *Traditions and Hearthside Stories* (Truro).

Boulay, J. du (1974) *Portrait of a Greek Mountain Village* (Oxford).

Bouteiller, M. (1958) *Sorciers et jeteurs de sort* (Paris).

Bovenschen, S. (1977) 'Die aktuelle Hexe, die historische Hexe und der Hexenmythos. Die Hexe: Subject der naturaneignung und Object der Naturbeherrschung', in *Aus der Zeit der Verzweiflung: Zur Genese und Aktualität des Hexenbildes* (Frankfurt am Main): 259–312.

Boyd, A. (1991) *Blasphemous Rumours: Is Satanic Ritual Abuse Fact or Fantasy? An Investigation* (London).

Bracelin, J. (1960) *Gerald Gardner: Witch* (London).

Briggs, K. (1970–1971) *A Dictionary of British Folk-Tales in the English Language* (London).

Brockie, W. (1886) *Legends and Superstitions of the County of Durham* (Durham).

Bromley, D. G. (1991) 'Satanism: the new cult scare', in J. T. Richardson et al., eds (1991): 49–72.

Brown, S. (1982) 'Friendly Societies and their symbols and rituals', *Group for Regional Studies in Museums Newsletter*, 10: 7–11.

Brown, T. (1970) 'Charming in Devon', *Folklore*, 81: 37–47.

Burne, C. (1888) *Shropshire Folk-Lore* (London).

Burnett, D. (1991) *Dawning of the Pagan Moon* (Eastbourne).

Burrow, J. (1966) *Evolution and Society* (Cambridge).

Campbell, J. K. (1964) *Honour, Family and Patronage: A Study of Institutions and Moral Values in a Greek Mountain Community* (Oxford).

Camus, D. (1986) 'Le malheur-sorcier. Mis en scène', *Le monde Alpin et Rhodanien*, 14: 173–92.

Camus, D. (1988) *Pouvoirs Sorciers: Enquête sur les pratiques actuelles de sorcellerie* (Paris).

Camus, D. (1989) 'Sorcellerie et ethnology', in *Anthropologie sociale et ethnologie de la France* (Louvain-la-Neuve): 405–16.

Caro Baroja, J. (1965) *The World of the Witches* (Chicago).

Carpenter, E. (1889) *Civilisation: Its Cause and Cure* (London).

Carter, I. (1979) *Farmlife in North-East Scotland, 1840–1914* (Edinburgh).

Cartwright, E. (1947) *Masonic Ritual* (London).

Cavendish, R. (1975) *The Powers of Evil in Western Religion, Magic and Folk Belief* (London).

Cerullo, M. (1973) *The Back Side of Satan* (Carol Stream, IL).

Chapman, J. (1993) *Quest for Dion Fortune* (York Beach, ME).

Chesterton, G. (1905) *Heretics* (London).

Christian, W. A. (1972) *Person and God in a Spanish Valley* (New York and London).

Clodd E. (1896) 'Presidential address', *Folklore*, 7: 47–8.

Cohn, N. (1970) 'The myth of Satan and his human servants', in M. Douglas, ed. *Witchcraft: Confessions and Accusations*, ASA Monographs 9 (London): 3–16.

Cohn, N. (1975) *Europe's Inner Demons* (St Albans).

Cole, S. (1991) *Women of the Praia: Works and Lives in a Portuguese Coastal Community* (Princeton).

Cotton, I. (1995) *The Hallelujah Revolution* (London).

Coulton, G. (1923) *Five Centuries of Religion*, vol i (Cambridge).

Courtney, M. (1890) *Cornish Feasts and Folklore* (Truro).

Cranston, S. (1993) *HPB* (New York).

Crowley, A. (1969) *The Confessions of Aleister Crowley: An Autohagiography*, J. Symonds and K. Grant, eds (Harmondsworth).

Crowley, A. (1973) *Magick*, J. Symonds and K. Grant, eds (London).

Crowley, A. (1979) *The Confessions*, 2nd edn (London).

Crowther, P. and Crowther, A. (1965) *The Witches Speak* (Douglas).

Cuningham, S. (1990) *Wicca: A Guide for the Solitary Practitioner* (St Paul, MN).

Cutileiro, J. (1971) *A Portuguese Rural Society* (Oxford).

Daras, H. (1964) *Onderzoek naar de sagenmotieven in het hart van de Antwerpse Kempen*, unpublished doctoral thesis, Catholic University Leuven.

Daras, H. (1983) 'De macht van de geestelijken', *Neerlands Volksleven*, 33: 127–67.

Davidson, T. (1956) 'The Horseman's Word', *Gwerin*, 2: 67–74.

Davies, J. (1911) *Folk-Lore of West and Mid-Wales* (Aberystwyth).

Davies, O. (1995) *The Decline in the Popular Belief in Witchcraft and Magic*, unpublished PhD thesis, University of Lancaster.

Davies, O. (1997a) 'Urbanization and the decline of witchcraft: an examination of London', *Journal of Social History*, 30: 597–617.

Davies, O. (1997b) 'Cunning-Folk in England and Wales during the eighteenth and nineteenth centuries', *Rural History*, 8: 91–107.

Davies, R. T. (1947) *Four Centuries of Witch-Beliefs* (London).

Dégh, L. and Vázsonyi, A. (1972) 'Legend and belief', in D. Ben-Amos, ed. *Folklore Genres* (Austin): 93–123.

Dekker, T. (1991) 'Witches and sorcerers in twentieth century legends', in M. Gijswijt-Hofstra and W. Frijhoff, eds (1991): 183–95.

Dhuibhne, É. ní (1993) ' "The old woman as hare": structure and meaning in an Irish legend', *Folklore*, 104: 77–85.

Dingeldein, H. J. (1983) 'Spuren fortlebenden Hexenglaubens: Zu einer Geschichte aus dem hessischen Odenwald und ihren Hintergründen', *Hessische Blätter für Volkskunde*, 14/15: 18–30.

Dingeldein, H. J. (1985) ' "Hexe" und Märchen: Überlegungen zum Hexenbild in den Kinder- und Hausmärchen der Brüder Grimm', in S. Früh and R. Wehse, eds *Die Frau im Märchen* (Kassel): 50–9.

Dionisopoulos-Mass, R. (1976) 'The evil eye and bewitchment in a peasant village', in C. Maloney, ed. *The Evil Eye* (New York): 42–62.

Dömötör, T. (1972) 'Zwei Zauberer aus Südungarn', in K. Beitl, ed. *Volkskunde: Fakten und Analysen. Festgabe für Leopold Schmidt zum 60. Geburtstag* (Vienna): 381–90.

Dömötör, T. (1973) 'Die Hebamme als Hexe', in L. Röhrich, ed. *Probleme der Sagenforschung* (Freiburg im Breisgau): 177–89.

Dömötör, T. (1982) *Hungarian Folk Beliefs* (Bloomington).

Dundes, A. (1992) 'Wet and dry, the evil eye: an essay in Indo-European and Semetic worldview', in A. Dundes, ed. *The Evil Eye: A Casebook* (Madison): 257–312.

Dyer, T. (1876) *British Popular Customs* (London).

Edgell, D. (1992) *The Order of Woodcraft Chivalry, 1916–1949* (Lewiston).

Ellis, W. (1993) 'The Highgate Cemetry vampire hunt: the Anglo-American connection in Satanic cult lore', *Folklore*, 104: 13–39.

Ellmann, R. (1949) *Yeats: The Man and the Masks* (London).

Ellmann, R. (1954) *The Identity of Yeats* (London).

Evans, G. (1960) *The Horse in the Furrow* (London).

Evans, G. (1966) *The Pattern under the Plough* (London).

Evans, G. (1972) *The Leaping Hare* (London).

Evans, G. (1975) *The Days That We Have Seen* (London).

Evans, G. (1987) *Spoken History* (London).

Evans, I. (1930) *Woodcraft and World Service* (London).

Eyen, C. van (1989a) *Heksengeloof in Kaggevinne anno 1988. Een volksver-haalstudie*, unpublished doctoral thesis, Catholic University Leuven.

Eyen, C. van (1989b) 'Heksengeloof in Kaggevinne anno 1988. Een volksverhaalstudie', *Ethnologia Flandrica*, 5: 63–103.

Farrar, J. (1984) *The Witches' Way* (London).

Farrar, J. and Farrar, S. (1981) *Eight Sabbats for Witches* (London: Hale).

Favret-Saada, J. (1971) 'La malheur biologique et sa répétition', *Annales: E.S.C.*, 26: 873–88.

Favret-Saada, J. (1980) *Deadly Words. Witchcraft in the Bocage* (Cambridge/ Paris).

Favret-Saada, J. (1986) 'L'invention d'une thérapie: la sorcellerie bocaine 1887–1970', *Le Débat. Histoire, Politique, Société*, 40: 29–46.

Favret-Saada, J. (1989) 'Unbewitching as therapy', *American Ethnologist*, 16: 40–56.

Favret-Saada, J. (1990) 'About participation', *Culture, Medicine and Psychiatry*, 14: 189–99.

Favret-Saada, J. and Contreras, J. (1981) *Corps pour corps. Enquête sur la sorcellerie dans le Bocage* (Paris).

Fenrir.

Finkelhor, D., Williams, L. and Burns, N. (1988) *Nursery Crimes* (New York).

Foster, G. M. (1965) 'Peasant society and the image of limited good', *American Anthropologist*, 67: 293–315.

Foster, G. M. (1972) 'The anatomy of envy: a study in symbolic behavior', *Current Anthropology*, 13: 165–202.

Fraser, R. (1990) *Sir James Frazer and the Literary Imagination* (London).

Fraysse, C. J. B. (1961) 'Au pays de Baugé (Maine-et-Loire): La thérapeutique populaire et les sorciers guérisseurs', *Arts et traditions populaires*, 9: 100–8.

Freeman, S. T. (1979) *The Pasiegos: Spaniards in No Man's Land* (Chicago and London).

Friesen, J. (1991) *Uncovering the Mystery of MPD* (San Bernardino, CA).

Frijhoff, W. (1991) 'Witchcraft and its changing representation in eastern Gelderland, from the sixteenth to twentieth centuries', in M. Gijswijt-Hofstra and W. Frijhoff, eds (1991): 167–80.

Gaboriau, P. (1985) 'La sorcellerie actuelle dans le Choletais', in *Histoire des faits de la sorcellerie* (Angers): 177–86.

Gaboriau, P. (1986) 'Les "bon côtés" du malheur. Les bénéfices psychologiques de la sorcellerie', *Le monde Alpin et Rhodanien*, 14: 173–92.

Gaboriau, P. (1987) *La pensée ensorcellée. La sorcellerie actuelle en Anjou et en Vendée* (Les Sables-d'Olonne).

Galt, A. H. (1982) 'The evil eye as synthetic image and its meanings on the island of Pantarella, Italy', *American Ethnologist*, 9: 664–81.

Garrison, V. and Arensberg, C. M. (1976) 'The evil eye: envy or risk of seizure? Paranoia or patronal dependency?', in C. Maloney, ed. *The Evil Eye* (New York): 286–327.

Geldof, W. (1979) *Volksverhalen uit Zeeland en de zuidhollandse eilanden* (Utrecht).

Gerhard, E. (1849) *Über Metroon und Götter-Mutter* (Berlin).

Gijswijt-Hofstra, M. (1997) *Vragen bijeen onttoverde wereld* (Amsterdam).

Gijswijt-Hofstra, M. and Frijhoff, W., eds (1991) *Witchcraft in the Netherlands, from the Fourteenth to the Twentieth Century* (Rijswijk).

Gilbert, R. (1983) *The Golden Dawn: Twilight of the Magicians* (Wellingborough).

Gilmore, D. D. (1987) *Aggression and Community: Paradoxes of Andalusian Culture* (New Haven and London).

Gomme, G. (1892) 'Presidential address', *Folklore*, 3: 4–12.

Gomme, G. (1893) *Ethnology in Folklore* (London).

Gomme, G. (1894) 'Presidential address', *Folklore*, 5: 66–73.

Gosden, P. (1961) *The Friendly Societies in England, 1815–1875* (Manchester).

Gottschalk, G. (1995) 'Hexen- und Zaubereisagen aus dem Westmünsterland', in M. Saatkamp and D. Schlüter, eds *Van Hexen un Düvelslüden. Über Hexen, Zauberei und Aberglauben im niederländischen-deutschen Grenzraum* (Vreden): 161–82.

Grätz, M. (1988) *Das Märchen in der deutschen Aufklärung* (Stuttgart).

Green, M. (1991) *A Witch Alone* (London).

Greenwood, S. (1995) 'The magical will, gender and power', in Harvey and Hardman, eds (1995): 191–203.

Grimm, J. (1883) *Teutonic Mythology*, trans. J. Stallybrass (London).

Gubbins, J. K. (1946) 'Some observations on the evil eye in modern Greece', *Folklore*, 57: 195–98.

Guggino, E. (1994) ' "Le corps est fait de syllabes". Discours de magiciens', *Ethnologie française*, 25: 629–41.

Guillatt, R. (1996) *Talk of the Devil* (Melbourne).

Gutch, E., ed. (1901) *County Folk-Lore II: North Riding of Yorkshire, York and Ainsty* (London).

Hamilton, M. (1995) *The Sociology of Religion* (London).

Hardie, M. M. (1992) 'The evil eye in some Greek villages of the Upper Haliakmon valley in West Macedonia', in A. Dundes, ed (1992) *The Evil Eye. A Casebook* (Madison): 107–23.

Hardwick, C. (1872) *Traditions, Superstitions and Folk-Lore* (Manchester).

Hargrave, J. (1919) *The Great War Brings It Home* (London).

Hargrave, J. (1927) *The Confession of the Kibbo Kift* (London).

Harmening, D. and Bauer, D., eds (1991) *Hexen heute. Magische Traditionen und neue Zutaten* (Würzburg).

Harper, G. (1974) *Yeats's Golden Dawn* (London).

Harrison, J. (1903) *Prolegomena to the Study of Greek Religion* (Cambridge).

Harvey, G. (1995a) 'Satanism in Britain today', *Journal of Contemporary Religion*, 10: 353–66.

Harvey, G. (1995b) 'Heathenism: a north European pagan tradition', in G. Harvey and C. Hardman, eds (1995): 49–64.

Harvey, G. (1997) *Listening People, Speaking Earth* (London).

Harvey, G. and Hardman, C., eds (1995) *Paganism Today* (London and San Francisco).

Hauschild, T. (1980) 'Johann Kruses Beitrag zur Erforschung des neuzeitlichen Hexenglaubens', *Mitteilungen aus dem Museum für Völkerkunde Hamburg*, NF 10: 139–57.

Hauschild, T. (1981) 'Hexen in Deutschland', in H. P. Duerr, ed. *Der Wissenschaftler und das Irrationale* I. (Frankfurt am Main): 537–64.

Hauschild, T. (1982) *Der böse Blick. Ideegeschichtliche und sozialpsychologische Untersuchungen*, rev. edn (Berlin).

Hazlitt, W. (1931) *Complete Works*, ed. E. Howe (London).

Heelas, P. (1982) 'Californian self-religions and socializing the subjective', in E. Barker, ed. *New Religious Movements: A Perspective for Understanding Society* (New York): 69–85.

Henderson, H. (1962) 'A slight case of devil worship', *New Statesman*, 14 June: 696–8.

Henningsen, G. (1982) 'Witchcraft in Denmark', *Folklore*, 93: 131–7.

Henningsen, G. (1989) 'Witch persecution after the era of the witch trials: a contribution to Danish ethnohistory', *Arv. Scandinavian Yearbook of Folklore 1988*, 44: 103–53.

Herzfeld, M. (1981) 'Meaning and morality: a semiotic approach to evil eye accusations in a Greek village', *American Ethnologist*, 8: 560–74.

Herzfeld, M. (1986) 'Closure as cure: tropes in the exploration of bodily and social disorder', *Current Anthropology*, 27: 107–20.

Heupers, E. (1979, 1981, 1984) *Volksverhalen uit Gooi- en Eemland en van de westelijke Veluwe*, i–iii (Amsterdam).

Hooke, S. (1937) 'Time and custom', *Folklore*, 48: 17–24.

Hörandner, E. (1987) ' "Hexenbilder" – Zum Nachleben der Hexenvorstellungen in Märchen und Sage, Glaube und Brauch', in H. Valentinitsch, ed. *Hexen und Zauberer. Die grosse Verfolgung – ein europäisches Phänomen in der Steiermark* (Graz/Vienna): 351–4.

Howe, E. (1972) *The Magicians of the Golden Dawn* (London).

Howkins, A. (1986) 'The discovery of rural England', in R. Collis and P. Dodd, eds *Englishness: Politics and Culture, 1880–1920* (London): 62–88.

Hunt, R. (1881) *Popular Romances of the West of England* (Truro).

Hutton, R. (1991) *The Pagan Religions of the Ancient British Isles* (Oxford).

Hutton, R. (1996) *The Stations of the Sun: A History of the Ritual Year in Britain* (Oxford).

Irvine, D. (1973) *From Witchcraft to Christ* (Cambridge).

Jalby, R. (1971) *Le folklore du Languedoc. Ariège–Aude–Lauraguais–Tarn* (Paris).

Jalby, R. (1974) *Sorcellerie et Médicine populaire en Languedoc* (Nyons).

Jarcke, K.-E. (1828) 'Ein Hexenprozess', *Annalen der deutschen und ausländischen Criminal-Rechts-Pflege* (Berlin), 1: 450.

Jayran, S. (1987) *Which Craft?* (London).

Jennings, H. (1887) *The Rosicrucians: Their Rites and Mysteries* (London).

Jenkins, R. P. (1977) 'Witches and fairies: supernatural aggression and deviance among the Irish peasantry', *Ulster Folklife*, 23: 33–56.

Johns, J. (1969) *King of the Witches: The World of Alex Sanders* (London).

Jonas, R. (1993) 'Zauber einer Landschaft. Ethnographie auf einem sensiblen Gebiet', *Kea. Zeitschrift für Kulturwissenschaften*, 5: 55–69.

Jones, B. (1956) *Freemasons' Guide and Compendium* (London).

Jones, P. and Matthews, C. (1990) *Voices from the Circle* (Wellingborough).

Juliard, A. (1994) 'Le malheur des sorts. Sorcellerie d'aujourd'hui en France', in R. Muchembled, ed. *Magie et sorcellerie en Europe du Moyen Age à nos jours* (Paris): 267–315.

Katschnig-Fasch, E. (1987) 'Hexenglaube in der Gegenwart – Versuch einer Begegnung', in Helfried Valentinitsch, ed. *Hexen und Zauberer. Die grosse Verfolgung – ein europäisches Phänomen in der Steiermark* (Graz and Vienna): 379–89.

Kaufmann, O. (1960) 'Oberbergische Volkserzählungen, i: Berichte über Hexen und Hexenmeister', *Reinisch-westfälische Zeitschrift für Volkskunde*, 7: 83–109.

Kelly, A. (1991) *Crafting the Art of Magic* (St Paul, MN).

Kieckhefer, R. (1989) *Magic in the Middle Ages* (Cambridge).

King, F. (1970) *Ritual Magic in England: 1887 to the Present Day* (London).

King, F. (1971) *Astral Projection, Ritual Magic and Alchemy* (London).

King, F. (1973) *The Secret Rituals of the O.T.O.* (London).

Koenig, S. (1937) 'Magical beliefs and practices among the Galician Ukrainians', *Folklore*, 48: 59–91.

Kooijman, H. (1988) *Volksverhalen uit het grensgebied van Zuid-Holland, Utrecht, Gelderland en Noord-Brabant* (Amsterdam).

Kovács, Z. (1977) 'Das Erkennen der Hexen in der Westeuropäischen und der Russischen Tradition', *Acta Ethnographica Hungarica*, 26: 241–84.

Kruse, J. (1951) *Hexen unter uns? Magie und Zauberglaube in unserer Zeit* (Hamburg).

Kurotschkin, A. V. (1992) 'Hexengestalt in der Ukrainischen Folkloretradition', *Acta Ethnographica Hungarica*, 37: 191–200.

La Fontaine, J. S. (1998) *Speak of the Devil: Tales of Satanic Abuse in Contemporary England* (Cambridge).

Lamb, G. (1977) *Magic, Witchcraft and the Occult* (London and New York).

Lancelin, C. (1911) *La sorcellerie des Campagnes* (photomechanical reprint; Paris, 1968).

Laplantine, F. (1978) *La médicine populaire des campagnes françaises aujourd'hui* (Paris).

Larner, C. (1984) *Witchcraft and Religion: The Politics of Popular Belief* (Oxford).

LaVey, A. (1969) *The Satanic Bible* (New York).

LaVey, A. (1972) *The Satanic Rituals* (New York).

Leask, J. (1933) 'How Willo o' Iver Tuack became a Horseman', *Old Lore Miscellany of Orkney, Shetland, Caithness and Sutherland*, 9: 75–81.

Lehnert-Leven, C. (1995) 'Hexenmotive in den "Sagen und Geschichten aus der Westeifel"', in G. Franz, F. Irsigler and E. Biesel, eds *Hexenglaube und Hexenprozesse im Raum Rhein-Mosel-Saar* (Trier): 131–141.

Levack, B. (1987) *The Witchhunt in Early Modern Europe* (London and New York).

Liddell, E. and Howard, M. (1994) *The Pickingill Papers* (Chieveley).

Liu, T. P. (1994) '*Le patrimoine magique*: reassessing the power of women in peasant households in nineteenth-century France', *Gender & History*, 6: 13–36.

Lisón Tolosana, C. (1994) *Sorcellerie, structure sociale et symbolisme en Galice* (Paris).

Longman Medway, G. (in preparation) *The Lure of the Sinister Or the Unnatural History of Satan-Hunting*.

Lorint, F. E. and Bernabé, J. (1977) *La sorcellerie paysanne. Approche anthropologique de l'Homo Magus, avec une étude sur la Roumanie* (Brussels).

Luhrmann, T. (1989) *Persuasions of the Witch's Craft* (Oxford).

Lüthi, M. (1979) *Märchen* (Stuttgart).

Lykiardopoulos, A. (1981) 'The evil eye: towards an exhaustive study', *Folklore*, 92: 221–30.

McCormick, D. (1968) *Murder by Witchcraft* (London).

McPherson, J. (1929) *Primitive Beliefs in the North-East of Scotland* (London).

Maple, E. (1960a) 'Cunning Murrell', *Folklore*, 71: 36–43.

Maple, E. (1960b) 'The witches of Canewdon', *Folklore*, 71: 241–9.

Maple, E. (1962) 'The witches of Dengie', *Folklore*, 73: 178–83.

Marsh, J. (1982) *Back to the Land: The Pastoral Impulse in England, from 1880 to 1914* (London).

Martino, E. de (1963) *Italie du Sud et magie* (Paris).

Martino, E. de (1982) *Katholizismus Magie Aufklärung. Religionswissenschaftliche Studie am Beispiel Süd-Italiens* (Munich).

Mathisen, S. R. (1993) 'North Norwegian folk legends about the secret knowledge of the magic experts', *Arv. Nordic Yearbook of Folklore*, 49: 19–27.

Medway, G. (ms) *The Lure of the Sinister or The Unnatural History of Satan-Hunting*.

Melton, J. G. (1993) *Encyclopaedia of American Religions*, 4th edn (Detroit/ Washington/London).

Merchant, C. (1980) *The Death of Nature* (San Francisco).

Merivale, P. (1969) *Pan the Goat-God: His Myth in Modern Times* (Cambridge, MA).

Migliore, S. (1997) *Mal'uocchiu: Ambiguity, Evil Eye, and the Language of Distress* (Toronto).

Mone, F.-J. (1839) 'Uber das Hexenwesen', *Anzeiger für Kunde der teutschen Vorzeit* (Baden), 8: 271–5, 444–5.

Moody, E. (1974) 'Magical therapy: contemporary satanism', in I. Zaretsky and M. Leone, eds *Religious Movements in Contemporary America* (Princeton, NJ): 355–82.

Mouchketique, L. (1992) 'Les croyances démonologique du folklore de la contrée limitrophe de l'Ukraine et de la Hongrie', *Acta Ethnographica Hungarica*, 37: 201–13.

Mulhern, S. (1991) 'Satanism and psychotherapy: a rumour in search of an Inquisition', in J. T. Richardson *et al.*, eds (1991): 145–72.

Murray, M. (1921) *The Witch-Cult in Western Europe* (London).

Murray, M. (1933) *The God of the Witches* (London).

Murray, M. (1963) *My First Hundred Years* (London).

Nathan, D. and Snedeker, M. (1995) *Satan's Silence* (New York).

Neave, D. (1991) *Mutual Aid in the Victorian Countryside, 1830–1914* (Hull).

Newman, L. (1940) 'Notes on some rural and trade initiation ceremonies in the eastern counties', *Folklore*, 51: 32–42.

Nicholson, M. (1939) *Mountain Gloom and Mountain Glory* (Ithaca, NY).

Nildin-Wall, B. and Wall, J. (1993) 'The witch as hare or the witch's hare: popular legends and beliefs in Nordic tradition', *Folklore*, 104: 67–76.

Ofshe, R. (1992) 'Inadvertent hypnosis during interrogation: false confession due to dissociative state; misidentified multiple personality and the satanic cult hypothesis, *International Journal of Clinical and Experimental Hypnosis*.

Ofshe, R. and Watters, E. (1994) *Making Monsters* (New York).

Owen, E. (1887) *Welsh Folk-Lore* (Oswestry).

Palmer, K. (1976) *The Folklore of Somerset* (London).

Parker, J. (1993) *At the Heart of Darkness* (London).

Parkin, D. ed. (1985a) *The Anthropology of Evil* (Oxford).

Parkin, D. (1985b) 'Entitling evil: Muslims and non-Muslims in coastal Kenya', in D. Parkin, ed. (1985a): 224–43.

Partner, P. (1981) *The Murdered Magicians* (Oxford).

Paton, C. (1873) *Freemasonry: Its Symbolism, Religious Nature and Law of Perfection* (London).

Paul, C. (1993) '"Und da waren plötzlich über Nacht die Pferde gezopft". Vom Hexenglauben in einem oberschwäbischen Dorf', *Kea. Zeitschrift für Kulturwissenschaften*, 5: 103–18.

Pazder, L. and Smith, M. (1980) *Michelle Remembers* (New York).

Pearson, K. (1897) *The Chances of Death and Other Studies in Evolution* (London).

Pelling, H. (1976) *A History of British Trade Unionism*, 3rd edn (Harmondsworth).

Penneman, T. (1972) *Bekende heksen en tovenaars. Proeve van geïntegreerd sagenonderzoek in de arrondissementen Eeklo en Gent* (Sint-Niklaas).

Pina-Cabral, J. de (1986) *Sons of Adam, Daughters of Eve: The Peasant Worldview of the Alto Minho* (Oxford).

Pinies, J.-P. (1983) *Figures de la sorcellerie Languedocienne. Brèish, endevinaire, armièr* (Paris).

Pintschovius, H.-J. (1991) '"Heute wie zu allen Zeiten . . ." – Hexerei vor deutschen Gerichten', in D. Harmening and D. Bauer, eds (1991): 79–85.

Pitt-Rivers, J. A. (1971) *The People of the Sierra* (Chicago and London).

Pócs, É. (1967) 'Binde- und Lösungszauber im Ungarischen Volksglauben', *Acta Ethnographica Hungarica*, 16: 79–140.

Pócs, É. (1989a) 'Hungarian *Táltos* and his European parallels', in M. Hoppál and J. Pentikäinen, eds *Uralic Mythology and Folklore* (Budapest and Helsinki): 251–276.

Pócs, É. (1989b) *Fairies and Witches at the Boundary of South-Eastern and Central Europe* (Helsinki).

Poole, H. (1951) *Gould's 'History of Freemasonry'*, 3rd edn (London).

Porter, E. (1969) *Cambridgeshire Customs and Folklore* (London).

Powell, F. (1903) 'Charles Godfrey Leland', *Folklore*, 14: 162–3.

Purkiss, D. (1996) *The Witch in History: Early Modern and Twentieth-Century Representations* (London).

Raven Banner, The.

Regardie, I. (1937–40) *The Golden Dawn* (London).

Rhys, J. (1900) *Celtic Folk-Lore* (Oxford).

Richardson, A. (1985) *Dancers to the Gods* (Wellingborough).

Richardson, A. (1986) *Priestess: The Life and Magic of Dion Fortune* (Wellingborough).

Richardson, J. T., Best, J. and Bromley, D. G., eds (1991) *The Satanism Scare* (New York).

Risso, M. and Böker, W. (1964) *Verhexungswahn. Ein Beiträg zum Verstandniss von Wahnerkrankungen süditalienischer Arbeiter in der Schweiz* (Basel and New York).

Roberts, J. (1972) *The Mythology of the Secret Societies* (London).

Rockwell, J. (1978) 'Animals and witchcraft in Danish peasant culture', in J. R. Porter and W. M. S. Russell, eds *Animals in Folklore* (Ipswich): 86–95.

Roeck, F. (1966) 'Hedendaags heksengeloof in de provincie Antwerpen', *De Noordgouw*, 6: 143–60.

Röll, J. (1991) 'Zaubereiannoncen', in Harmening, D. and Bauer, D. eds (1991): 87-95.

Romanucci-Ross, L. (1991) 'Creativity in illness: methodological linkages to the logic and language of science in folk pursuit of health in central Italy', in L. Romanucci-Ross, D. E. Moerman and L. R. Tancredi, eds *The Anthropology of Medicine: From Culture to Method* (New York, Westport, London): 5–19.

Rose, E. (1989) *A Razor for a Goat* (Toronto); first publ. 1962.

Rowe, L. and Cavender, G. (1991) 'Cauldrons bubble, Satan's trouble, but witches are okay': media constructions of satanism and witchcraft, in J. T. Richardson *et al.*, eds (1991): 263–75.

Rudkin, E. (1934) 'Lincolnshire Folklore', *Folklore*, 45: 247–9.

Russell, J. B. (1991) 'The historical Satan', in J. T. Richardson *et al.*, eds (1991): 41–8.

Ryall, R. (1989) *West Country Wicca* (Custer, WA).

Ryan, R. (1976) *Keats: The Religious Sense* (Princeton, NJ).

Salzmann, Z. and Scheufler, V. (1974) *Komárov: A Czech Farming Village* (New York, etc).

Sanders, I. T. (1949) *Balkan Village* (Lexington).

Sanders, M. (1976) *Maxine: The Witch Queen* (London).

Schäfer, H. (1955) *Hexenmacht und Hexenjagd. Ein Beitrag zum Problem der kriminellen Folgen des Hexenaberglaubens der Gegenwart* (Hamburg).

Schäfer, H. (1959) *Der Okkulttäter (Hexenbanner – Magische Heiler – Erdenstrahler)* (Hamburg).

Scherf, W. (1987) 'Die Hexe im Zaubermärchen', in R. van Dülmen, ed.

Hexenwelten. Magie und Imagination vom 16.-20. Jahrhundert (Frankfurt am Main): 219–52.

Schiffmann, A. C. (1988) 'The witch and the crime: the persecution of witches in twentieth-century Poland', *Arv. Scandinavian Yearbook of Folklore 1987*, 43: 147–65.

Schipflinger, A. (1944) 'Bauerndoktoren und Hexenglaube im Brixental', *Wiener Zeitschrift für Volkskunde*, 49: 13–26.

Schmidt, L. (1972) *Volkskunde von Niederösterreich, ii* (Horn).

Schöck, I. (1978) *Hexenglaube in der Gegenwart. Empirische Untersuchungen in Südwestdeutschland* (Tübingen).

Schöck, I. (1987) 'Hexen heute. Traditioneller Hexenglaube und aktuelle Hexenwelle', in R. van Dülmen, ed. *Hexenwelten. Magie und Imagination vom 16.-20. Jahrhundert* (Frankfurt am Main): 282–305.

Schöck, I. (1991) 'Hexenglaube – noch heute?', in Harmening and Bauer, eds (1991): 41–54.

Scott, W. (1943) *The Athenians* (London).

Scott, W. (1944) *Shelley at Oxford* (London).

Sebald, H. (1986) 'Justice by magic: witchcraft as social control among Franconian peasants', *Deviant Behavior* 7: 269–87.

Sharp, C. (1912–24) *The Morris Book, Pts 1–5* (London).

Simpson, J. (1973) *The Folklore of Sussex* (London).

Simpson, J. (1994) 'Margaret Murray: who believed her and why?', *Folklore*, 105: 89–96.

Sinason, V., ed. (1994) *Treating Survivors of Satanist Abuse* (London).

Sinason, V. and Hale, R. (1994) 'Internal and external reality: establishing parameters', in V. Sinason, ed. (1994): 274–85.

Sinninghe, J. R. W. (1943) *Katalog der niederländische Märchen-, Ursprungs-sagen-, Sagen- und Legendenvarianten* (Helsinki).

Slade, A. (1754) *The Free Mason Examin'd* (London).

Smith, E. (1984) *A Dictionary of Classical Reference in English Poetry* (Cambridge).

Smith, K. C. (1978) 'The role of animals in witchcraft and popular magic: with special reference to Yorkshire', in J. R. Porter and W. M. S. Russell, eds *Animals in Folklore* (Ipswich): 96–110.

Spretnak, C., ed. (1982) *The Politics of Women's Spirituality* (New York).

Starhawk (1979) *The Spiral Dance* (San Francisco).

Starhawk (1982) *Dreaming the Dark* (Boston).

Starhawk (1987) *Truth or Dare* (San Francisco).

Stevenson, D. (1988a) *The Origins of Freemasonry* (Cambridge).

Stevenson, D. (1988b) *The First Freemasons* (Aberdeen).

Stewart, C. (1991) *Demons and the Devil: Moral Imagination in Modern Greek Culture* (Princeton).

Strangways, A. (1933) *Cecil Sharp* (Oxford).

Stratford, L. (1988) *Satan's Underground* (Eugene, OR).

Sutcliffe, R. (1996) 'Left-hand path ritual magick: an historical and philosophical overview', in G. Harvey and C. Hardman, eds (1995) 109–37.

Symonds, J. (1971) *The Great Beast* (London).

Szendrey, Á. (1955) 'Hexe – Hexendruck', *Acta Ethnographica Hungarica*, 4: 129–69.

Taylor, D. (1985) 'Theological thoughts about evil', in D. Parkin, ed. (1985a): 26–41.

Thomas, A. (1993) *In Satan's Name*, 'Viewpoint', ITV: 29 June.

Thomas, C. (1953) 'Present-day charmers in Cornwall', *Folklore*, 64: 304–5.

Thomas, K. V. (1971) *Religion and the Decline of Magic* (Harmondsworth).

Thomas, K. V. (1983) *Man and the Natural World* (London).

Thompson, S. (1946) *The Folktale* (Bloomington).

Tillhagen, C.-H. (1969) 'Finnen und Lappen als Zauberkundige in der skandinavischen Volksüberlieferung', in *Kontakte und Grenzen, Probleme der Volks- Kultur- und Sozialforschung. Festschrift für Gerhard Heilfurth zum 60. Geburtstag* (Göttingen): 129–43.

Tongue, R. (1965) *Somerset Folklore* (London).

Torrens, R. (1973) *The Secret Rituals of the Golden Dawn* (Wellingborough).

Treiber, A. (1991) 'Die Faszination des Ursprungs', in D. Harmening and D. Bauer, eds (1991): 145–52.

Trevelyan, M. (1909) *Folk-Lore and Folk-Stories of Wales* (London).

Ucko, P. (1968) *Anthropomorphic Figurines of Predynastic Egypt and Neolithic Crete, with Comparative Material from the Prehistoric Near East and Mainland Greece* (London).

Udal, J. (1922) *Dorsetshire Folklore* (Hertford).

Unverhau, D. (1990) 'Frauenbewegung und historische Hexenverfolgung', in Blauert, A. ed. *Ketzer, Zauberer, Hexen. Die Anfänge der europäischen Hexenverfolgungen* (Frankfurt am Main): 241–83.

Valiente, D. (1962) *Where Witchcraft Lives* (London).

Valiente, D. (1973) *An ABC of Witchcraft Past and Present* (London).

Valiente, D. (1975) *Natural Magic* (London).

Valiente, D. (1978) *Witchcraft for Tomorrow* (London).

Valiente, D. (1989) *The Rebirth of Witchcraft* (Custer, WA).

Valkyrie.

Varga, L. (1939) 'Sorcellerie d'hier. Enquête dans une vallée ladine', *Annales d'histoire sociale*, 1: 121–32.

Victor, J. S. (1991) 'The dynamics of rumour-panics about satanic cults', in J. T. Richardson *et al.*, eds (1991): 221–36.

Vordemfelde, H. (1924) 'Die Hexe im deutschen Volksmärchen', in *Festschrift Eugen Mogk zum 70. Geburtstag* (Halle an der Saale): 558–74.

Vuorela, T. (1967) *Der böse Blick im Lichte der finnischen Überlieferung* (Helsinki).

Waardt, H. de (1991) *Toverij en samenleving. Holland 1500–1800* (The Hague).
Wagner, E. (1970) 'Hexenglaube in Franken heute. Problematik und Ergebnisse einer Umfrage', *Jahrbuch für fränkische Landesforschung*, 30: 343–56.
Ward, J. (1921) *Freemasonry and the Ancient Gods* (London).
Warnke, M. with Balsiger, D. and Jones, L. (1972) *The Satan-Seller* (South Plainfield, NJ).
Weiser-Aall, L. (1931) 'Hexe', *Handwörterbuch des deutschen Aberglaubens, iii* (Berlin and Leipzig): col. 1827–920.
Whitlock, R. (1992) 'Horse sense and nonsense', *Guardian Weekly*, 8 March: 6.
Widdowson, J. (1973) 'The witch as a frightening and threatening figure', in V. Newall, ed. *The Witch Figure* (London and Boston): 200–20.
Wiener, M. (1981) *English Culture and the Decline of the Industrial Spirit* (Cambridge).
Williams, P. H. (1938) *South Italian Folkways in Europe and America: A Handbook for Social Workers, Visiting Nurses, School Teachers and Physicians* (New Haven).
Williams, R. (1973) *The Country and the City* (London).
Wittmann, A. (1933) *Die Gestalt der Hexe in der deutschen Sage* (Bruchsal).
Wytzes, C.-A. (1995) *Ik zie, ik zie wat jij niet ziet. . . . De beeldvorming van de informanten van Engelbert Heupers en Dam Jaarsma uit respectievelijk Soest en Harkema Opeinde over heksen, tovenaars en toverij aan het eind van de 19de eeuw en het begin van de 20ste eeuw,* unpublished doctoral thesis, Rotterdam Erasmus University.

Yeats, W. (1926) *Autobiographies* (London).
Youatt, W. (1859) *The Horse*, ed. E. Gabriel (London).

Zammit-Maempel, G. (1968) 'The evil eye and protective cattle horns in Malta', *Folklore* 79: 1–16.
Zender, M. (1977) 'Glaube und Brauch. Fest und Spiel', in G. Wiegelmann, M. Zender and G. Heilfurt, *Volkskunde. Eine Einführung* (Berlin): 132–97.
Zentai, T. (1976) 'The figure of the "Szépasszony" in the Hungarian folk belief', *Acta Ethnographica Hungarica*, 23: 251–74.

Index

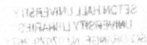